Sanskrit Parsing
Based on the Theories of Śābdabodha

Sanskrit Parsing

Based on the Theories of Śābdabodha

Amba Kulkarni

Foreword by

Rajeev Sangal

INDIAN INSTITUTE OF ADVANCED STUDY
Shimla

PRINTWORLD
Publishers of Indian Traditions

Cataloging in Publication Data — DK
[Courtesy: D.K. Agencies (P) Ltd. <docinfo@dkagencies.com>]

Kulkarni, Amba, author.
Sanskrit parsing : based on the theories of śābdabodha/ Amba Kulkarni; foreword by Rajeev Sangal
pages cm
Includes passages in Sanskrit (roman).
Includes bibliographical references and index.
ISBN 9788124609880

1. Sanskrit language – Parsing. 2. Parsing (Computer grammar) 3. Sanskrit language – Semantics. I. Title.

LCC PK435.K85 2019 | DDC 491.20285635 23

ISBN: 978-81-246-0988-0
First published in India, 2019

Published by:
The Secretary
Indian Institute of Advanced Study
Rashtrapati Nivas, Summerhill, Shimla - 171 005
Phones: (0177) 283 1379; Fax: 283 1389
e-mail: proiias@gmail.com
Website: www.iias.org

and

D.K. Printworld (P) Ltd.
Regd. office: "Vedaśrī", F-395, Sudarshan Park
(Metro Station: ESI Hospital), New Delhi - 110015
Phones: (011) 2545 3975; 2546 6019
e-mail: indology@dkprintworld.com
Website: www.dkprintworld.com

Printed by: D.K. Printworld (P) Ltd., New Delhi

Dedicated in memory of my Father and Teacher

Anantpur Bacce Padmanabharao

who introduced me to
the Language of Mathematics and
the mathematically precise grammar of a language,
and was a source of inspiration
for all my endeavours

Foreword

SANSKRIT holds an important place in the development of theories of language. First, as a language it is rich in lexical and grammatical derivational processes, dealing with word and morpheme level to sentence level and beyond. Second, theories which were developed to analyse Sanskrit language were themselves rich and awe-inspiring. Their goal was to bring precision and clarity in the utterance which was a unique endeavour of its time in 500 BCE. The theories were designed to fix meaning, namely, the meaning of Sanskrit utterance should be clear, precise, and unambiguous for all time to come. Metaphorically, the Sanskrit grammarians and theorists were solving the Y10K or Y100K problem![1]

The study of language played the same role in the Indian civilization as was played by the study of geometry in the Greek civilization. Both encouraged precision of thought and formalization in reasoning. The former was clearly a much tougher domain. The success achieved therein influenced the entire civilization.

These theories of language influenced the study of language and linguistics across the world. Sanskrit language, its vocabulary, and affixes (*pratyaya*) were adopted in Tibetan language a millennium earlier. Later, many of the ideas travelled via the Arab world to Europe. In the nineteenth century, Sanskrit as a wonderful language was rediscovered by Europe, particularly the German and later the British scholars. Subsequently, language typological studies (Greenberg 1963) of the West were influenced by theories of language and grammar developed by the Sanskrit grammarians.

---

[1] Compare this with the Y2K problem: Computer software needed to be fixed to remove ambiguity, caused due to use of only the last two digits of a year. The problem appeared or would have appeared in the year 2000, within a span of mere forty years of the software being written. The contrast between, forty years and 10,000 years (Y10K) is too stark not to be noticed.

In the twentieth century, Pāṇinian model was discovered and rediscovered in a variety of ways. The ideas of formal generative grammar introduced by Chomsky in the 1950s were not only present in Pāṇini but already developed to a high order (Cardona 1976, 1988). At the same time, the Pāṇinian model was much closer to semantics, with, for example, a developed theory of *kāraka* (arguments of verbs) and *samāsa* (compounding). It used "case" or the more generalized concept of *vibhakti*, anticipating Fillmore (1968) by two millennia, and that too complete with the derivational (generative) process. The idea of Minimalism is inherent in the organization of Pāṇini's *Aṣṭādhyāyī* (Deshpande 1985; Kiparsky 1982). What was not realized earlier was that Pāṇini defined operations on a technical representation and through that showed the computational process in derivation of sentences of the language, much like what modern computational linguistics was/is trying to do (Bharati et al. 1995).

Today, there is a young new technology called Natural Language Processing (NLP) with applications as wide as Machine Translation, Information Extraction and Retrieval, Question–Answering, Dialogue Systems, etc. Language theories from Sanskrit suddenly find a new fertile ground for their application. This makes the book even more timely.

The Sanskrit theories relate directly with language processing. In this sense, the theories are almost tailor-made for NLP. They deal with information and meaning in a central way. They address the question: How can one go from the information contained in words and their coming together in a sentence, to the meaning or *vivakṣā* (intension) in the speaker's mind? Thus, human communication or conveying of meaning comes at the centre.

The author of this book presents the Indian Grammatical Tradition (IGT) with detailed references very faithfully. Every concept is introduced in the larger setting of information and meaning, is defined referring to the traditional sources, and is connected with the larger task of language processing. In this fashion, the theories become more lucid and useful at the same time, without sacrificing faithfulness.

After setting the stage in the first chapter, the author introduces the *śabda-śakti* (word meaning) and *śābdabodha* (theories of verbal cognition) in Chap. 2. These are central to the theories of language in the IGT. The different types of meaning of a word in IGT are not just intuitively easy to comprehend, but also simplify the theory conceptually. The author's treatment is scholarly. Theories of *śābdabodha* show the different types of concerns in language analysis, from the perspectives of Vaiyākaraṇas (Grammarians), Naiyāyikas (Logicians), and the Mīmāṁskas (Discourse/Pragmaticians).

Śābdabodha in IGT contains the key elements for a program in Computational Linguistics. These are *ākāṅkṣā* (expectancy), *sannidhi* (planarity), and *yogyatā* (congruity). They allow linguistic data to be prepared and parsing to be done elegantly. My hope is that in time to come, these will permit the integration of theory-based approaches with theory-bereft approaches (viz. Statistical and Neural-based NLP). The theory will bring out the essence so that it can be handled by machine almost directly. For the phenomena, where the required concomitant knowledge is very hard to compile, it can be left for the "theory-bereft" approaches. Finally, the author presents the algorithms for parsing which is a result of complementing the traditional theories with modern efficient algorithms.

The strength of the book lies in its faithful and clear presentation of the theories of language from IGT, the identification of the key elements, and finally their use in constructing efficient algorithms. The book not only documents the salient pieces of work carried out over the last quarter century under Computational Paninian Grammar (CPG), but provides the first comprehensive exposition of the ideas involved. It will serve as an important milestone of achievements so far.

Hopefully, the book will also open up the frontier of applying concepts from Sanskrit parsing to modern Indian languages on a bigger scale, and indeed to all languages of the world.

References

Bharati, Akshar, Vineet Chaitanya and Rajeev Sangal, 1995, *Natural Language Processing: A Paninian Perspective*, New Delhi: Prentice Hall of India.

Cardona, George, 1976, *Panini: A Survey of Research*, The Hague: Mouton & Co.

———, 1988, *Panini: His Work and Its Traditions*, vol. 1: *Background and Introduction*, Delhi: Motilal Banarsidass.

Deshpande, Madhav M., 1985, *Ellipses and Syntactic Overlapping: Current Issues in*

Paninian Syntactic Theory, Pune: Bhandarkar Oriental Research Institute.

Fillmore, Charles J., 1968, "The Case for Case", in *Universals of Linguistic Theory*, ed. E. Bach and R.T. Harms, pp. 1-88, New York: Holt Rinehart and Winston.

Greenberg, Joseph, 1963, *Universals of Language*, Cambridge, MA: MIT Press.

Kiparsky, P., 1982, *Some Theoretical Problems in Pāṇini's Grammar*, Poona: Bhandarkar Oriental Research Institute.

IIIT Hyderabad **Rajeev Sangal**

24 April 2019

Preface

THIS book is an outcome of my fellowship at the Indian Institute of Advanced Study, Shimla during 2015-17. I was always fascinated by the rich Indian grammatical tradition, especially the minute attention paid to the information coding in a language string. In 2006 when I joined the Department of Sanskrit Studies at the University of Hyderabad, I decided to restrict my work to the Sanskrit Computational Linguistics, taking as much help as possible from this rich tradition. Immediately after developing a morphological analyser and a *sandhi* splitter, I decided to venture into the development of a sentential parser. While all the machine translation systems used several other modules such as part of speech (POS) tagger and chunker before calling the parser, I decided to call the parser right after the morphological analyser. The main reason behind this decision was that when I looked at various Indian literature there was no discussion on any kind of POS tagger or chunker. However there were discussions on various factors that help in verbal cognition. The main focus of all these discussions was the flow of information in a sentence. And this was essentially what I was looking for in order to build automatic language processors. So I decided to follow the tradition as closely as possible in the development of my parser, even at the risk of going against the current trends of using machine-learning algorithms, which I believe deserve a place only when one exhausts almost all the information sources discussed in Indian traditional grammar.

The first parser was developed in 2009 by my student N. Shailaja as a part of her MPhil dissertation. She used C Language Integrated Production System (CLIPS),[1] a tool for building an expert system, for writing her rules. This first parser was further enhanced by Sheetal Pokar, Pavankumar Satuluri and Madhvachar, with funding from the Department of Information Technology (DeitY), under its Technology

---

[1] http://www.clipsrules.net/

Development for Indian Languages (TDIL) programme. This parser had two components. The first one was formation of a graph, for which we used the CLIPS environment, and the second part was a constraint solver. This constraint solver was written in MINION.[2] I noticed that the constraint specifications represented in matrix form for the MINION constraint solver resulted in a large-sized sparse matrix, which slowed down the performance of the system. This prompted me to re-examine the design of the constraint solver which resulted in a graph-based depth first traversal algorithm implemented in Perl.[3] Though I had a working module for a morphological analyser, the coverage of the derivational morphology was not satisfactory. Gérard Huet's "The Sanskrit Heritage Site"[4] had good coverage of morphology as well as the best implementation of a *sandhi* splitter. Therefore I thought of taking advantage of existing resources instead of improving my own morphological analyser and *sandhi* splitter. When I started interlinking this module with the segmenter of the Heritage site, I thought it would be better to implement my parser in OCaml[5] (in which the Heritage platform is developed) for better integration. I also noticed that the depth first traversal algorithm written in Perl could be improved further by noting down the compatibility conditions in the beginning. This observation along with the functional aspect of OCaml resulted in the redesigning of my algorithm further so as to make it natural from the functional programming point of view. And this was the fourth *avatāra* of the parser. My student Sanjeev Panchal encoded various Pāṇinian *sūtra*s in OCaml, while I wrote the constraint solver to extract dependency tree from a graph following the edge-centric binary join.

The development of these parsers is largely influenced by the theories of *śābdabodha* (verbal cognition). These theories discuss in great detail the information encoding in a language string. They provided me answers to questions such as where is the information encoded, how much information is encoded, what do the words signify, what role do various significative powers of a word have in

2 http://www.constraintmodelling.org/minion

3 http://www.perl.org

4 http://sanskrit.inria.fr

5 https://ocaml.org

the understanding of a text and so on. Different schools, in Indian tradition, have discussed these questions. The major challenge before me was to decide which school to follow. Second, the examples discussed were few in number, often just one or two. It was therefore challenging for me to understand their stand based on these examples and the commentaries on these texts. I followed two different approaches. When I knew of a relevant concept discussed in the Śāstras, I would try to understand it and then use it appropriately to solve the problem. When I did not know where to look for the solution, I would first arrive at the solution on the basis of empirical evidence and then look for the theoretical support for it in the Śāstras. In the case of *ākāṅkṣā* and *sannidhi*, I followed the first approach. But in the case of *yogyatā*, since I could find hardly one or two pages of material on *yogyatā* with only one stock example, I, with the help of my student Sanjeev, came up with observations based on the data. These observations provided us clues for what and where to look for in the Śāstras. Of course whatever approach we followed we tested our implementation on a corpus, drawn from various classical Sanskrit texts. In all the grammatical texts which we referred to, what I found useful was that the theories of verbal import were objective. And it is this objectivity that guarantees automatic processing.

Students of Sanskrit, especially of Vyākaraṇa, Nyāya and Mīmāṁsā, hear that the theories of *śābdabodha* are useful computationally. But the lack of any text describing the importance of *śābdabodha* leaves them clueless. During the last few years, I travelled all over India delivering lectures on the importance of *śābdabodha* from computational point of view, and I found that it generated a new enthusiasm among Sanskrit students. This also made me think over preparing a short monograph describing this importance in detail. I also met several teachers who were interested in offering a course on the contemporary relevance of Indian theories of *śābdabodha*, but due to lack of any teaching material, they could not.

On the other hand there are students and researchers working in the field of computational linguistics focusing on Indian languages. There are very few grammar books for Indian languages, and hardly any of these is as complete as Pāṇini's grammar for Sanskrit. Since most of the Indo-Aryan languages have originated from Sanskrit,

Pāṇini's grammar definitely provides good insights for handling various linguistic problems of them. After the book by the Akshar Bharati group *Natural Language Processing: A Paninian Perspective*, though much research took place in this field, no textbook was produced that can help a student. Texts by Kunjunni Raja, B.K. Matilal, Veluri Subba Rao, Subramania Iyer, to name a few, written from the perspective of providing an overview of the contribution of Indian grammarians, are useful for researchers. But for students of computational linguistics, they do not provide any direct insights. There are several excellent translations of the original work, such as the one by Mahāmahopādhyāya Ganganath Jha of the *Śābara-Bhāṣya* on Mīmāṁsā *sūtra*s, or the translations of Patañjali's *Mahābhāṣya*, and a lot of secondary literature on these topics. But all this material is beyond the reach of the students of computational linguistics since these texts are written from a different perspective.

With these two strata of readers in mind, I decided to write down my understanding of these theories from a computational viewpoint. This book is the result of that exercise. The first chapter provides an overview of various computational tools for Sanskrit and then introduces the main theme of this book, viz. the dependency parsing. The second chapter introduces the Indian theories of word meaning and sentence meaning briefly, discussing various conditions of knowing the meaning of a sentence. The third chapter is my main contribution which provides interpretation of the concepts discussed in the second chapter from the computational perspective and provides computational models to implement them. The fourth chapter discusses the three different dependency parser algorithms I built, with the help of my students, each one being an improvement over the previous one.

I have tried to provide a glimpse of parallel concepts employed in the contemporary computational linguistics so that the students of linguistics in general and of computational linguistics in particular should find it easy to connect the concepts presented here with what they are familiar with. At the same time, the students of Sanskrit grammar should find the third chapter interesting where they would know the nature of problems a computational linguist is facing and see the practical demonstration of application of the Indian theories to solve the contemporary problems. I hope this book will provide confidence to the students and researchers from both the disciplines to access the relevant material on the other discipline.

What I have presented is my understanding of the concepts in the Indian grammatical tradition. If there are any errors in my understanding, or errors in the presentation, I am solely responsible for them. I would, in such cases, like to know about them so that I can rectify them and correct my understanding. I hope this book will be useful to students of computational linguistics and also Sanskrit students to understand the rich Indian grammatical tradition and its relevance to the field of computational linguistics.

Contents

Foreword vii

Preface xi

Acknowledgements xxi

1. Introduction **1**

1.1 Sanskrit Computational Tools: Current Status 2

1.1.1 Word Generators 3

1.1.2 Word Analysers 4

1.1.3 Lexical Resources 6

1.1.4 Tools Based on Data-driven Approaches 7

1.2 Sanskrit Parser 7

1.2.1 Constituency Structure 8

1.2.2 Dependency Structure 10

1.2.3 Parsing and Theories of Verbal Cognition 12

2. Understanding Texts : Indian Theories **15**

2.1 Word Meaning 16

2.1.1 Abhidhā (Primary Denotation) 18

2.1.2 Lakṣaṇā (Implication) 19

2.1.3 Vyañjanā (Suggestion) 22

2.2 Necessary Conditions for Verbal Cognition 23

2.2.1 Ākāṅkṣā (Expectancy) 24

2.2.2 Sannidhi (Proximity) 26

2.2.3 Yogyatā (Congruity) 27

2.2.4 Tātparya (Purport) 28

2.3 Vākyārtha (Sentential Meaning) 30

2.4 Structure of Verbal Cognition 33

2.5 Understanding Texts: Commentary Tradition 36

2.5.1 Canonical Word Order 39

2.6 Conclusion 40

3. Śābdabodha Theories and Sanskrit Parsing **41**
3.1 Ākāṅkṣā: Establishing Relations 41
3.1.1 Where Is the Information? 42
3.1.2 What Kind of Information? 47
3.1.3 Repository of Relations 51
3.1.4 How Is the Information Encoded? 52
3.2 Sannidhi: Planarity Constraint 54
3.2.1 Projectivity Principle 55
3.2.2 Weak Non-projectivity (Planarity) 57
3.2.3 Empirical Evaluation 59
3.2.4 Conclusion 67
3.3 Yogyatā: Semantic Restrictions 68
3.3.1 Selection Restriction 69
3.3.2 Śabda-śakti (Level of Signification) 70
3.3.3 Yogyatā as a Filter 73
3.3.4 Modelling Yogyatā 76
3.3.5 Evaluation 88
3.4 Conclusion 90

4. Sanskrit Parsing **93**
4.1 Introduction 93
4.1.1 Dependency Parse Structure 95
4.2 Design of a Parser 100
4.2.1 Establishing Directed Edges 104
4.2.2 Defining the Constraints 107
4.3 Solving the Constraints 109
4.3.1 Constraint Satisfaction Problem 110
4.3.2 Vertex-centric Traversal 114
4.3.3 Edge-centric Binary Join 121
4.4 Compact Display of Multiple Solutions 125
4.5 Conclusion 127

5. Conclusion **135**

Appendices 139

A. Evaluation of Parsers : Various Parameters 141
Measure of Correctness of Parse 141
A.1 Precision and Recall 142

B. Classification of Lakṣaṇā 145

C. List of Relations in Pāṇinian Grammar 151
D. List of Relations Used in the Sanskrit Parser 155
Glossary 159
Bibliography 163
Index 175

Acknowledgements

I WAS very fortunate to be a fellow at the Indian Institute of Advanced Study, Shimla during 2015-17. At the outset, I thank the selection committee and the then Director Prof. Chetan Singh for giving me an opportunity to work in this prestigious Institute at the feet of the Himalayas. The conducive atmosphere in the Institute for carrying out research, the serene skies, the evening sunsets and the dense pine and *devadāra* trees touching the skies provided me the right kind of environment to carry out my work without any disturbances. Thanks are also due to my parent institute, the University of Hyderabad, for granting me leave for the above period.

Some of the material in this book was earlier published in the form of conference/seminar papers in their proceedings, or as a journal article. I thank the publishers for giving me permission to use the relevant parts in this book, with or without modification. The publications from which I have used the material are the following:

1. Kulkarni, A., S. Pokar and D. Shukl, 2010, "Designing a Constraint Based Parser for Sanskrit", in *Fourth International Sanskrit Computational Linguistics Symposium*, ed. G.N. Jha, pp. 70-90, Springer-Verlag, LNAI 6465.
2. Bharati, A. and A. Kulkarni, 2010, "Information Coding in a Language: Some Insights from Paninian Grammar", *Dhīmahi, Journal of Chinmaya International Foundation Shodha Sansthan*, I(1): 77-91.
3. Kulkarni, A., 2013, "A Deterministic Dependency Parser with Dynamic Programming for Sanskrit", in *Proceedings of the Second International Conference on Dependency Linguistics (DepLing 2013)*, pp. 157-66, Prague, Czech Republic: Charles University in Prague Matfyzpress Prague Czech Republic.
4. Kulkarni, A. and K.V. Ramakrishnamacharyulu, 2013, "Parsing Sanskrit Texts: Some Relation Specific Issues", in *Proceedings*

of the 5th International Sanskrit Computational Linguistics Symposium, ed. M. Kulkarni, New Delhi: D.K. Printworld.

5. Kulkarni, A.P., P. Shukla, P. Satuluri and D. Shukl, 2015, "How Free Is the 'Free' Word Order in Sanskrit", in *Sanskrit Syntax*, ed. P. Scharf, pp. 269-304, The Sanskrit Library.
6. Sanjeev, P. and A. Kulkarni, 2018, "Yogyatā as an Absence of Incongruity", in *Computational Sanskrit & Digital Humanities*, ed. H. Gérard and A. Kulkarni, New Delhi: D.K. Publishers.

I thank all my fellow friends at the Indian Institute of Advanced Study, who participated in my presentations and gave valuable suggestions concerning my work. Special thanks are due to Dr Terry Varma, Prof. Madhavan and Dr Lalitha Raja who read earlier drafts of my manuscripts meticulously, and discussed various aspects, to Prof. Nirmal Sengupta and Prof. Vijay Varma for valuable discussions on related topics, and to Amit Datta and Ayswarya Sankaranarayanan, who shared my study at the Institute, for exposing me to the wonderful creative world of artists.

I also thank the anonymous reviewers who reviewed my intermediate and the final drafts of the manuscript and provided useful feedback on the manuscript.

I thank my teachers, colleagues, friends and students who took trouble to go through my draft manuscript and provided useful suggestions. While there is a danger of leaving somebody out, I still would like to put on record the names: Prof. Rajeev Sangal, Prof. K.V. Ramakrishnamacharyulu, Prof. B.N. Patnaik, Prof. Korada Subrahmanyam, Prof. Peter Scharf, Prof. Dipti Misra Sharma, Prof. Srinivas Varakhedi, Prof. Rajaram Shukla, Prof. Tirumala Kulkarni, Prof. Lalit Kumar Tripathi, Dr Sukhada, Dr Arjuna and Sanjeev Panchal. I thank my research assistants and students Dr Shailaja, Dr Sheetal Pokar, Dr Pavankumar Satuluri, Dr Madhvachar for implementation of earlier versions of *ākāṅkṣā* module and Sanjeev Panchal for the current implementation of both the *ākāṅkṣā* and *yogyatā*. Thanks are also due to Dr Preeti Shukl and Dr Pavankumar Satuluri who worked with me on the problem of word order and *sannidhi* violation in Sanskrit.

Prof. Vineet Chaitanya deserves special mention. Most of the concepts discussed here have either originated from him, or he was the sounding board for them. Discussions with him on various aspects brought clarity to my thoughts. Prof. Gérard Huet, not only went through my ever-evolving manuscript at several times, but also raised several intriguing questions which helped me broaden my vision and improve the implementation of the software as well as the content of the manuscript.

I thank Prof. Rajeev Sangal, my teacher and the leader of the computational linguistics community in India, who along with Prof. Vineet Chaitanya, is pioneer in demonstrating the utility of the Indian grammatical theories for Natural Language Processing and in particular Machine Translation, for writing the foreword.

I also thank Shri Susheel Mittal ji of the D K Printworld for readily accepting to print the book and also for providing all the necessary assistance.

Finally, I thank my sons Achyut and Kedar who kept me free from any botherations and always provided the needed emotional support for carrying out my work with more enthusiasm.

1

Introduction

LANGUAGE technology plays an important role in the digital era. The last half century has seen an exponential growth in the fields of computational linguistics and language technology. Software related to machine translation, information retrieval, information extraction, search engines, question answering systems, etc. are available and constantly being enhanced. With mobile phones becoming as powerful as computers, mobile apps are being developed in several language-related areas including language learning and language games. Such tools are not only useful for modern languages, but also play a crucial role in making classical language texts easily accessible. For example, the Perseus Digital Library Project[1] provides access to a digital corpus of classical languages such as Latin, Greek and Arabic, with support for linguistic analysis and contextual reading. Sanskrit has received good attention from scholars as well as enthusiasts from all over the world. In addition to several websites serving as repositories of Sanskrit texts, in the field of computational linguistics we find individual as well as collaborative efforts during the last two decades with their linguistic software available online for public usage.[2]

While earlier efforts towards the development of many such linguistic tools were based on linguistic theories specially developed from the computational perspective, the last decade has seen the use of machine-learning techniques, deep-learning and big data replacing linguistic theories. The main reason behind the preference for machine learning and similar techniques over pure linguistic approaches is the cost involved in developing the language resources needed for disambiguation at various levels, and the complexity involved in the representation of such knowledge. Machine-learning and deep-

1 http://www.perseus.tufts.edu/hopper/about

2 http://sanskrit.uohyd.ac.in/scl; http://sanskrit.inria.fr; http://www.sanskritreader.de; http://sanskrit.jnu.ac.in; and http://sanskritlibrary.org

learning techniques with the help of big data can capture the nuances of languages very effectively and in recent years have shown promise in the field of word-sense-disambiguation, an important module in any machine-translation system. But the disadvantage of these techniques is that whatever a machine learns cannot be controlled or modified or improved manually. In order to improve the performance of a machine, we end up needing more actionable, relevant and smart data that help reduce the unreliability.

When it comes to classical languages such as Sanskrit, we definitely want our software to produce "reliable" and "faithful" translations as well, in addition to quick translations which may be useful to get a rough idea about what the text in the source language is. Quick translations help one to judge the relevance of the text one wants to get translated before venturing into getting it translated manually. Faithful translator or an accessor, on the other hand, provides complete access to the original text, giving one confidence about the reliability of the translation. Thus, on the one hand, for classical languages we need a machine-translation system developed using fast, actionable, reliable and smart (FARS) data to provide a quick gist and on the other hand, we need complete and faithful access to the original text.

1.1 Sanskrit Computational Tools: Current Status

Sanskrit assumes a unique status when it comes to the field of linguistic analysis with its more than 2,500-year long and still extant grammatical tradition. Sanskrit grammar enjoys a similar status in India as mathematics in the West. Pāṇini's grammar is an important milestone in the Indian grammatical tradition. Unlike grammars of other languages, it is almost complete and, together with the theories of *śābdabodha* (verbal understanding), this grammar provides a complete system for language analysis as well as generation. It is therefore natural to explore the use of these theories for building computational tools for language analysis that can provide complete and faithful access to the original Sanskrit texts. At the same time, we also see tools that are developed with state-of-the-art technology such as machine learning. In what follows, we give a brief summary of the various efforts in the development of Sanskrit computational tools, both grammar-based as well as non-grammar-based or data-driven.

1.1.1 WORD GENERATORS

In the recent past there have been several efforts to implement the rules of the *Aṣṭādhyāyī* computationally simulating the process of rule selection and the derivation process in the *Aṣṭādhyāyī* by Goyal, Kulkarni and Behera (2009), Misra (2009), and Subbanna and Varakhedi (2009, 2010). Pavankumar Satuluri (2016) developed a compound generator following the procedure described in the *Aṣṭādhyāyī*. He was not only interested in being faithful to the derivation process as described in the *Aṣṭādhyāyī*, but was also interested in its computational complexity. Krishna and Goyal (2016) describe a *taddhita* (secondary derivatives) generator that represents a *sūtra* from the *Aṣṭādhyāyī* as an object. They discuss the problems related to multiple inheritance and conflict resolution techniques. Patel and Katuri (2016) describe an "NLP order of *sūtra*s" and implement the *subanta* (nominal inflections) generation rules as arranged in the *Siddhāntakaumudī*. In a similar effort, Swami Shivamurthy Taralabalu[3] has developed a noun generator. Scharf et al. (2015) programmatically determine *ātmanepada* vs *parasmaipada* verbal terminations. In the recent developments, Sohoni and M.A. Kulkarni (2018) have developed a simulator where they translate each Pāṇinian *sūtra* as a Haskell module. In another effort, Sarada Susarla, Tilak Rao and Sai Susarla (2018) have developed an interpreter for *sūtra*s in the *Aṣṭādhyāyī*, where each *sūtra* is represented as a record in JSON format. Scharf (2009a) has examined how to model various features of Pāṇinian grammar. Recently Scharf (2016) described an XML annotation scheme to represent the interpretation of *sūtra*s in an unambiguous way so that one can translate them into a computer program to build a simulator. All these efforts tried to follow the grammar *in toto*, and for some of them, the motive behind the development of this software was also to interpret Pāṇini's grammar from the computational point of view and implement them programmatically.

There are some other efforts where we notice a deviation from Pāṇini in the implementation of generators for Sanskrit words. The Heritage engine developed by Huet (2016) is one such instance, where he is interested in representing the tight coupling of word and meaning in the derivation process, but his system deviates from Pāṇini in the implementation. Kulkarni and Shukl (2009) follow a paradigm

---

3 http://www.taralabalu.org/panini/

model, used in pedagogy, for noun generation. For verb generation they use a ready-made verb-form tables, and an efficient finite state transducer[4] is used for computational processing.

1.1.2 WORD ANALYSERS

A word, for computational purpose, is defined as a string of characters separated by white spaces. In Sanskrit, due to the influence of oral tradition, the consecutive words are joined together. At the join, the phonemes, optionally, undergo a change termed as *sandhi*.[*] So the task of word analysers, in the case of Sanskrit, is twofold. The first task is to identify the word boundaries, and undo the *sandhi* operation, and the second task is to analyse such split words.

A generative grammar of any language provides rules for generation. For analysis, we require a mechanism by which we can use these rules in a reverse way. The reversal in some cases is easy and also deterministic. For example, subtraction is an inverse operation of addition and is deterministic. The reversal, however, may not always be deterministic. Let us see a simple example of non-deterministic reversal with which all of us are familiar. The multiplication tables or simple method of repetitive addition provides a mechanical way for multiplication. Given a product, to find its factors is a reverse process. Multiplication of two numbers, say 4 and 3, produces a unique number 12. But its decomposition into two factors is not unique. 12 may be decomposed into two factors as either {6, 2} or {4, 3} in addition to a trivial decomposition {12, 1}. Thus the inverse process may at times involve non-determinism. Depending upon the context, if one factor is known, the other factor gets fixed. For example, if you are interested in distributing 12 apples among 2 children, then one of the factors being 2, the other factor, viz. 6, is determined uniquely.

This is true of a generative grammar as well. To give an example, look at the following two *sūtra*s of Pāṇini.

---

4 http://wiki.apertium.org/wiki/Lttoolbox

* संहिता एकपदे नित्या नित्या धातु-उपसर्गयोः।
नित्या समासे वाक्ये तु सा विवक्षाम् अपेक्षते।।

Sandhi is to be done always i. if the resultant is used as a one word, ii. in between a root and its prefix, and iii. in a compound. In a sentence it is discretionary.

- *anabhihite* (A 2.3.1[5])
- *kartṛkaraṇayos tṛtīyā* (A 2.3.18)

These two *sūtra*s together, in case of a passive voice (*karmaṇi prayogaḥ*), assign a third case suffix (*vibhakti*) to both the *kartṛ* (agent) as well as *karaṇa* (instrument) *kāraka*. Here is an illustrative sentence:

> Skt: *rāmeṇa bāṇena vāliḥ ahanyata* । (1)
> Gloss: By_Rāma with_an arrow Vāli was_killed.
> Eng: Vāli was killed by Rāma with an arrow.

Now, when a hearer (who knows Sanskrit grammar) listens to this utterance, he notices two words ending in the third case suffix and that the construction is in the passive voice. But unless he knows that *rāma* (Rāma) is the name of a person and *bāṇa* (arrow) is used as an instrument, he may fail to get the correct reading. In the absence of such "extra-linguistic" knowledge, there are two possible interpretations, viz. either *rāma* is *kartṛ* and *bāṇa* is *karaṇa*, or *bāṇa* is *kartṛ* and *rāma* is *karaṇa* leading to non-determinism.[6]

We come across non-determinism with the process of segmentation as well. As mentioned earlier, in the case of Sanskrit compound words, *sandhi* between the components of a compound is mandatory. Further, there is a tendency to write Sanskrit text as a continuous string (*saṁhitāpāṭha*), due to the influence of an oral tradition. During the *sandhi* process, the phonemes at the juncture undergo changes. And in order to process such a *sandhi*ed text, one needs to split the string into meaningful components. Pāṇini describes rules for the formation of *sandhi* when two phonemes pronounced are in proximity. These rules are for the generation of a *sandhi*ed string. Segmentation is the reverse process, and this also involves non-determinism. For example, the compound word *rāmālayaḥ* results from a *sandhi* of two components *rāma* and *ālayaḥ*. But since *ā* may also result from the *sandhi* of two *a*s, or two *ā*s, or one *a* and another *ā*, there are four different ways a word can be split at *ā*. This results in multiple possible splits, with a constraint that each such split component should be meaningful.

---

[5] A *sūtra* number has three parts: *adhyāya* (chapter), *pāda* (a quarter/fourth part) and *sūtra* (concise formula) number.

[6] There are two more possibilities, since both have the same gender number and *vibhakti*, one can be an adjective of the other.

Huet (2002) extends the finite state technology to represent *sandhi* transitions on a decorated trie where the nodes are decorated with the possible morphological analysis and optionally with the information of transitions due to *sandhi*. Such a decorated trie structure is used for segmentation. Goyal and Huet (2013) further provided an interactive user interface to select the correct segmentation in a given context. This interface is an excellent example of sharing the load between man and machine. The machine carries out part of the task – the task of splitting a given text at all possible places taking into account the *sandhi* rules and the constraint that it splits the string only into morphologically valid strings. But since a machine does not have the knowledge of word meanings, the task of deciding whether the split is meaningful or not is left to a human being who is reading/accessing the text. Anil Kumar, Mittal and Kulkarni (2010) built a segmenter that prioritizes the possible solutions on the basis of statistical evidence. Both Huet and Anil Kumar use a word analyser to prune out unmeaningful splits. These word analysers provide all possible analyses. For building the morphological analysers finite state transducers are used which provide the best performance.

1.1.3 LEXICAL RESOURCES

Several lexical resources for Sanskrit have been developed and are being developed. The knowledge structure of the *Amarakośa* was explored by Nair (2011) and linked with the Vaiśeṣika ontology.[7] SanskNet[8] – a WordNet for Sanskrit – was developed at IIT Bombay under the leadership of Malhar Kulkarni (Kulkarni et al. 2010). Scharf (2009b) determined the canonical forms of the verbal roots expected by Pāṇini in the *Aṣṭādhyāyī*. He made the *dhātupāṭha* as commented upon in the *Mādhavīya Dhātuvṛttisaiddhāntikānukramaṇī*, an important work describing the verbal roots, their forms, accents and meanings, available online.[9] A concordance[10] of three major *dhātuvṛttis* – *Mādhavīyadhātuvṛtti*, *Kṣīrataraṅgiṇī* and *Dhātupradīpa* – was produced by Shailaja (2014).

[7] http://sanskrit.uohyd.ac.in/amarakosha/index.html

[8] http://www.cfilt.iitb.ac.in/wordnet/webswn/wn.php

[9] http://www.sanskritlibrary.org/Sanskrit/Vyakarana/Dhatupatha/index2.html

[10] http://sanskrit.uohyd.ac.in/scl/dhaatupaatha/index.html

1.1.4 TOOLS BASED ON DATA-DRIVEN APPROACHES

All these efforts are grammar-based and make only superficial use of corpus as well as statistical and machine-learning methods. Among the use of machine-learning approaches and use of corpus statistics the work by the German scholar Hellwig (2009b, 2010) is worth mentioning. He built *n*-grams[11] of inflected forms from a Sanskrit corpus, and used these *n*-grams to develop a part of speech (POS) tagger and has demonstrated very promising results. He also provides the Digital Corpus of Sanskrit[12] with a search facility for collection of lemmatized Sanskrit texts. This website also provides automatic segmentation and tagging of Sanskrit texts. Hellwig (2009a) described a statistical parser for analysing Sanskrit. There were a few other efforts also that use the existing corpus for improving the segmented output. Natarajan and Charniak (2011) proposed *sandhi* splitting based on the Dirichlet process and obtained better results than Mittal (2010) who used Optimality Theory by defining the posterior probability function to choose the most probable split among the valid splits. Anil Kumar (2012) developed a compound word analyser for Sanskrit that shows possible constituency analyses and possible compound type(s). He uses both grammatical rules as well as makes use of corpus for prioritizing the solutions based on statistical evidences, and posterior probability.

The recent trend is to use the deep learning and neural network models for automatic segmentation. Krishna, Satuluri and Goyal (2017) proposed the first model that performs both word segmentation and morphological analysis for Sanskrit. This was further improved by Reddy et al. (2018) with a seq2seq model with attention.

1.2 Sanskrit Parser

Parsing unfolds a linear string of words into a structure which shows explicitly the relations between words. This structure is dictated by the grammar. There are two distinct ways to look at a language string from the structural point of view: as a constituency structure and as a dependency structure.

---

11 *n*-grams is a contiguous sequence of *n* items from a given sequence of text or speech.

12 http://kjc-fs-cluster.kjc.uni-heidelberg.de/dcs/index.php

1.2.1 CONSTITUENCY STRUCTURE

A constituency structure shows how a sentence is constituted by combining the words in it. A constituency is a relation between a constituent and the larger unit that it is part of. The grammar that describes the structure of a sentence in terms of its constituents organized hierarchically is called a constituency grammar or a phrase structure grammar. *Figure* 1.1 shows the constituency structure[13] of a sentence "The king gives a cow to a brāhmaṇa" as a parse tree.

A constituency parse tree consists of two types of nodes: terminal and non-terminal. The terminal nodes, which are the leaf nodes of a tree, correspond to the words in a sentence. All other nodes are the non-terminal nodes. The non-terminal nodes immediately above the leaf nodes represent the POS category of the word at the leaf node. One or more POS nodes get connected into phrasal nodes. These phrasal nodes correspond to constituent phrases.

Thus *V* is the POS of "gives" and *PP* is the prepositional phrase comprising to a "brāhmaṇa". The constituency parse structure is sometimes also represented as a bracketed expression. The bracketed expression for the above sentence is

$$[[\text{ The king }]_{NP}[\text{ gives }[\text{ a cow }]_{NP}[\text{ to a brāhmaṇa }]_{PP}]_{VP}]_{S}$$

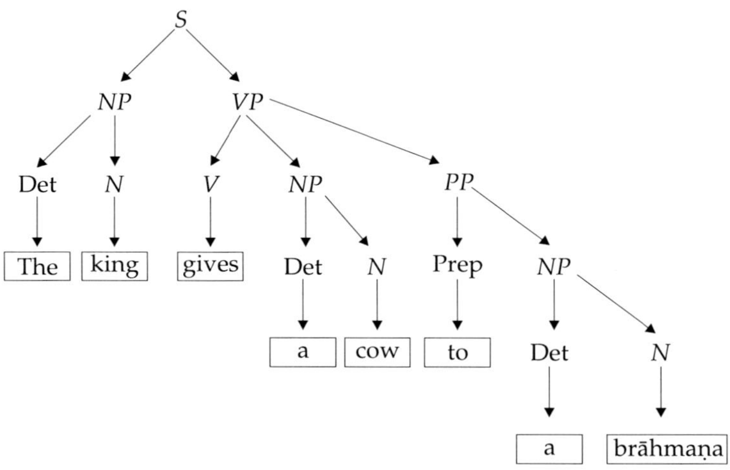

fig. 1.1: Constituency tree of an English sentence "The king gives a cow to a brāhmaṇa."

[13] This tree does not follow any particular theoretical framework.

For positional languages such as English the constituency tree is very important as it shows the syntactic structure of a sentence and the boundaries of phrases constituting various semantic units.

The structure of Sanskrit compounds can best be described by a constituency tree. Sanskrit compounds are typically binary and recursive in nature. They can go any level deep. *Figure* 1.2 shows the constituency structure of the following compound from the *Pañcatantra*.

> Skt: *pravara-mukuṭa-maṇi-marīci-mañjarī-caya-carcita-caraṇa-yugalam*।[14]
>
> Gloss: Excellent-crown-gem-radiant-cluster-heap-cover-foot-pair.
>
> Eng: The one whose feet are covered by the heap of a cluster of radiance from the gem of the excellent crown.

This compound has nine components. The intermediate nodes and

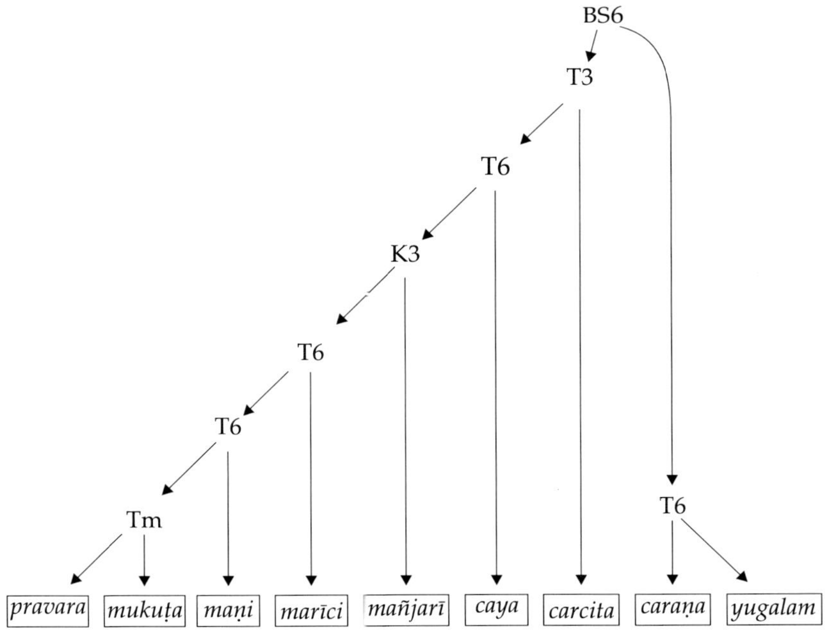

fig. 1.2: Constituency tree of a Sanskrit compound

the root nodes of the compound structure, in fact, do not stand for

[14] Another variant of this compound with ten components is: *pravara-nṛpa-mukuṭa-maṇi-marīci-mañjarī-caya-carcita-caraṇa-yugalam.*

the phrase label, as in the constituency tree of an English sentence, but these intermediate labels, viz. T6, T7,[15] etc. stand for the type of compound.[16] The type of a compound shows the dependency relation between the two heads. For example, the relation T6 between *caraṇa* (foot) and *yugalam* (pair) stands for a genitive relation, giving the meaning "pair of foot".

1.2.2 DEPENDENCY STRUCTURE

For the sentential parse of Sanskrit sentences, such a constituency parse makes little sense. Sanskrit is morphologically rich and to a large extent has free word order. There is also a strong tradition of Pāṇinian grammar for Sanskrit, which happens to be the oldest dependency grammar. In dependency grammar, constituency structure does not have any role. On the other hand, the grammatical relations between the words are important. A dependency parse shows the dependency relations between various words in a sentence. The dependency relations are directional from the *viśeṣya* (head/modified) to the *viśeṣaṇa* (dependents/modifiers). These relations are also labelled. The label denotes the role of the dependent node with respect to the head node. The head and the dependents are also termed modified and modifier respectively. In every sentence, there is one morpheme which is the head of the entire sentence. This is called the root of the dependency structure. It is called *mukhya-viśeṣya* (chief qualificand) in Indian grammar. The dependency parsed structure is represented as a tree and hence the dependency parse is also called a dependency tree. The dependency tree is a directed, labelled acyclic graph.

1. It has a single node called a root node.
2. All nodes except the root node have exactly one incoming arrow.
3. The root node does not have any incoming arrow.

The structure of a Sanskrit sentence is best represented by a dependency tree (see Chap. 4 for detailed reasoning).

A dependency parse of

---

15 "T" stands for *tatpuruṣa* – an endocentric compound, and the numbers 6 and 7 stand for the case. Thus T6 stands for an endocentric genitive compound.

16 Another variant analysis is where *mukuṭa* and *maṇi* form one constituent with T6 and then *pravara* joins them.

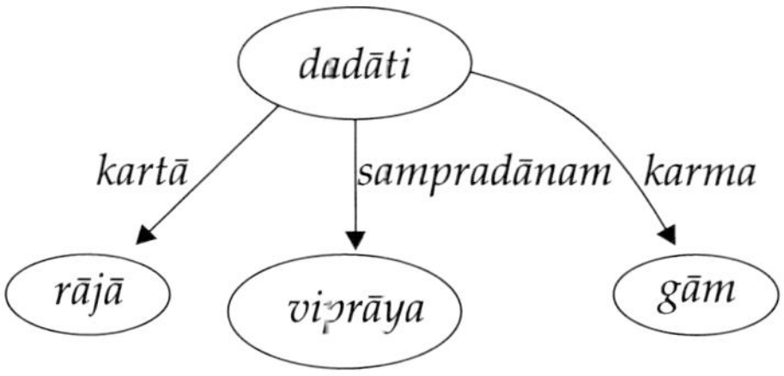

fig. 1.3: Dependency tree of a Sanskrit sentence: *rājā viprāya gām dadāti*

Skt: *rājā viprāya gām dadāti.* (2)

Gloss: King {nom.} brāhmaṇa {dat.} cow {acc.} give {pr. tense, 3p, sg}

Eng: The king gives a cow to a brāhmaṇa.

is shown in *fig*. 1.3 as a dependency tree. The relation labels *kartṛ* (agent[17]), *karman* (goal) and *sampradāna* (beneficiary, recepient) are the semantic relations expressing the role of the substantives in relation to the verb. The root of the parse tree here is the main verb.[18]

The importance of dependency trees over the constituency trees was well recognized by the computational linguistic community. The dependency analysis is preferred over the constituency not only from the evaluation point of view (Lin 1998) but also because of its suitability (Marneffe et al. 2006) for a wide range of NLP tasks such as machine translation, information extraction, question answering and logical deductions and inferences. Naturally, we notice that during the last decade there is an upsurge in the use of dependency structure in computational parsing of several languages such as English, French, Chinese and Japanese. The parsed structure of the sentence, "The king gives a cow to a brāhmaṇa", following Universal Dependencies,[19] is shown in *fig*. 1.4.

The first parser for Sanskrit was built by Bhattacharyya (1986) as a part of his MTech thesis at IIT Kanpur in 1987 using

---

[17] These are not faithful translations but just rough translations of case relations, to indicate the nature of the relation.

[18] Strictly speaking the relations are between the denotations of nominal stem (*prātipadika*) and the verbal root (*dhātu*) which are realized by their suffixes. But for the ease of reading the diagram, we represent these relations between words.

[19] http://universaldependencies.org/

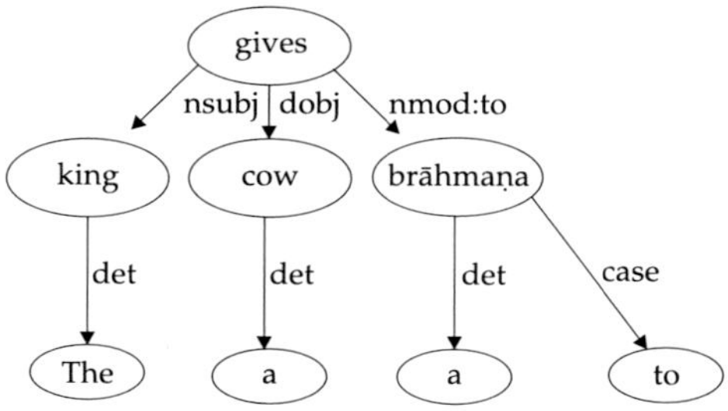

fig. 1.4: Dependency tree of an English sentence: The king gives a cow to a brāhmaṇa

integer programming. Later, in the early 1990s, the team led by Lakshmitatachar (Ramapriya and Saumyanarayana 2001) developed a generator that could generate the expressions of verbal cognition following different Indian schools, for Bhandarkar's Sanskrit primer, at the Academy of Sanskrit Research in Melkote. Huet (2007, 2009) has a shallow parser that uses the minimal information of transitivity of a verb as a subcategorization frame and models it as a graph-matching algorithm. The main purpose of this shallow parser is to filter out non-sensical segmentations.

1.2.3 PARSING AND THEORIES OF VERBAL COGNITION

In order to develop a dependency parser, we need to know answers to the following questions:

1. How does one know which word relates to which other in a sentence?
2. Where is the information of word relations encoded?
3. How is this information encoded?
4. What is the semantics associated with such a relation?
5. Is there any repository of relation names?
6. Do the word meanings have any role to play in establishing the relations?
7. Does the relation between the words have any role in the decision of the word meaning?
8. What is the expressive capacity of a word?

Answers to these questions are found in the Indian theories of verbal cognition. The dependency grammar of Pāṇini was further strengthened by the development of theories of verbal import that provide the structure of sentential meaning mentioning minute details such as what are the sources of information and how the information flows in a sentence. The theories discuss the importance of three factors, viz. *ākāṅkṣā* (expectancy), *yogyatā* (mutual congruity) and *sannidhi* (proximity) as essential factors for any verbal understanding. Further these theories also deal with the question of what the meaning of "meaning" is? Three levels of signification of words, viz. *abhidhā* (primary), *lakṣaṇā* (secondary) and *vyañjanā* (suggestive) are suggested with several subdivisions. In addition, these theories describe minute details such as which part of a sentence expresses what kind of information and how this information relates one word to the other. Vaiyākaraṇas (grammarians), Naiyāyikas (logicians) and Mīmāṁsakas (exegesists) developed their own theories of verbal cognition. Subbarao (1969) provides detailed diagrammes showing the *śābdabodha*s of all the three schools providing all the details of the sources of information and the information flow in the process of cognition, according to each of these schools. These theories provide a sound base for sentential analysis.

The Navya-Naiyāyikas (neo-logicians), further, have developed a technical language for expressing the verbal understanding unambiguously. This language is known as the technical language of Navya-Nyāya. All the schools use this language to express the verbal cognition through this language. For example, the Vaiyākaraṇas' (grammarians') *śābdabodha* of (2) is

> *rājakartṛka-gokarmaka-viprasampradānaka-dānānukūla-vyāpāraḥ* ।
>
> An activity of giving (*dāna*) whose agent (*kartṛ*) is a king, whose goal (*karman*) is a cow and whose recipient (*sampradāna*) is a brāhmaṇa.

The exegesists' (Mīmāṁsakas') *śābdabodha* is

> *rājakartṛka-gokarmaka-viprasampradānaka-dānānukūla-bhāvanā* ।
>
> A productive activity (*bhāvanā*) of giving (*dāna*) whose agent (*kartṛ*) is a king, whose goal (*karman*) is a cow and whose recipient (*sampradāna*) is a brāhmaṇa.

There is only a slight difference between a Vaiyākaraṇa's *śābdabodha* and that of a Mīmāṁsaka. The Mīmāṁsakas are interested in the speech act and not merely the verbal import. According to them the verbal suffix denotes the *bhāvanā* which is qualified by an activity expressed by the verbal root resulting in a productive activity (*ārthī-bhāvanā*). Thus the verbal suffix is the *mukhya-viśeṣya* (chief-qualificand), whereas according to the Vaiyākaraṇas the verbal root is the *mukhya-viśeṣya*.

For a Naiyāyika, the structure of the verbal cognition resulting from this utterance is different. For him, generally, a word in nominative case is the *mukhya-viśeṣya*. The Naiyāyika's (logician's) *śābdabodha* is

> *gokarmaka-viprasampradānaka-dānānukūla-kṛtimān rājā* ।
>
> A king who is the agent (*kartṛ*) of an activity of giving (*dāna*), whose goal (*karman*) is a cow and whose recipient (*sampradāna*) is a brāhmaṇa.

These theories discuss in detail the sources of information for establishing various relations, justifying such establishments providing supportive theoretical basis and arguments when they differ from other schools. Though these theories differ in the *mukhya-viśeṣya* and in the minor details such as the source of information in some cases, they unanimously accept major relations used in the Pāṇinian grammar to mark the relations between words. The hair-splitting analysis and due attention paid to the sources of information in a language string made us look at these theories from the computational perspective.

In the following chapters, we describe the role of the theories of *śābdabodha* in building a Sanskrit parser. In the next chapter we briefly describe the essential factors that aid the process of *śābdabodha*, together with the theories of word meaning and sentence meaning in order to understand the process of verbal cognition as described in the Indian tradition. Later we discuss the relevance of these theories from the view of processing the information mechanically. Finally we describe the three different models of Sanskrit parsers based on these theories, each successive model being an improvement over the earlier one.

2

Understanding Texts : Indian Theories

LANGUAGE is a means of communication. Communication is a two-way process where a speaker expresses his thoughts through a language string and the listener deciphers this language string into the underlying encoded thoughts. These two processes are the processes of generation and analysis. The process of generation, given all the necessary parameters to produce an utterance, is typically deterministic. There are some cases where the language allows alternative expressions leaving the choice open to the speaker.[1] Barring such a few cases, once a speaker makes all the choices for various parameters, a generator produces a single linguistic utterance that represents the thoughts of the speaker. Such a linguistic utterance may have ambiguity. One source of ambiguity is the homophonous, homonymous and polysemous words. Another source of ambiguity may be due to mapping of a two-dimensional structure of word relations to a linear structure. *Sandhi* process is another potential source for introducing ambiguities. When a listener receives a language string, which is a unidimensional representation of the speaker's thoughts, he has to reconstruct a thought from the linguistic utterance, which may be ambiguous, by relating the words through their meanings together. While doing so, the knowledge of the grammar of a language, the meaning of the words, context, shared knowledge, etc. play a crucial role in understanding/deciphering the message encoded in a linguistic expression. How does one understand a linguistic utterance? The theories of *śābdabodha* deal with this question.

The term *śābdabodha* stands for the cognition (*bodha*) arriving out of a language string (*śabda*). A sentence is composed of words and these words have the *śakti* (potential) to express meaning. Given a

---

1 For example, in the *Aṣṭādhyāyī*, the *mahāvibhāṣā* (a general alternative) corresponding to the *samāsa* (compounds) provides a choice to the speaker for use of a compounded form or its paraphrase.

sentence, from the word meanings, how does one decide whether the sentence is meaningful or not? If it is meaningful, how does one get the sentence meaning? Where is the information about the relation between the words encoded? And what is the structure of the cognition arising from the words in a sentence? These are the concerns of the theories of *śābdabodha*.

In this chapter we present the relevant views on word meaning and sentence meaning from the Indian theories. Only those concepts that are needed in order to understand the following chapters are presented here briefly. Interested readers may refer to Kunjunni Raja (1963) for more elaborate treatment of the subject. First we discuss the views on the meaning of a word. Then we describe the essential factors that are useful in knowing the meaning of a sentence. This is followed by a brief discussion on two dominant views on sentential meaning. Next the structure of the *śābdabodha* according to different schools is presented. Finally we provide a brief introduction to the procedure a commentator follows in order to explain any text.

2.1 Word Meaning

What is the meaning of "meaning"? What are the relations between the thoughts in the mind of a speaker, the referent in the real world and the word itself? These are some of the questions that have been bothering the philosophers in the East as well as in the West. In the West, Ferdinand de Saussure had assumed a direct relationship between the significant (word) and the signifié (meaning). There was a major criticism on this position by C.K. Ogden and I.A. Richards and also A.H. Gardiner for the omission of clear reference to the things/referents of the words. Ogden and Richard proposed a triangle showing the relations between a word as a symbol, its referent in the real world and the corresponding mental image or a thought or a reference. According to them a word symbolizes a thought or a reference that refers to the actual referent in the world. Thus for them a word stands for a referent only through a thought.

All Indian schools of thought assume a direct relationship between the *pada* (word) and *padārtha*[2] (literally word-meaning). Kunjunni Raja (1963), taking into consideration the Indian theories, argues that it is

2 *padasya arthaḥ = pada-arthaḥ = padārthaḥ*

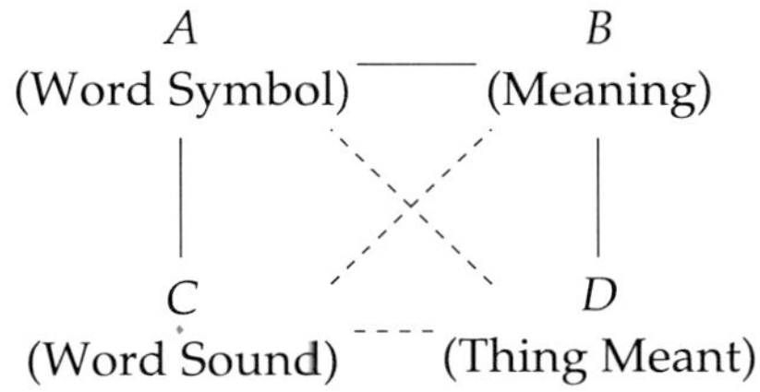

fig. 2.1: Kunjunni Raja's word-meaning rectangle

further necessary to distinguish between a word and its utterance. An utterance is a particular instance or a token of the type that corresponds to the symbolic word. The relation between an utterance, a symbolic word, its mental image/thought and the thing meant or the word in the real world is represented by him as shown in *fig*. 2.1. In this figure, a solid line shows a direct relation and a dotted line shows an indirect one.

The direct relation between word and its meaning in Indian thoughts as well as de Saussure's analysis of the relation between significant and signifié correspond to the top side of the square, viz. *AB*. △ *ABD* is the triangle proposed by Ogden–Richards. The vertex *C* represents the actual sounds of the word uttered. This is the *vaikṛta-dhvani*. This sound, which is attributed with personal variations, when abstracted gives us the *prākṛta-dhvani*, that is devoid of any personal variations. This *prākṛta-dhvani*, represented by the vertex *A* in the square, still consists of individual sound units, and is not yet cognized as an integral unit. In the next step, the *prākṛta-dhvani* (the whole utterance) is considered to be an integral unit representing an indivisible language-symbol. These three stages are the threefold nature of the revelation of speech, as explained by Bhartṛhari: *paśyantī*, *madhyamā* and *vaikharī*, corresponding respectively to *sphoṭa*, *prākṛta-dhvani* and *vaikṛta-dhvani* (Kunjunni Raja 1963).

A *pada*, according to a Vaiyākaraṇa, is a sequence of characters that end in either a nominal or a verbal suffix.[3] As such each *pada* consists of at least two parts – a stem and a suffix. For example, *gacchati* (goes) consists of two parts a root *gam* (to go) and a verbal suffix *ti* (third person singular present tense marker). In the case of a primary derivative *dhāvantam* (running), there are three units, viz. a

3 *suptiṅantam padam* – A 1.4.14

verbal root *dhāv* (to run), a *kṛt* suffix *śatṛ* (present participial marker) followed by a nominal suffix *am* (an accusative marker). Each of these parts is a meaningful unit – a morpheme. When a Vaiyākaraṇa describes a *śābdabodha* (verbal cognition), he meticulously describes the connection between meanings of each of these morphemes leading to the sentential meaning. These morphemes are termed *pada* by a Naiyāyika. According to a Naiyāyika, the essential nature of a *pada* is its significative power or *śakti*.[4] This significative power, we saw above, is the relation between a word and its meaning. It is also termed as *vṛtti*. Three types of *vṛtti*s are discussed in the Indian grammatical tradition. They are *abhidhā*, *lakṣaṇā* and *vyañjanā*. When the relation between word and its meaning is direct, it is called *abhidhā*. When the relation is indirect, based on the similarity or natural extension of the primary sense, the relation is called *lakṣaṇā*.[5] *Vyañjanā* is the relation between a word and its meaning other than its literal meaning or any extension thereof.

2.1.1 ABHIDHĀ (PRIMARY DENOTATION)

Abhidhā is the primary relation of the word with the sense resulting from the denotative capacity of the word. Based on the nature of these meanings, the primary meaning is further classified into four subcategories.

1. *Rūḍha* (*Conventional*). A *rūḍha* meaning is one which is conventional in nature. It is a convention that a word is being used in that sense. For example, *ghaṭa* to mean "a pot" and *paṭa* to mean "a cloth". This comes close to the notion of arbitrariness of a relation between the sound of a word and its meaning in the modern linguistics.
2. *Yaugika* (*Etymological*). All the derived words such as *kṛdanta*s (verbal nouns), *taddhitānta*s (secondary derivatives) and *samāsa*s (compounds) where the meaning of a derived word is compositional, fall under this category. Example of a *kṛdanta* is *gāyaka* (a singer), of a *taddhitānta* is *manuṣyatā* (humanity) and of a *samasta-pada* is *vidyālaya* (literally, an abode of knowledge;

---

[4] *śaktam padam* – *Tarkasaṁgraha*, 48

[5] There is a school which distinguishes between the similarity and the extension through some relation. The former is called *gauṇī* and the latter *lakṣaṇā*.

a school). In the *Bṛhaddevatā*, these are further classified into *dhātujam* (derived from a verbal root), *dhātuja-jātam* (derived from a derivative of a verbal root), *samastārthajam* (derived from a compound), *vākyajam* (derived from a sentence as in *iti ha āsa = itihāsa*), and finally *nirvācyam* (a confused derivation as in *siṁha* (a lion) being derived from *hiṁsa* (to kill)).

3. *Yogarūḍha* (*Etymological but Restricted by Convention*). Words whose etymological meaning is restricted by convention fall under this category. For example, the word *paṅkaja* etymologically refers to anything that is born out of mud.[6] But its usage is restricted only to a lotus. As such this meaning is termed as *yogarūḍha*. Some *taddhitānta* and *samasta-pada*s would fall under this category.
4. *Yaugikarūḍha* (*Both Etymological and Conventional Independently*). Words which express etymological as well as conventional meaning independently belong to this category. *Udbhid*, for example, when taken in an etymological sense means that which breaks or bursts through. And *udbhid*, conventionally, is the name of a sacrifice in Vedic rituals.

2.1.2 LAKṢAṆĀ (IMPLICATION)

The function of a word, denoting a referent different from its primary one but related to it, is called *lakṣaṇā*. This implied meaning is further classified as follows:

1. *nirūḍha-lakṣaṇā* (natural/unintentional implication)
2. *prayojanavatī-lakṣaṇā* (intentional implication)
   a. *śuddhā* (pure)
      i. *ajahad* (inclusive)
      ii. *jahad* (exclusive)
      iii. *jahad–ajahad* (partially inclusive)
   b. *gauṇī* (qualitative implication)
      i. *sāropā* (superimposition)
      ii. *sādhyavasānā* (intro-susceptive)

---

[6] *paṅkāt jāyate iti*।

Nirūḍha-lakṣaṇā (*Natural Implication*)

If the original, primary or etymological meaning of a word totally disappears and the actual meaning in use is more or less the only meaning it is used for, then such a usage is called *nirūḍha-lakṣaṇā*. For example, the word *kuśala* has the etymological meaning *kuśān lāti iti* (the one who brings the *kuśa* grass). But this word is being used in the sense of an expert. It was a very skilful job to cut the *kuśa* grass and bring it. So not everybody could do it. And thus over a period of time the meaning got generalized to "an expert/skilful person", not necessarily in cutting the *kuśa* grass but expert in any job. Another such word is *dvirepha* literally meaning two "*r*"s. The word *bhramara* has two "*r*"s, and hence sometimes it is referred to as *dvirepha*. Such an extension will make sense only if such usages are in vogue. Otherwise communication will break down. We notice that this class of *nirūḍha-lakṣaṇā* is very close to the class of *yogarūḍha* discussed earlier. Kunjunni Raja (1963) points to a fine distinction between *yogarūḍha* and *nirūḍha-lakṣaṇā*. According to him the former restricts the meaning while the latter one generalizes it. In the case of *paṅkaja* the meaning is restricted from "anything that grows in the mud" to the lotus, whereas in the case of *kuśala* the meaning is generalized from "anybody who is expert in cutting the grass" to "an expert in any activity".

The Mīmāṁsakas have a different connotation of *nirūḍha-lakṣaṇā*. For them this is a technical term used for words which are polysemous with one primary meaning and the other one secondary. For example the verbal suffix *tiṅ* denotes *bhāvanā* as the primary meaning and the expressed *kāraka* such as *kartṛ* or *karman* as the secondary meaning. This secondary meaning is called *nirūḍha lakṣya*.

Prayojanavatī-lakṣaṇā (*Intentional Implication*)

When a word does not have any connotation for the intended meaning, but the motive of the speaker is to use the word for the intended meaning, such a usage is called *prayojanavatī*. Of course a speaker cannot use any word to intend anything at his whim. Only under certain conditions can the extended meaning be properly conveyed to the listener. A speaker has some purpose (or intention) in his mind when he uses a word in its extended sense. Hence this type of extension is called *prayojanavatī*. This extension can be of two types: either through the quality of the referent or through the referent itself. When the extension depends on a quality the referent possesses, the extended meaning is termed as *gauṇī*, and when it depends on the referent itself, it is termed as *śuddhā*. The *śuddhā* and *gauṇī* are further classified as below:

1. *Śuddhā-lakṣaṇā* (*Pure Implication*). Depending on whether the extended meaning includes the primary meaning or not, the extension of meaning further is of three types.
   a. *Ajahad-lakṣaṇā* (*Inclusive Implication*). When the denotative meaning is also included in the extended meaning of a word, it is termed as *ajahad-lakṣaṇā* (that extended meaning which does not leave the original meaning). For example, in the sentence *kākebhyaḥ dadhi rakṣa* (protect the curd from the crows), what is intended is to protect the curd not only from crows but also from all the animals and birds that will spoil the curd. Thus here while *kāka* refers to the extended meaning, it still includes its primary meaning "crow".
   b. *Jahad-lakṣaṇā* (*Exclusive Implication*). When a word denotes only an extended meaning and the denotative meaning has no role to play in the interpretation, it is a case of *jahad-lakṣaṇā* (that extended meaning which leaves the original meaning). For example, *gaṅgāyām ghoṣaḥ* (literally, village on Ganges). Here *gaṅgā* no more refers to the river, but refers only to its bank.
   c. *Jahad–ajahad-lakṣaṇā* (*Implication with Partial Inclusion*). Sometimes, only a part of the meaning is included with the extended meaning. Such a meaning is termed *jahad–ajahad-lakṣaṇā*. In example such as *paṭo dagdhaḥ* (cloth is burnt), *paṭa* refers to only a part of the cloth and not complete. Another example of this type is *tat-tvam-asi* (thou art that). *Tat* refers to the Universal Soul. But when *tat* is equated with *tvam*, the equality is with the Universal Soul devoid of all qualifications such as omnipresence. Thus while *tat* retains its meaning, part of it is also stripped off. Hence it is an example of implication with partial inclusion.
2. *Gauṇī-lakṣaṇā* (*Secondary Implication*). *Gauṇī-lakṣaṇā* is of two types, viz. *sāropā* and *sādhyavasānā*. The type of *lakṣaṇā*, where

there is an imposition of some quality of one object on the other, it is called *sāropā*. For example, *mukham candraḥ iva* (moon-like face). When the imposition is total, it is called *sādhyavasānā*. The standard example is *ayam candraḥ* (this is moon), where *ayam* points to the face of a beautiful woman.

The nature of extension is also further studied by the Indians. Depending upon the nature of the extension, various classifications of *lakṣaṇā* have been proposed. See Appendix B for details.

2.1.3 VYAÑJANĀ (SUGGESTION)

In addition to the primary and extended meanings, rhetoricians and grammarians accept a third category, viz. suggestive meaning or the *vyaṅgyārtha*. An oft-quoted example is *gato 'stam arkaḥ* (the sun has set).

> *gato 'stam arko bhātindur yānti vāsāya pakṣiṇaḥ* ।
> *ity evam ādi kim kāvyam vārttām enām pracakṣate* ॥
> – *Kāvyālaṁkāra* II.77

> The sun has set, the moon shines, the birds go home to rest. In such and similar examples, there is no poetry. These are simple cases of *vārttā*. – Masson 1979

While on the face of it, a sentence such as *gato 'stam arkaḥ* looks like a simple sentence, there is suggestive meaning hidden behind it. In Mammaṭa's *Kāvyaprakāśa* we find a brilliant explanation of the sentence *gato 'stam arkaḥ*, explaining how suggestions depend on the listener, the speaker and the context (Masson 1979), as listed below:

1. A general would understand that

   The time for destroying the enemy has approached.

2. A woman eager to meet her lover might be told by her confidante the time has come to

   Go to meet your lover.

3. Friends of a woman ready to meet her lover would mean

   Your lover has almost arrived.

4. One worker would say this to another worker in the sense

   Let us stop working now.

5. A servant speaking to a brāhmaṇa would mean

It is time to perform your sandhyā.

6. A mother may say this to a child to mean
   Don't go far.
7. A householder, speaking to a cow-herder would mean
   Bring the cows home.
8. A friend on a hot day would say this to another friend to mean
   Now it is no longer hot.
9. The owner of a shop, saying this to his servant, may mean
   It is now time to put away the goods.

From these examples we see that the suggestive meaning is different for different speakers, listeners and contexts. These meanings thus have a sociocultural aspect. The suggested meanings depending upon various circumstances are practically endless. And these are over and above the literal and the metaphoric meanings.

The importance of suggestive meaning for a human being has been noticed since time immemorial. Literal meaning is just a part of the meaning. Many a time in discourse, the suggestive meaning plays an important role, as we saw above. Unless one looks at the suggestive meaning, one may even not understand the significance of the speech.

Naiyāyikas and Mimāṁsakas are more confined to the literal meaning of the text. According to Naiyāyikas, suggestive meaning is arrived at through the process of inference. Discourse analysis through the process of inference can lead to the suggestive meaning. Both Mīmāṁsakas and Naiyāyikas want accuracy and precision in the use of words. They want objectivity in the analysis. Suggestive meanings on the other hand are subjective. They do not have any boundaries and are limited only by the poet's imagination.

2.2 Necessary Conditions for Verbal Cognition

The process of cognition arising from a linguistic utterance is studied in detail by the Indians under the theories of *śābdabodha*. Kumārila Bhaṭṭa, a Mīmāṁsaka, in his *Tantravārttika* (Sastri 1903) discusses three factors that explain how various isolated words which comprise a sentence result in the syntactic unity of a sentence giving rise to the sentential meaning.

ākāṅkṣā sannidhānaṁ ca yogyatā ceti ca trayam ।
sambandhakāraṇatvena kḷptaṁ nānantaraśrutiḥ ॥
– *Tantravārttikam*, vol. I, p. 455

Mutual expectancy (*ākāṅkṣā*), proximity (*sannidhi*) and congruity (*yogyatā*) constitute the grounds of relationship; mere immediate sequence is not a ground of relationship.
– Kunjunni Raja 1963: 156

Ākāṅkṣā (expectancy), *yogyatā* (congruity) and *sannidhi* (proximity) are the three essential factors for *śābdabodha*. To this, later another factor, viz. *tātparya* (the intention of the speaker or the purport of the sentence) was added. In what follows, we describe in brief each of these four factors.

2.2.1 ĀKĀṄKṢĀ (EXPECTANCY)

We first come across the term *ākāṅkṣā* in the definition of a *vākya* (sentence) in Jaimini's *Mīmāṁsāsūtra* 2.1.46:

arthaikatvāt ekam vākyam sākāṅkṣam cet vibhāge syāt ।

A group of words forms a sentence

1. if, when separated, the words have mutual expectancy, and
2. if the group of words denote a single meaning/if it serves a single purpose.*

Thus *ākāṅkṣā*, expressed through syntax, among words is a necessary condition for a group of words to form a sentence. Literally *ākāṅkṣā* is the desire on the part of a listener to know (*jñātum icchā*) the other words in a sentence are needed for complete understanding. Now if *ākāṅkṣā* is the curiosity (*jijñāsā*) on the part of a listener then after listening to a verbal form such as *ānayati* (brings), a listener will have a curiosity to know who brings, what he brings, how he brings and so on. Further if the object of bring is, say, a cow, the listener may have further curiosities such as to find out which coloured cow to bring, what is the purpose of bringing her and so on. There is no end to such curiosities. These curiosities are more of a psychological nature than of a syntactic one.

The Naiyāyikas made a clear distinction between the psychological

---

* The word *artha* is ambiguous between "meaning" and "purpose". Hence two interpretations.

and the syntactic expectancy. *Ākāṅkṣā*, according to Naiyāyikas, is the syntactic expectancy a word has in order to correlate with another. For example, in the word *dvāraṁ* (to the door), the stem *dvāra* (door) denotes an object in the real world and the *am* suffix (an accusative marker) marks an expectancy of a verb whose *karman* (object) can be *dvāra*. This expectancy which arises from the knowledge of the suffix is a syntactic one, and it allows one to connect the word *dvāram* with a verb, say, *pidhehi* (close). This expectancy is not one way, but mutual. It is also not psychological. It is based on the usages of the verbs in a sentence and is thus syntactic in nature. As another illustration, consider two verbs *gamḷ* (to go) and *caraṁ* (to wander). Both the verbs *gamḷ* and *caraṁ* are used in the sense of motion (*gamḷ gatau* and *caraṁ gatau*). However the verb *gamḷ* is *sakarmaka* (transitive) while *caraṁ* is *akarmaka* (intransitive). This requirement of a *karman* (object) for *gamḷ* is not psychological, but is based on the usage of the verb.

The expectancies which are mutual, direct and natural are termed *niyata* or *utthita-ākāṅkṣā* (restricted or risen expectancy) (Kunjunni Raja 1963). The expectancy between a verb and the words denoting *kāraka*s or between relational words falls under this category.[7] In contrast to mutual expectancy, the expectancy that is unilateral is called *aniyata* or *utthāpya-ākāṅkṣā* (unrestricted or to be raised). This is aroused only if necessary. So it is potential. For example, in a phrase such as *white cow*, the *ākāṅkṣā* of *white* for a substantive is natural, but the *ākāṅkṣā* of *cow* to have an adjective is potential. It gets aroused only in the presence of an adjective such as *white*. Even a noun in apposition may arouse an expectancy. The example discussed in the *Rāmarudrī* commentary on the *Dinakarī* commentary on the *Nyāyasiddhāntamuktāvalī* is *udayati candraḥ kumudabāndhavaḥ* (Jere 2002) (rises the moon, the friend of a lotus that opens its petals during night and closes them in the morning). After hearing *udayati candraḥ* (the moon rises) all the expectancies are fulfilled. And thus understanding is complete. Now when one hears *kumudabāndhavaḥ* (friend of a lotus) then this word needs to be related to one of the words uttered earlier because there cannot be freely hanging words in a meaningful sentence. This word has an expectancy of a substantive and thus it gets related to *candraḥ*. Both these cases are examples of unilateral expectancy.

---

7 *Niyatākāṅkṣā: yathā kriyākārakapadānām parasparākāṅkṣā* (Jere 2002).

2.2.2 SANNIDHI (PROXIMITY)

Sannidhi is defined in the *Tarkasaṁgraha* as an utterance of words without any gap (*padānām avilambena uccāraṇam*) (*Tarkasaṁgraha* 47), or as the presentation of word meanings without any intervention (*a-vyavadhānena pada-janya padārtha-upasthitiḥ*). From the text processing point of view, the latter definition is important. If some unrelated words intervene between related words, then such an utterance does not produce any verbal cognition. To make the point clear, Viśvanātha Pañcānana, in his *Nyāyasiddhāntamuktāvalī* (Joshi 1985), gives the following example:

> Skt: *giriḥ bhuktam agnimān devadattena* ।
>
> Gloss: Hill {m, sg, nom.} is_eaten fiery {m, sg, nom.} Devadatta {ins.}.
>
> Eng: Hill is fiery. (It) is eaten by Devadatta.

The words *giriḥ* (hill) and *agnimān* (fiery) have mutual expectancy so do *bhuktam* (eaten) and *devadattena* (by Devadatta). *Bhuktam*, being a past participle in the neuter, expects a *kartṛ* in the instrumental case and a *karman* in the neuter nominative. But this group of four words does not have a neuter nominative. So we interpret either the verb *bhuj* (to eat) in this context to be an intransitive or consider the example to be a case of the ellipsis of the *karman kāraka*. In either case this group of four words corresponds to two independent sentences whose arguments are intertwined. *Bhuktam* intervenes between the words *giriḥ* and *agnimān* which have mutual expectancy. Similarly *agnimān* intervenes between the related words *bhuktam* and *devadattena*. This intervention forms an obstacle to verbal cognition.

The condition of not having intervention is only a necessary condition in the process of *śābdabodha*. For, even non-intervention may give rise to more than one *śābdabodha*s: one of them as a true cognition (*pramātmaka-jñāna*) and the other one as a false cognition (*bhramātmaka-jñāna*) as explained by Viśvanātha Pañcānana in the *Nyāyasiddhāntamuktāvalī* (Joshi 1985) with the following example:

> Skt: *nīlaḥ ghaṭaḥ dravyam paṭaḥ* ।
>
> Gloss: Blue {nom.} pot {nom.} thing {nom.} cloth {nom.}.

This may lead to two cognitions, as described below:

1. The pot is blue, and the cloth is a thing.
2. The cloth is blue, and the pot is a thing.

There are three situations possible: The first one in which only the pot is blue, the other one only the cloth is blue and the third one in which both the pot and the cloth are blue. In the first two situations then, only one among these cognitions would lead to a true cognition and the other one to a false cognition, while in the third situation, both the cognitions would be true. The notion of true cognition and false cognition is thus context dependent. The notion of *sannidhi* on the other hand depends only on the expectancies and the compatibility of the meanings of the words involved.

2.2.3 YOGYATĀ (CONGRUITY)

Yogyatā is suitability or compatibility. Here the term is being used in the sense of mutual compatibility or fitness of meanings of related words in a linguistic utterance. *Yogyatā* is defined in the *Tarkasaṁgraha* as the *artha-abādhaḥ*[8] (absence of obstruction in meaning). In the *Paramalaghumañjūṣā* it is defined as *paraspara-anvaya-prayojaka-dharmavattvam* (a property of promoting mutual relationship), in the Śabda section of the *Tattvacintāmaṇi* it is defined as *bādhaka-pramā-virahaḥ* (lack of hindrance of valid cognition) and the *Vākyārthamātṛkāvṛtti* defines it as *sambandha-arhatvam* (ability to establish a relation). Thus we see that while some have defined it as a positive property, others have defined it in terms of absence. Each of these definitions, therefore, will have different implications in its usage. We will look at some aspects of these implications from the computational point of view in Chap. 3.

The pair of examples discussed in the literature for explaining the concept of *yogyatā* is *payasā siñcati* "(He) sprinkles with water" vs *vahninā siñcati* "(He) sprinkles with fire". The previous one satisfies *yogyatā* while the latter one lacks it. There are different opinions with respect to the verbal cognition in the absence of *yogyatā*. Naiyāyikas insist on *yogyatā* as one of the essential factors in the process of verbal cognition, since for them *śabda* is a means of valid cognition. Vaiyākaraṇas, on the other hand, admit that even in the absence of *yogyatā*, verbal cognition does take place. The basic difference between the two opposite opinions is due to the differences in their basic axioms. For a Naiyāyika, linguistic expressions are the representations of reality whereas for a Vaiyākaraṇa it is the representation of a

[8] All these definitions are listed in Jhalkikar's *Nyāyakośa*, p. 675.

mental creation. The position of Mīmāṁsakas is not different from that of the Vaiyākaraṇas. In the *Ślokavārttika* 1.1.2.6, Kumārila Bhaṭṭa clearly states:

> *atyantāsaty api hy arthe jñānam śabdaḥ karoti hi* ।
> *abādhāt tu pramām atra svataḥ prāmāṇyaniścalām* ॥
>
> When the meanings are inconsistent, that is, there is lack of *yogyatā* among the meanings, the overall meaning will still be conceivable. When the meanings are consistent, that is, when there is congruity among the meanings of various words in a sentence, the sentence produces not only a verbal cognition but also a valid cognition.
>
> – Kunjunni Raja, *Indian Theories of Meaning*, p. 165, n 2

Thus we see that a distinction is made between a verbal cognition and a valid cognition. The verbal cognition needs to be valid for the *śabda* to be a means of valid cognition (*pramāṇa*). The sentence *vahninā siñcati* though cannot produce a valid cognition, one may still imagine another possible world where fire is in liquid form. Alternately, if the incongruity may be explained by resorting to a secondary meaning, *vahninā siñcati* would lead to a valid cognition. There is yet another class of incongruity as in the case of *square circle* or *vandhyā-suta* (son of a barren woman) where the meanings are logically inconsistent and in no way one can assign metaphorical interpretation to them leaving them inconceivable.

Thus there are three different situations:

1. The word meanings are mutually congruous (*payasā siñcati*).
2. The word meanings are not mutually congruous, but the meanings are conceivable (*vahninā siñcati*)
   a. either through the metaphoric meaning,
   b. or in a possible world.
3. The word meanings are logically inconsistent/contradictory (*square circle*).

2.2.4 TĀTPARYA (PURPORT)

According to Gaṅgeśopādhyāya and Viśvanātha, *tātparya* is the fourth factor essential for verbal cognition.[9] It is the meaning of a sentence what a speaker intends it to mean (and not what a speaker has in his

[9] *vaktur icchā tu tātparyam* – (Śabdakhaṇḍa, *Bhāṣāpariccheda* 84) Joshi 1985: 198.

mind). A speaker may intend a listener to understand the same text differently in different contexts. While the context helps a listener in deciding the intended sense, sometimes the speaker may use intonation to communicate the intended meaning. *Tātparya* is also used to explain the meaning of a sentence that is over and above the sum total of the meaning of its constituent words. Vedāntins and Mīmāṁsakas, being engaged in the interpretation of the Vedic texts which they consider to be authorless (*apauruṣeya*), formulate their theory of verbal cognition without any reference to the speaker. According to them, it is the meaning conveyed by the capacity of words themselves that helps in determining the intended meaning of the passage.

Naiyāyikas discuss various cases of *tātparya* and the sources that help in deciding the *tātparya* in each case:

1. The first case is the one where a homonymous word is used leading to ambiguity. The example is

   Skt: *saindhavam ānaya* ।

   Gloss: Salt/Horse {acc.} bring.

   Here the context determines the speakers' intended meaning. If you are having lunch, it means salt, and in the context of a war, it refers to a horse. Of course, in the context of a dinner in the battlefield, it may mean either!

2. The second case is where the sentence is ambiguous syntactically. The example discussed in the literature is

   Skt: *ayam eti putraḥ rājñaḥ puruṣaḥ apasāryatām* ।

   Gloss: Here comes a_son of_a_king man should_be_removed

   which is ambiguous between "Here comes the son of a king, the man should be removed" and "Here comes the son, the king's man should be removed", depending on whether the word *rājñaḥ* is connected with *putraḥ* or with *puruṣaḥ*. Again it is the context in which this sentence is uttered that removes the ambiguity.

3. The third case arises when a speaker intends the secondary meaning, while the primary meaning makes full sense, as in the case of *kākebhyaḥ dadhi rakṣatām* (protect the curd from the crow). Here the meaning of *kāka* as a crow makes perfect sense.

But what is intended is not only the protection of the curd from a crow, but from all those animals and birds who would spoil the curd. Thus, this is a case where the speaker's intention plays a more prominent role than the context.

Nāgeśa, a Vaiyākaraṇa, in his *Laghumañjūṣā* has accepted *tātparya* as one of the factors in the process of verbal cognition and, according to him, the clues for deciding the intended meaning are provided by the context.

Mīmāṁsakas refer to six *liṅga*s (indicators) for deciding the intended meaning. They are:

1. *upakrama–upasaṁhāra* (consistency in the meaning from the beginning to the end),
2. *abhyāsa* (repetition of the main topic),
3. *apūrvatā* (novelty in the subject matter),
4. *phala* (result intended),
5. *arthavāda* (corroborative/eulogistic remarks), and
6. *upapatti* (arguments in favour of the main topic).

Use of these indicators ensures that the intended meaning can be objectively inferred using the context.

Some Ālaṁkārikas (rhetoricians) include *tātparya* in suggestive meaning.[10] Thus, a sentence *gato 'stam arkaḥ* (the sun has set) may mean different things to listeners in different contexts, as seen earlier. For a child playing in a playground, it may mean "now it is getting dark, and it is time to stop playing and go home", for a brāhmaṇa, it may mean "it is time to do the *sandhyā-vandana* (a ritual at dusk)", and for a young person it may mean "it is time to meet his/her lover".

Here we note that, while Naiyāyikas, Vaiyākaraṇas and Mīmāṁsakas rely on the literal meaning, the Ālaṁkārikas use the word *tātparya* to refer to the suggestive meaning.

2.3 Vākyārtha (Sentential Meaning)

When we hear a sentence, we get a unitary meaning from it. There are two different approaches to the study of sentential meaning in Indian

---

[10] *tātparyārthaḥ ca vyaṅgyārtha eva – Pratāparudrīya* II under v 5 (Kumārasvāmin 1909)

tradition. They are *khaṇḍa-pakṣa* (analytic approach) and *akhaṇḍa-pakṣa* (gestalt view). According to the *khaṇḍa-pakṣa*, the words in a sentence have autonomous status and the word meanings contribute towards the sentential meaning. In the *akhaṇḍa-pakṣa* view, the words in a sentence do not have any relevance. The sentence is an indivisible and integral linguistic unit. One gets the meaning of a sentence by *vākya-sphoṭa*. This is like a gestalt effect. The words in a sentence are just pointers to arrive at the correct meaning. From the computational perspective, the *khaṇḍa-pakṣa* provides us a better and economic model, since we can compose the meaning of a sentence from those of its constituting units.

Under this approach of *khaṇḍa-pakṣa* and from the point of view of understanding, information needed for deciphering any sentence falls under three categories:

1. a relation between a word and its meaning,
2. relations between the words in a sentence, and
3. generating the overall meaning of a sentence using the above information.

Earlier we have seen three types of relations between a word and its meaning. In the next chapter we will see how to connect the words in a sentence. Now we look at what Indian grammatical theories of meaning have to say about the third factor. The third factor deals with an important aspect of the theory of verbal comprehension and the major debate on whether the sentence meaning is the collection of the word meanings that comprise it or it is the sense we get from the collection of related words. The former theory is known as Abhihitānvayavāda and the latter is known as Anvitābhidhānavāda. The Mīmāṁsā system is known for the science of sentence interpretation (Vākyaśāstra). Whether the sentential meaning arises from the words constituting it or from the meanings of the words in a sentence is debated by the Mīmāṁsakas. This debate resulted in two prominent schools – Prābhākara and Bhāṭṭa – led by Prabhākara Mīmāṁsaka and Kumārila Bhaṭṭa, respectively.

The Prābhākara school argues that the words convey their individual meaning as a connected entity in syntactic relation to other words in a sentence. Thus the sentence meaning is the sum total of the meanings of such connected words. Or in other words, a word in a sentence does not convey its own meaning in isolation, but it conveys the meaning only in the context, as related to other word(s) in the sentence. This theory cites an example of a child learning a language through observation and the process of inclusion and exclusion (*āvāpa-udvāpa* or *anvaya-vyatireka*). They believe that every word expresses its meaning only as related to the other words in a sentence. One cannot comprehend a word in isolation. What a word conveys is its meaning in relation to the other words. Thus for example, in the sentence *gām ānaya* (bring a cow), the meaning of the verb *bring* is in relation to the object of bringing, viz. a cow. If the object of bringing changes, the meaning of the verb *bring* also changes accordingly, since bringing a cow will be different from, say, bringing salt, as far as the action is concerned. In bringing a cow, you may tie a rope to the cow and pull her, but you will bring salt in a box. Thus the meaning conveyed by the words is that of the whole sentence, each word contributing its meaning in syntactic connection with the other. For establishing the syntactic connection and deciding the compatibility of the meanings, they do use the conditions of *ākāṅkṣā*, *yogyatā* and *sannidhi*. This school of thought explaining the sentence meaning is known as Anvitābhidhānavāda, since the connected words (*anvita*) convey the meaning expressed by such a connection (*abhidhāna*).

The Bhāṭṭa school claims that the words in a sentence express their individual meanings and then the three factors, viz. *ākāṅkṣā*, *yogyatā* and *sannidhi*, condition them further to generate the sentential meaning. Thus according to this theory, when a sentence is heard, the listener isolates the words from one another and gets the meaning of each word. Then the expectancy (*ākāṅkṣā*) connects the words, provided the meanings are mutually congruous (*yogya*) and further the constraint of proximity (*sannidhi*) checks that there is no violation of the principle of proximity in the association of words. This school of thought discussing the sentence meaning is known as Abhihitānvayavāda.

We notice that the process of arriving at the sentential meaning following the Mīmāṁsā schools is a bottom-up process, since they are Khaṇḍapakṣavādins (believers in the analytical method). Both of these schools accept the three conditions for arriving at the sentential meaning mentioned above. We have followed this bottom-up process for building an automatic sentential parser. Since we are aiming at developing a parser that shows the relations between the words in a sentence, and not at making the computer understand a sentence, we use the word meanings only when required and as much required. We start with the meaningful units in a sentence. Some of these meaningful units termed function words (*vibhakti*s) establish the relations between the content words (*prātipadika/dhātu*). Such a relation results in the composite meaning of the related words together. This process of relating words to each other in composite units is continued until all the words in a sentence are related in a single composite unit.

The compositionality of word meanings is discussed by Patañjali in the Samarthāhnika of the *Mahābhāṣya*. Though he is discussing the meaning of compound words, many of the issues are the same for inflected words in a sentence. Patañjali discusses four different types of *sāmarthya*,[11] viz. *saṅgatārtha* (united meaning), *saṁsṛṣṭārtha* (collective meaning), *samprekṣitārtha* (considered meaning) and *sambaddhārtha* (related meaning). The analogies he gives for these four meanings are: oil with ghee (which are impossible to separate from each other, once mixed), wood fire (where we can separate one log of wood from the other), a cow tied to a nail with a rope (the two things the cow and the nail are easily separable) and a relation of a father with his son (where we see two distinct entities, with an invisible bond between them). We see a difference in the separability of the items involved in these four cases. Similarly, Patañjali says, in the case of compounds also, we see a spectrum in the compositionality of the meaning of a compound and that of its components. At one extreme, we have compound words whose meaning is completely new, where it is hard to find the traces of the meaning of individual components, and at the other end we have compounds whose meaning is totally composed of the meanings of its parts. The situation with the sentence is similar. There are cases where the sentential meaning is completely compositional and cases where it is totally non-compositional.

2.4 Structure of Verbal Cognition

Śābdabodha is the cognition arising from the meaning of a sentence. In

11 *saṅgatārtham samartham saṁsṛṣṭārtham samartham samprekṣitārtham samartham sambaddhārtham samartham iti* – under A 2.1.1 in MBh

the *Nyāyasiddhāntamuktāvalī* it is defined as the result[12] of an activity of remembrance of the meaning of words where the cognition of words act as an instrument. In the process of *śābdabodha*, first of all, a word is cognized. This cognition of a word acts as an instrument for the activity of remembrance of its meaning. The knowledge of the relation between a word and its meaning assists in this activity. This activity produces the verbal cognition. We have seen above various factors involved in the production of the verbal import of a sentence. Now we will see the structure of the verbal import. The verbal import in all the three schools, viz. Vyākaraṇa, Nyāya and Mīmāṁsā, is represented as a modifier–modified relation. All the three schools differ in some minor details regarding the chief qualificand and also the nature of information coded in various morphemes. We describe here the Vaiyākaraṇas' (grammarians') and Naiyāyikas' (logicians') *śābdabodha* with an example.[13]

Consider a sentence

Skt: *rāmaḥ vanam gacchati* ।

Gloss: Rāma {nom.} forest {acc.} goes.

Eng: Rāma goes to the forest.

In the verbal cognition, first, every word is cognized as made up of two morphemes: a *prakṛti* (stem/root) and a *pratyaya* (suffix). Thus the above sentence is composed of six morphemes, viz. *rāma*, *su*, *vana*, *am*, *gam* and *ti*. Then through the denotative capacities of these morphemes, one gets the meaning of each part. Each nominal stem (*prātipadika*) denotes three aspects,[14] viz. *jāti* (genus), *vyakti* (an individual) and *liṅga* (gender). Thus *rāma* denotes a person by name Rāma with masculine gender. *Vana* denotes a "forest" with neuter gender. A verbal root denotes an activity favourable to the result

[12] *padajñānam tu karaṇam dvāram tatra padārthadhīḥ* ।
śābdabodhaḥ phalam tatra śaktidhīḥ sahakāriṇī ॥ (*Śabdakhaṇḍa*, *Bhāṣāpariccheda* 81) (Joshi 1985: p. 171)

[13] For more details about the differences among various schools, and also for more varied examples, please refer to Subbarao (1969), Deshpande (2007) and Scharf (1990).

[14] There are differences of opinion among different schools regarding what information each nominal stem codes. We do not go here into the details, since it is outside the scope of this book. Interested readers may refer to Subbarao (1969) for more details.

(*phala-anukūla-vyāpāra*). Thus *gam* denotes an activity favourable to the contact with the desired region (*uttaradeśa-saṁyoga-anukūla-vyāpāra*), in this case a forest. The verbal suffix *ti* denotes the doer of the activity (*kartṛ*) in addition to the number (*saṅkhyā*), person (*puruṣa*) and tense (*kāla*).

The suffix *am* denotes the locus of the result of the activity (*phalāśraya*), viz. the forest. And the suffix *su* has the same denotation as that of *rāma*. Now mutual expectancy, meaning congruity and proximity come into play. The expectancy of the verb *gam* to have distinct loci for the result of the action and the activity of the action, i.e. for *phala* and *vyāpāra*, respectively, demands two distinct nouns satisfying this expectancy. The nominal suffix *am* represents the accusative case and thus denotes the *karman* (*phalāśraya*), and the verbal suffix *ti* marks the locus of the doer of the action. *Su* has the same denotation as that of *rāma*, which agrees in number and person with the denotation of *ti*, thus establishing a relation of non-difference (*abheda*) between the locus of the doer of the activity and *rāma*. For each such connection it is ensured that the connected meaning is congruous and there is no violation of proximity. The collection of all these meanings results in the following *śābdabodha*.

eka-vana-abhinna-āśrayaka-uttara-deśa-saṁyoga-anukūlaḥ ।
eka-rāma-abhinna-āśraya-nirūpakaḥ vartamāna-kālikaḥ vyāpāraḥ ॥

An activity qualified by present tense, which takes place in Rāma, and the result of which is the contact with a forest.

Figure 2.2[15] shows the dynamics of information flow giving rise to the verbal import described above. The morphemes are shown in ovals and their denotations are shown in squares connected by dotted lines. The solid lines joining the meanings of various morphemes produce the verbal import.

The Naiyāyikas' *śābdabodha* for the same sentence is

eka-vana-karmaka-uttara-deśa-saṁyoga-anukūla-vyāpāra-janaka-vartamāna-kālika-kṛtimān rāmaḥ

Rāma is the locus of the present activity whose result is the contact with a forest.

---

[15] This and the following figure are adapted from the diagrammatic representations of *śābdabodha* in the Appendix of Subbarao (1969).

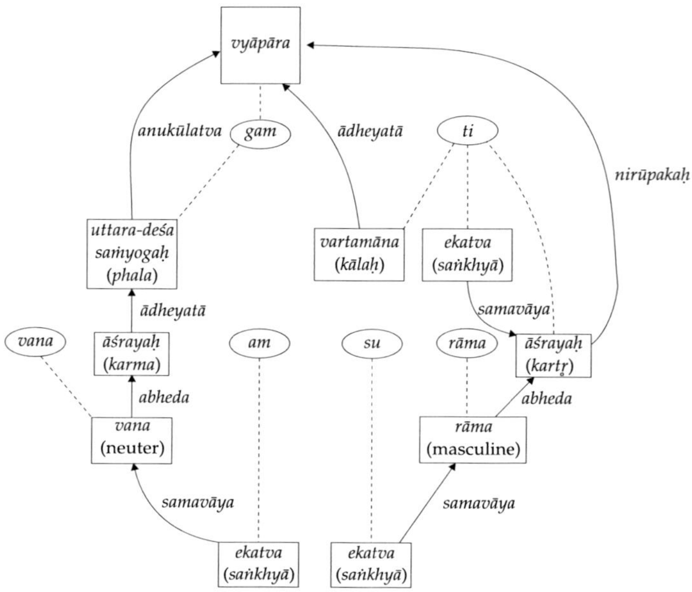

fig. 2.2: Grammarian's verbal import

The information flow is shown in *fig*. 2.3. The six morphemes in this *śābdabodha* are the same as those of Vaiyākaraṇas' *śābdabodha*. However, the modifier–modified relations are different. The major difference between the two *śābdabodha*s is the *mukhya-viśeṣya* (chief qualificand). For the grammarians, the chief qualificand is the activity denoted by the verb, while for the logicians, the chief qualificand is the substantive in nominative case.

2.5 Understanding Texts: Commentary Tradition

Free word order in Sanskrit had a key role in the emergence of the poetic style, rather than prose, as a natural style for Sanskrit compositions. Authors who have written Sanskrit prose also have taken advantage of the free word order to present texts that are consistent with the intended metre or are interesting from the aesthetics point of view. But it is also true that it is difficult to understand poetry compared to prose. This is evident from the fact that we notice the commentators, especially commenting on the *kāvya* (poetic) literature, first rewrite the verse in prose in some default word order and then comment on it. The issue of word order is not only restricted to the verse style, but even in prose we find a lot of stylistic variation in the word order.

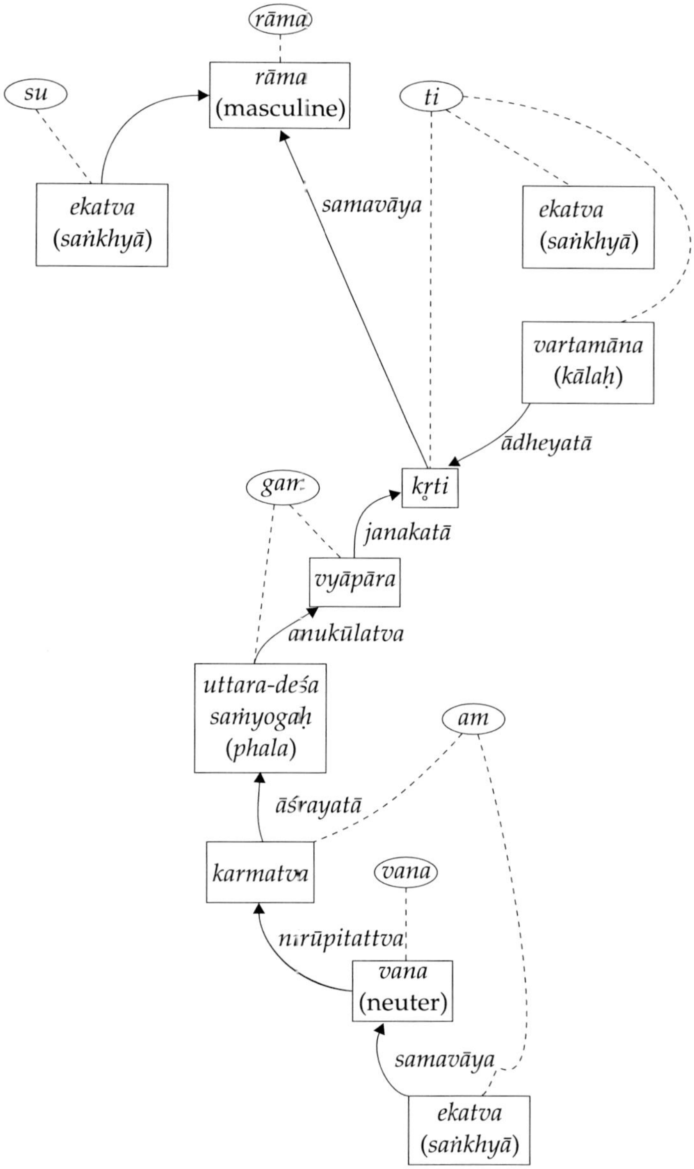

fig. 2.3: Logician's verbal import

For example, in order to bring certain point to focus, the author may bring it to the front thereby changing the default word order. This deviation from the normal word order adds an extra load on the part of the readers in understanding the poetry. In order to understand such texts, one needs special training for interpreting these texts. We come across commentaries on several of such Sanskrit poetic texts, which make their understanding easier. These commentaries follow a certain well-defined structure while explaining any *śloka*. According to the *Parāśara Purāṇa*[16] a commentary has the following five components:

1. Segmentation (*padaccheda*),
2. word analysis and its meaning (*pada-paricaya* and *padārtha-ukti*),
3. compound word analysis (*vigraha*),
4. sentential analysis (*vākya-yojanā*), and
5. answers to objections (*ākṣepeṣu samādhāna*).

In the Indian tradition, we see two methods followed by commentators while dealing with sentence-level analysis of *śloka*s (Tubb and Boose 2007). The first one is the *daṇḍa-anvaya* (also known as *anvayamukhī*). In this method, first the commentator arranges the words in the *śloka* in a prose form, following a default word order typically encountered in prose, described by the following verses:

ādau kartṛpadaṃ vācyaṃ dvitīyādipadaṃ tataḥ ।
ktvātumunlyap ca madhye tu kuryād ante kriyāpadam ॥
– *Samāsacakra, Kārikā* 4; Bhagirath 1901: 12

Starting with *kartṛ*, followed by other words, placing the non-finite verbal forms such as *ktvā, tumun, lyap* in between, place the main verb at the end.

viśeṣaṇaṃ puraskṛtya viśeṣyaṃ tadanantaram ।
kartṛ-karma-kriyā-yuktam etad anvaya-lakṣaṇam ॥
– *Samāsacakra, kārikā* 10; ibid.: 13

Starting with adjectives, targeting the headword, in the order of *kartṛ–karma–kriyā* (subject–object–verb) gives an *anvaya* (the natural order of words in a sentence).

And then the commentator further explains this *anvaya*, providing the morphological analysis of difficult words, explaining the compounds, providing grammatical details wherever necessary, supplying ellipsed

---

16 *padacchedaḥ padārthoktir vigraho vākyayojanā* ॥
ākṣepeṣu samādhānaṃ vyākhyānaṃ pañcalakṣaṇam ।
– *Parāśara Purāṇa* 18.17-18

words, explaining the meanings of some rare usages and finally paraphrasing the complete *śloka* in his own words, sometimes even providing the *śābdabodha*, following the theories described above.

The second method is known as *khaṇḍa-anvaya* (also known as *katham-bhūtinī*), where the commentator starts with the verb and the expectancies associated with the verb, and goes on filling these slots with the nominal forms in the *śloka*. Once the basic skeleton with all the expectancies is ready, then the commentator connects the *viśeṣaṇa*s (adjectives) to their *viśeṣya*s (headwords), providing flesh to the skeleton.

In both these approaches, the aim of the commentator is to unfold the encoded meaning. While doing so, the commentator takes clues from the theories of *śābdabodha*.

2.5.1 CANONICAL WORD ORDER

A commentator paraphrases the prose or poetry being commented upon in some default word order, called the *daṇḍānvaya*, or simply an *anvaya*, as described above.

Aralikatti (1991) has shown that the unmarked word order in Sanskrit is SOV. That is, all the arguments of a verb are placed to the left of the verb starting with the *kartṛ*, then *karman* followed by other arguments, the attributive adjectives are placed to the left of the noun they qualify and the predicate is at the end of the sentence. The subordinate clauses, if any, are before the predicate.

Taking clue from the verses described above describing the default prose word order and also learning from Aralikatti (1991), we define a sentence to be in "canonical word order" if it satisfies the following criterion:

> All the modifiers are placed to the left of the word they modify.

This is equivalent to the following:

1. The adjectives are to the left of the substantives they qualify.
2. All the arguments of a verb (either in finite form or in non-finite form) are to its left.
3. All the non-finite forms that modify the finite verb form are to its left.

This implies that the main verb[17] is always the last word of a sentence.

2.6 Conclusion

In this chapter we looked at three levels of meaning, viz. *abhidhā*, *lakṣaṇā* and *vyañjanā*, a word expresses. Then we saw the role of various factors such as *ākāṅkṣā*, *yogyatā*, *sannidhi* and *tātparya* that helps one to connect the words in a sentence through their meanings. This results into the *śābdabodha*. Two prevalent theories of sentential meanings were discussed and finally we also looked at the commentary tradition. We notice that these theories provide precise sources for each and every piece of information coded in a language string and describe the flow of information. In the next chapter, we shall discuss the importance of these concepts from mechanical processing point of view.

[17] The main verb can be either in finite form, or in a participial form with either of the suffixes: *kta*, *ktavatu* (Speijer 1886, reprint 2009), or any of the *kṛtya* suffixes, viz. *anīyar*, *tavyat*, *tavya*, *yat*, *kyap*, *ṅyat* or *kelimer*.

3

Śābdabodha Theories and Sanskrit Parsing

In this chapter we will see how the concepts of *ākāṅkṣā*, *yogyatā*, and *sannidhi* are useful in building a sentential parser for Sanskrit.

3.1 Ākāṅkṣā: Establishing Relations

Ākāṅkṣā[1] (desire), as we saw earlier, is the expectancy a word has for another word. This expectancy establishes a relation between two words. In order to connect a word with another, we should know where exactly is this information of expectancy coded? What is the semantics associated with such a relation? Is this information coded explicitly or is it implicit? If it is implicit, how do we figure it out? How do we name such a relation? Is there any repository of relation names? We try to provide answers to these questions below.

---

1 The concept akin to *ākāṅkṣā* in the phrase structure grammar is subcategorization frames where a verb is subcategorized into intransitive, transitive and bi-transitive according to the structure of verb phrase it is associated with. This concept is similar to the concept of valency of the dependency grammar of Tesniére. The only major difference between valency and the subcategorization frame is, valency also counts the subject as one argument while the earlier subcategorization frames took the subject for granted. The modern computational frameworks such as Head-driven Phrase Structure Grammar (HPSG) or Tree Adjoint Grammar (TAG) mark subject as a dependent argument. These subcategorization frames provide the specifications of the number and the syntactic category of the arguments a verb takes. For example, the subcategorization frames for the verbs sleep, eat and give are given below:

sleep [NP _]

eat [NP _ (NP)]

give [NP _ NP NP]/[NP _ NP to NP],

where the argument in parenthesis is optional.

The subcategorization is normally discussed with reference to verbs. But such subcategorization frames are also needed for other lexical categories such as nouns, adjectives. These frames are part of speaker's knowledge of the word, based on its usage, and thus more a part of a lexicon than grammar.

3.1.1 WHERE IS THE INFORMATION?

The expectancy of a verb is encoded in its usage. Various *kāraka*s a verb expects are expressed by means of different case suffixes. The case suffixes of nouns express the role the noun has with respect to an activity expressed by a verb. Thus the case suffixes have an expectancy for a verb. These two together establish a relation between a noun and a verb corresponding to the various *kāraka* requirements of the verb. Sometimes the agreement features between a noun and a verbal form, or between two nouns mark a relation. Similarly certain indeclinables have an expectancy to relate to other words. The position of certain words in a sentence also provides us clues regarding the relations between the words in the sentence. We illustrate below these clues with examples:

1. *Usage.* The expectancy of a verb for nouns, satisfying the *kāraka* requirement, is encoded in its signification (*śakti*). Indian theories discuss eight different means of learning the usage of words:[2] *vyākaraṇa* (grammar), *upamāna* (analogy), *kośa* (dictionary), *āptavākya* (usage by a trustworthy person), *loka-vyavahāra* (popular usage), *vākyaśeṣa* (rest of the sentence or even an ellipsis), *vivṛti* (explanation) and *siddhapada-sannidhi* (known words in the proximity). Among these, analogy, known words in the proximity, rest of the sentence or even explanation can help in understanding the meaning of a verb. But none of these provides any clue for the expectancy of a verb. The four factors that are useful for knowing the expectancies of a verb are *vyākaraṇa, kośa, āptavākya* and *vyavahāra*. Grammar is associated with auxiliary databases such as a *dhātupāṭha* (list of verbal roots classified into classes). *Dhātuvṛtti*s (commentaries on the *dhātupāṭha*) sometimes provide information about the transitivity (roughly the property of being *sakarmaka / akarmaka*) of a verb. Similarly, the *kośa*s typically provide the information of transitivity of verbs. But the expectancy of other *kāraka*s is not available through *kośa*s or grammar, barring some exceptional cases. For example, we know that certain verbs

---

[2] *śaktigraham vyākaraṇopamānakośāptavākyād vyavahārataśca* ।
vākyasya śeṣād vivṛter vadanti sānnidhyataḥ siddhapadasya vṛddhaḥ ॥
– *Nyāyasiddhāntamuktāvalī*, Joshi 1985

with *lyuṭ* (gerund) suffix denote a *karaṇa-kāraka* (an instrument) associated with that verb, as in *lekhanī* (a writing instrument such as a pen/a pencil). From this, one can infer that the verb *likh* (to write) has an expectancy of a *karaṇa-kāraka*. It is the usage either through *vyavahāra* or *āptavākya* that really helps in deciding the expectancies of a verb. Sanka (2015) has collected such a list of expectancies of verbs from the corpus. She provides a list of frequently used verbs with their expectancies and also expectancies for verbs with prefixes, along with examples from the corpus.

2. *Suffixes*. These fall under two types: inflectional (*tiṅ*, *sup*) and derivational (*taddhita*, *kṛt* and *sanādi*). The former are either nominal or verbal. These suffixes provide us clues for establishing relations between words.

   (a) *Verbal Suffixes*. The verbal suffixes, both the inflectional and the derivational, themselves may express some *kāraka*s (either *kartṛ* or *karman*). For example, the verbal suffix *ti* in the finite verb form in the active voice as in *gacchati* (goes) expresses a *kartṛ-kāraka*, while the verbal suffix *te* in the finite verb form in the passive voice as in *gamyate* (has gone), expresses a *karma-kāraka*. The *śatṛ* (present participle) suffix in the primary derivative such as *gacchan* expresses a *kartṛ* and so on. The *kāraka* expressed through such suffixes is called *abhihita* (expressed). These verb forms, however, do not convey the complete information about the *kāraka* such as who the referent is. A substantive which is in agreement (agreeing in number and person) with the verb provides the referent. A *vārttika*[3] on the Pāṇinian *sūtra anabhihite* (2.3.1) (if not already expressed) explains *abhihita* as the one which is expressed either by *tiṅ* (a finite verbal suffix), *kṛt* (a non-finite verbal suffix), *taddhita* (derivational nominal suffix) or *samāsa* (compound). For example, in the sentence

   Skt: *rāmaḥ vanam gacchati* ।
   Gloss: Rāma {nom.} forest {acc.} goes.
   Eng: Rāma goes to the forest.

[3] *tiṅkṛttaddhitasamāsaiḥ parisaṅkhyānam* – Ma. Bhā. 2.3.1 vā

The verb being in the active voice (*kartari prayogaḥ*), the verbal suffix *ti* expresses the *kartṛ*. In the following sentence in the passive voice (*karmaṇi prayogaḥ*)

Skt: *rāmeṇa vanam gamyate* ।
Gloss: Rāma {instr.} forest {nom.} is_gone.

the *karman* is expressed by the verbal suffix. As such, in both cases, the *kāraka* which is expressed (*kartṛ* and *karman*, respectively) by the verb form gets a nominative case suffix and shows number and person agreement with the verb form.

Similarly, the derivational suffixes also express *kartṛ* and *karman-kāraka*. For example, in

Skt: *dhāvan aśvaḥ* ।
Gloss: Running horse.

The *kṛt* suffix *śatṛ* in *dhāvan* expresses the relation of *kartṛ*[4] and indicates the one which performs the action of *dhāv* (run).

(b) *Nominal suffixes*. They fall under three categories:

i. A case marker (*vibhakti*) indicating a *kāraka* relation. This marks a relation between a noun and a verb known as a *kāraka* relation. Sanskrit uses seven case suffixes to mark six *kāraka* relations, viz. *kartṛ*, *karman*, *karaṇa*, *sampradāna*, *apādāna* and *adhikaraṇa*. The genitive suffix, in addition to marking a *kāraka* relation,[5] is predominantly used to mark a noun–noun relation.

ii. *Upapada vibhakti*. In addition to the noun–noun relations expressed by the sixth case, there are certain words that mark a special kind of noun–noun relation. These words mark a relation of a noun with another noun, and in turn demand a special case suffix for the preceding noun. For example, the *upapada saha* demands a third case suffix for the preceding noun as in

---

4 *kartari kṛt* – A 3.4.68

5 *kartṛkarmaṇoḥ kṛti* – A 2.3.65

Skt: *rāmeṇa saha sītā vanam gacchati* ।
Gloss: Rāma {instr.} with Sītā forest {acc.} goes.
Eng: Sītā goes to the forest with Rāma.

iii. *Vibhakti*s indicating various other relations such as the following.

A. *Atyantasaṁyoga* (intimate and total contact) as in *māsam adhītaḥ* (he studied for a month without any break), where the accusative case in *māsa* indicates the intimate and total contact.

B. *Kriyāviśeṣaṇa* (adverbial usage) as in *vegena dhāvati* (he runs fast), where the third case in *vega* indicates the adverbial usage.

C. *Aṅgavikāra* (defect in a body-organ) as in *akṣṇā kāṇaḥ* (blind with an eye), where the third case in *akṣṇā* indicates the defect in a body organ.

D. *Nirdhāraṇa* (specifying one out of many) as in *nareṣu śreṣṭhaḥ* (best among the men). The sixth or seventh case marker is used to single out one out of many.

E. *Vibhakta* (distinct/different) as in *gopālāt śyāmaḥ avaraḥ* (Śyāma is inferior to Gopāla). Here the ablative case marker is used for differentiation.

F. *Karmapravacanīya* as in *vṛkṣam anu vidyotate vidyut* (there is lightening towards a tree), the word *anu* governs the *vibhakti* of the preceding noun *vṛkṣa* and thus indirectly marks the relation between the noun it governs and the verb.

3. *Agreement*. In Sanskrit we find two cases of agreement, viz. between two nominals, and between a noun and a verbal suffix. The first one is the case of adjectives, while the second one indicates the *kāraka* relation expressed through a verb, which we have already discussed. This agreement denotes the coreference and is termed *samānādhikaraṇa* relation. Agreement in gender, number and case suffix marks *sāmānādhikaraṇya* or the modifier–modified relation between two nouns as in

Skt: *śvetaḥ aśvaḥ dhāvati* ।
Gloss: White horse runs.

Eng: The white horse runs.

Skt: *aśvaḥ śvetaḥ asti* ।
Gloss: Horse white is.
Eng: The horse is white.

In both the above sentences, the words *aśvaḥ* and *śvetaḥ* have the same gender, number and *vibhakti* indicating *sāmānādhikaraṇya*.

However, there is a subtle difference between the information being conveyed. In the second sentence, the word *śvetaḥ* is a predicative adjective (*vidheya viśeṣaṇa*), while in the first it is an attributive adjective.

The other two instances of agreement involve verbal suffix. These cases, one involving a finite and the other involving a non-finite verbal suffix, are covered under 2(a) above.

4. *Certain Indeclinables*. Indeclinables mark various kinds of relations such as negation, adverbial (manner adverbs only) and coordination. Sometimes they also provide information about interrogation, emphasis, etc.

   For example, the relation of *na* with *gacchati* in the sentence

   Skt: *rāmaḥ gṛham na gacchati* ।
   Gloss: Rāma home not goes.
   Eng: Rāma does not go home.

   is that of negation (*pratiṣedha*). Similarly, the relation of *mandam* with *calati* in the sentence

   Skt: *rāmaḥ mandam calati* ।
   Gloss: Rāma slowly walks.
   Eng: Rāma walks slowly.

   is that of adverbial (*kriyā-viśeṣaṇa*). The relation of *eva* with *rāma* in the sentence

   Skt: *rāmaḥ eva tatra upaviśati* ।
   Gloss: Rāma only there sits.
   Eng: Only Rāma sits there.

   is that of emphasis (*avadhāraṇa*).

5. *Position*. Certain words such as *api* (also) in different positions

have different demands. In sentence initial position, *api* begins an interrogative sentence. In non-initial positions, it expects a noun or a pronoun before it.

For example, in the following sentence, *api* expects a sentence:

Skt: *api sītā gacchati* ।
Eng: Does Sītā go?

And in the following *api* is just an emphatic/inclusive marker:

Skt: *sītā api gacchati* ।
Eng: Sītā also goes.

3.1.2 WHAT KIND OF INFORMATION?

The relation between a verb and a noun that is instrumental in bringing about the action (or an event) denoted by the verb is termed a *kāraka* relation. Pāṇini specifies the semantic content of the *kāraka* relations through various *sūtra*s under the *adhikāra sūtra kārake* (A 1.4.23). The *kāraka* relations have a different status from the purely semantic relations such as thematic roles of Western linguistics. There is no one-to-one relation between thematic relations and *kāraka* relations. One *kāraka* corresponds to several semantic relations and one semantic relation may correspond to several *kāraka*s (Kiparsky 2009: 48). Below we illustrate with an example a few *kāraka* relations along with the semantics associated with them.

1. *Svatantraḥ kartā*. Pāṇini defines *kartṛ* as *svatantraḥ kartā* (A 1.4.54). To understand this *sūtra*, let us look at the three sentences:
   a. *Devadattaḥ pacati*. (Devadatta cooks.)
   b. *Sthālī pacati*. (A vessel cooks.)
   c. *Edhāḥ pacanti*. (The logs cook.)

   In the real world, *devadattaḥ*, *sthālī* (vessel) and *edhāḥ* (logs) are the agent, the locus and the instrument, respectively. But, according to Pāṇinian grammar, the relations of *devadattaḥ*, *sthālī* and *edhāḥ* with respect to the verbs they follow, in each of the three sentences above are all that of *kartṛ*. The *vārttika*s under Pāṇini's *sūtra kārake* (A 1.4.23), that explain why all these are *kartṛ*, go like this:[6]

[6] *adhiśrayaṇodakāsecanataṇḍulāvapanaidho 'pakarṣaṇakriyāḥ pradhānasya kartuḥ pākaḥ* ।
– Ma. Bhā. 1.4.23, vā 8
→

In the sentence *devadattaḥ pacati* (Devadatta cooks), the activity of cooking refers to the activity of Devadatta, viz. putting a vessel on the stove, pouring water in it, adding rice, supplying fuel, etc. and this activity refers to the activity of the *pradhāna kartṛ* (the chief doer of the activity). In the sentence *sthālī pacati* (a vessel cooks), the cooking activity refers to holding the rice and water till the rice cooks and this activity is that of a vessel. In the sentence *edhāḥ pacanti* (logs cook), the cooking activity refers to the supply of sufficient heat by a piece of firewood and thus refers to the activity of an instrument.

That is, in the sentence *devadattaḥ pacati*, the verb *pac* expresses the activities of Devadatta, viz. putting a vessel on the stove, pouring water in it, adding rice, supplying the fuel, etc. Let us denote this meaning of *pac* by pac_1. Among all the participants of the activity, Devadatta is the most independent one and hence is assigned the role of *kartṛ*. Now, when a speaker wants to highlight the activity of a vessel, undermining the role of Devadatta, he utters a sentence *sthālī pacati*. In this sentence, the verb *pac* expresses the activities of a vessel viz. holding the rice and water and supplying the heat uniformly. Let us denote this meaning by pac_2. For the activity denoted by pac_2, *sthālī* is the most independent of all the participants. And hence it is assigned the role of *kartṛ*. And finally, in the sentence *edhāḥ pacanti*, the speaker intends to highlight the action of the logs of supplying the fuel. Here the verb *pac* refers to the activities of the wood. Let us denote this by pac_3. For this activity, logs are the most independent of all participants and hence they are assigned the *kartṛ* role.

During the generation process, this *kartā*, in active voice, is expressed by the agreement of the noun in number and person with the verbal form, and is assigned a nominative case. Thus, in all the three examples listed above, the nominals *devadattaḥ*, *sthālī* and *edhāḥ* are in nominative case and show concord with

---

← *droṇam pacatyāḍhakam pacatīti sambhavanakriyā dhāraṇakriyā cādhikaraṇasya pākaḥ* ||
– Ma. Bhā. 1.4.23, vā 9

edhāḥ pakṣyantyā viklitter jvaliṣyantīti jvalanakriyā karaṇasya pākaḥ ||
– Ma. Bhā. 1.4.23, vā 10

the verb. It is important to note here that what is expressed by the agreement in number and person is just the *kartṛtva* (agenthood) of the *pradhāna kartṛ* (chief agent), *adhikaraṇa* (locus) and *karaṇa* (instrument), respectively.

From analysis point of view, the only information available through the linguistic expression is the concord between a noun and a verb. And this concord, as we saw above expresses the *kartṛ*. Thus only information that can be extracted from the language string is that a noun which shows concord with the verb and which is in nominative case is the *kartṛ*. The beauty of this analysis lies in the economy. Now one need not have to use any kind of "extra-linguistic" information to decide the relation. In order to decide the thematic role of each of these participants, we need to appeal to world knowledge, since the morphemes do not express these relations.

2. *Ṣaṣṭhī śeṣe* (A 2.3.50). The relation between *vṛkṣa* (tree) and *śākhā* (branch) in the phrase *vṛkṣasya śākhā* (branch of a tree), between *pitṛ* (father) and *putra* (son) in the phrase *pituḥ putraḥ* (son of a father) and between *rājan* (king) and *puruṣa* (man) in the phrase *rājñaḥ puruṣaḥ* (king's man) is marked by the genitive case suffix, and Pāṇini groups all of them under the *sūtra ṣaṣṭhī śeṣe* (sixth case in the remaining) (A 2.3.50). Semantically however the first relation is *avayava–avayavī-bhāva* (part–whole relation), the second one is *janya–janaka-bhāva* (parent–child relation) and the third one is *sva–svāmī-bhāva* (owner–possession relation). Again, in order to decide upon these semantic distinctions, one should know that *śākhā* is a part of a *vṛkṣa* or *puruṣa* can be a servant of a king. This, then requires world knowledge, organized in a specific way so that a machine can use it. However, one can mark a general relation, let us call it a *ṣaṣṭhī sambandha* (genitive relation), in the absence of any such knowledge.[7]

3. *Adhiśīṅsthāsām karma* (A 1.4.46). Here is another example where Pāṇini focuses on the information marked by a suffix. In the sentences:

[7] See the discussion under Sect. 3.3 (Yogyatā) for the usefulness of such knowledge.

Skt: *hariḥ vaikuṇṭham adhiśete* ।
Gloss: Hari {nom.} *vaikuṇṭha* {acc.} sleeps.
Eng: Hari sleeps in the *vaikuṇṭha*.

Skt: *muniḥ śilāpaṭṭam adhitiṣṭhati* ।
Gloss: Sage {nom.} stone_slab {acc.} sits.
Eng: A sage sits on a stone slab.

vaikuṇṭha and *śilāpaṭṭa* are in the accusative case and Pāṇini assigns them a *karman* role. However, semantically, both of them are the *ādhāra*s (loci) of the activities of the associated verbs, viz. *adhi-śīṅ* (to sleep) and *adhi-sthā* (to sit). Hence the Naiyāyikas, who want to map the *śabda jagat* (world of words) to *vyāvahārika jagat* (the real world), find it difficult to accept the *karmatva* of these words and they qualify this *karmatva* on the second case ending as *ādhārasya anuśāsanika-karmatva* (imposed *karmatva* of the locus) (Achyutanand 1991: 141). Thus, there is a disconnect between the real world and what is expressed through the words. But the grammarians restrict themselves to the "world of words" and do not venture into mapping it to the real world. Pāṇini had a choice. The first choice is to state this as an exception for assigning a *dvitīyā vibhakti* (accusative case marker) to the *adhikaraṇa kāraka*, which, by default takes *saptamī vibhakti* (locative case marker). And second choice is to assign a different *kāraka*, thereby not disturbing the *kāraka-vibhakti* mapping. Pāṇini chose the second alternative over the first one. It may be because, Pāṇini considered the thing that is a locus, is also the most desirable one to the *kartṛ*,[8] and hence gets a *karman* role. Thus we see that the information that is coded in a sentence may be different from the actual reality. During the analysis process, only the information coded in the language string would be extracted. The analysis of thematic relations is differed due to want of world knowledge.

4. *sahayukte 'pradhāne* (A 2.3.19). Here is the final example. In the sentence:

   Skt: *mātā saha bālakaḥ āgacchati* ।
   Gloss: mother {instr.} with child {acc.} comes.

[8] *kartuḥ īpsitatamam karma* – A 1.4.49

Eng: The child comes with her mother.

the agreement of the verb is with *bālakaḥ* and not with *mātā*. According to *Aṣṭādhyāyī* 2.3.19, *saha* is used with the *apradhāna* (subordinate) *kāraka*. Thus in this example, *mātā* (mother) is subordinate and *bālaka* (child) is the *pradhāna* (primary) *kartṛ*. However, from the semantic point of view, the situation is reversed. It is the mother who carries the child in her arms, or holds the finger of a child guiding her and thus *bālaka* is *apradhāna* (subordinate) and *mātā* is the *pradhāna-kāraka*. Thus again there is a mismatch between the reality and what the sentence actually encodes. And Pāṇini chooses to go with what is encoded in the text.

From all the above examples, it is clear that the *śabdajagat* (world of words) is different from the real world. To name the relations reflecting their role as experienced in the real world, extralinguistic information is needed. Since the extralinguistic information is not easily accessible and is open-ended, it is possible to mark only syntactico–semantic relations that depend solely upon the linguistic/grammatical information in a sentence, following the grammarians.

In our parser, in the first step, we decided to mark all those relations that can be extracted from the morphemes themselves, without appealing to real-world knowledge. Thus we mark *devadatta*, *sthālī* and *edhāḥ* as *kartṛ*. Similarly, we mark only the genitive relation and do not further subclassify it into *avayava–avayavī-bhāva*, *pitā–putra-sambandha*, etc. In the case of locus marked as a *karman* with the verbs *adhi-śīṅ*, *adhi-sthā*, etc. we mark the relation as a *karman* and in the case of *saha*, we mark the relation of *kartṛ* with *bālaka* and not with *mātā*. Though it is possible to capture the real-world semantics directly in some of the cases, we decided not to go for it, since the *kāraka* relations, as described by Pāṇini, give us a very clear level of marking the relations purely on the basis of what is encoded in a language string, without appealing to the world knowledge. This also helps us to keep the syntax separate from the semantics.

3.1.3 REPOSITORY OF RELATIONS

All the relations described above and many more are mentioned in the *Aṣṭādhyāyī* and various other books on the theories of *śābdabodha*, commentaries thereupon, and various other texts dealing with *vyākaraṇa*. All these relations described in the traditional grammar books have been compiled and classified by Ramakrishnamacharyulu (2009) under the two broad headings, viz. inter-sentential and intra-sentential relations. Appendix C provides a list of all these relations. These relations were critically examined from the point of view of their usability in an automatic sentential parser (Kulkarni and Ramakrishnamacharyulu 2013). A subset of a little more than thirty relations from this repository were chosen for developing a parser. Appendix D provides a list of these selected relations.

3.1.4 HOW IS THE INFORMATION ENCODED?

Relations are not always encoded explicitly. Sometimes they are coded through a language convention. For example, consider the following example where the verbal arguments are shared:

> Skt: *rāmaḥ dugdham pītvā śālām gacchati* ।
>
> Gloss: Rāma {nom.} milk {acc.} having_drunk school {acc.} goes.
>
> Eng: Having drunk milk, Rāma goes to school.

In this example, there are two verbs – *gam* and *pā*. Both these verbs are transitive and thus demand two arguments each, viz. *kartṛ* and *karman*. In the above example, we notice that there are only three nouns, two of which are in the accusative, thus being the *karman*s for the two verbs. But there is only one noun in the nominative. The nominative case suffix, as seen earlier, just expresses the *sāmānādhikaraṇya* (coreferentiality) with the finite verbal suffix. So with this, then, a relation between *gacchati* and *rāmaḥ* is established. Now the question is, how does Sanskrit mark the information that Rāma is also a *kartṛ* of the activity of drink? We find the clue in Pāṇini's *sūtra*

> *samānakartṛkayoḥ pūrvakāle* – A 3.4.21

which states that the suffix *ktvā* is used to denote the preceding of two actions that shares the same *kartṛ*. So in the above example, the *ktvā* suffix with the verb *pā* indicates that the action of drinking took place before the action of going and that the *kartṛ* of both the actions is the same. In order to understand which *kartṛtva* (agenthood) is marked, we get a hint in Bhartṛhari's *kārikā*.

Bhartṛhari in his *Vākyapadīyam* 3.7.81-82 states:

pradhānetarayor yatra dravyasya kriyayoḥ pṛthak ।
śaktir guṇāśrayā tatra pradhānaṃ anurudhyate ॥
– 3.7.81

When one and the same thing has the power (of being the object) in regard to two actions, the main one and the secondary one, the power in regard to the secondary action follows that in regard to the main one. – Iyer 1971: 198

pradhānaviṣayā śaktiḥ pratyayenābhidhīyate ।
yadā guṇe tadā tadvad anuktāpi prakāśate ॥
– 3.7.82

Where the power (of being the object) relating to the main action is expressed by the verbal suffix, then the one relating to the second action, though not expressed, is understood. – Iyer 1971: 198

The following sentences make this point clearer

Skt: *rāmaḥ dugdham pītvā śālāṃ gacchati* ।

Gloss: Rāma milk after_drinking to_school goes.

Eng: Rāma goes to school after drinking milk.

and

Skt: *rāmeṇa dugdham pītvā śālā gamyate* ।

Gloss: by_Rāma milk having_drunk school was gone.

Eng: The school was visited by Rāma after drinking milk.

From these two sentences, it is clear that the *vibhakti* of *rāma* is governed by the main verb *gam*. And hence, the information that *Rāma* is also the *kartṛ* of the verb *pā* is not expressed through any of the suffixes. The *ktvā* suffix expresses only the precedence relation (*pūrvakālīkatva*). And then, with the help of *Aṣṭādhyāyī* 3.4.21, we infer that *rāma* is also the *kartṛ* of the verb *pā*. Thus we see that language does not code all the relations explicitly. There are certain conventions of the language which facilitate certain implicit coding. Such an implicit coding may be different for different languages. And hence it is also necessary to extract such implicitly encoded information. As an illustration, let us look at the following sentence discussed by Kiparsky (2009: 36):

Skt: *vanāt grāmam adya upetya odanaḥ āśvapatena apāci* ।

Gloss: From_the_forest to_the_village today having_come rice by_Āśvapata was_cooked.

Eng: When Āśvapata came from the forest to the village today, he cooked some rice.
Literally: Having come from the forest to the village today, the rice was cooked by Āśvapata.

In English, it is the subject that is shared in such constructions. So if we look at the literal translation, we will notice that rice is the subject of the matrix clause and hence from the literal translation in English, an English reader would get the meaning that it is rice which came from the forest. English does not have a scheme to mark the sharing of an object of the matrix clause with the subject of the subordinate clause the phenomenon which we see in the above Sanskrit sentence. So unless we mark these implicit (shared) relations as well, the translation systems may produce wrong translations.

Another *sūtra* that deals with the sharing of arguments is

samānakartṛkeṣu (icchārtheṣu) tumun – A 3.3.158

which states that in case of verbs expressing desire, the infinitive verb in the subordinate clause will have the same *kartṛ* as that of the verb it modifies. Here also the primary information available from the non-finite verbal suffix *tumun* is the relation of purpose.[9]

Thus in the sentence,

Skt: *rāmaḥ gṛhaṁ gantum icchati* ।
Gloss: Rāma home {acc.} to_go wishes.
Eng: Rāma wants to go home.

Rāma is marked as a *kartṛ* of the verb *icchati* but is not marked as a *kartṛ* of *gantum* by any suffix. The sharing in the case of suffixes *ktvā* and *tumun* is the result of the precondition *samānakartṛkatva* in *Aṣṭādhyayī* 3.4.21, and 3.3.158 which act as argument-sharing rules respectively.

3.2 Sannidhi: Planarity Constraint

Sanskrit being inflectionally rich, the conventional wisdom about Sanskrit word order is that it is free. It is also a common understanding among the linguists that the freeness of word order in Sanskrit is clause-internal. That is, it is not possible to freely interleave the constituents from subordinate clauses with elements from the main

---

9 *tumunṇvulau kriyāyām kriyārthāyām* – A 3.3.10

clause or other subordinate clauses. Thus the mixing of elements from different clauses is not allowed. The examples discussed by Viśvanātha Pañcānana also point to the same constraint. In order to build a parser, this conventional wisdom needs to be formalized. It is necessary to know whether there are any exceptions to it, and if there are, what is their nature.

There have been several efforts in the domain of the dependency framework to study the relation between governance and precedence (Bodirsky, Kuhlmann and Möhl 2005; Havelka 2005; Nivre 2006). These studies have resulted in various types of constraints on dependency graphs. These constraints ban some word orders. The strongest among these is the projectivity principle. The less stringent ones are weak non-projectivity and well-nestedness.

3.2.1 PROJECTIVITY PRINCIPLE

The principle of projectivity states a constraint on the dependency tree which disallows certain dependency structures.

> A sentence is projective if and only if we can draw a dependency tree whose every node can be projected by a vertical line onto its word form in the surface string without crossing another projection or a dependency edge.

Hudson (1984: 98) calls this projectivity principle the "adjacency principle".

Consider the sentence

Skt: *śvetaḥ aśvaḥ dhāvati* ।

Gloss: White {nom.} horse {nom.} run {3p. sg.}.

Eng: White horse runs.

The following six word orders are possible with the same overall meaning:

(a) *śvetaḥ aśvaḥ dhāvati* ।

(b) *śvetaḥ dhāvati aśvaḥ* ।

(c) *aśvaḥ śvetaḥ dhāvati* ।

(d) *dhāvati śvetaḥ aśvaḥ* ।

(e) *aśvaḥ dhāvati śvetaḥ* ।

(f) *dhāvati aśvaḥ śvetaḥ* ।

Though all these word orders are acceptable and convey the same overall meaning, namely, "a white horse runs", (a) and (d) are more probable than the others. *Figure* 3.1 shows the projections of sentences (a) to (f). We notice that sentences (b) and (e) have the projection line (shown by dotted lines) crossing the governance relation (shown by solid lines) showing the violation of the projectivity principle. Let us look at another example (g).

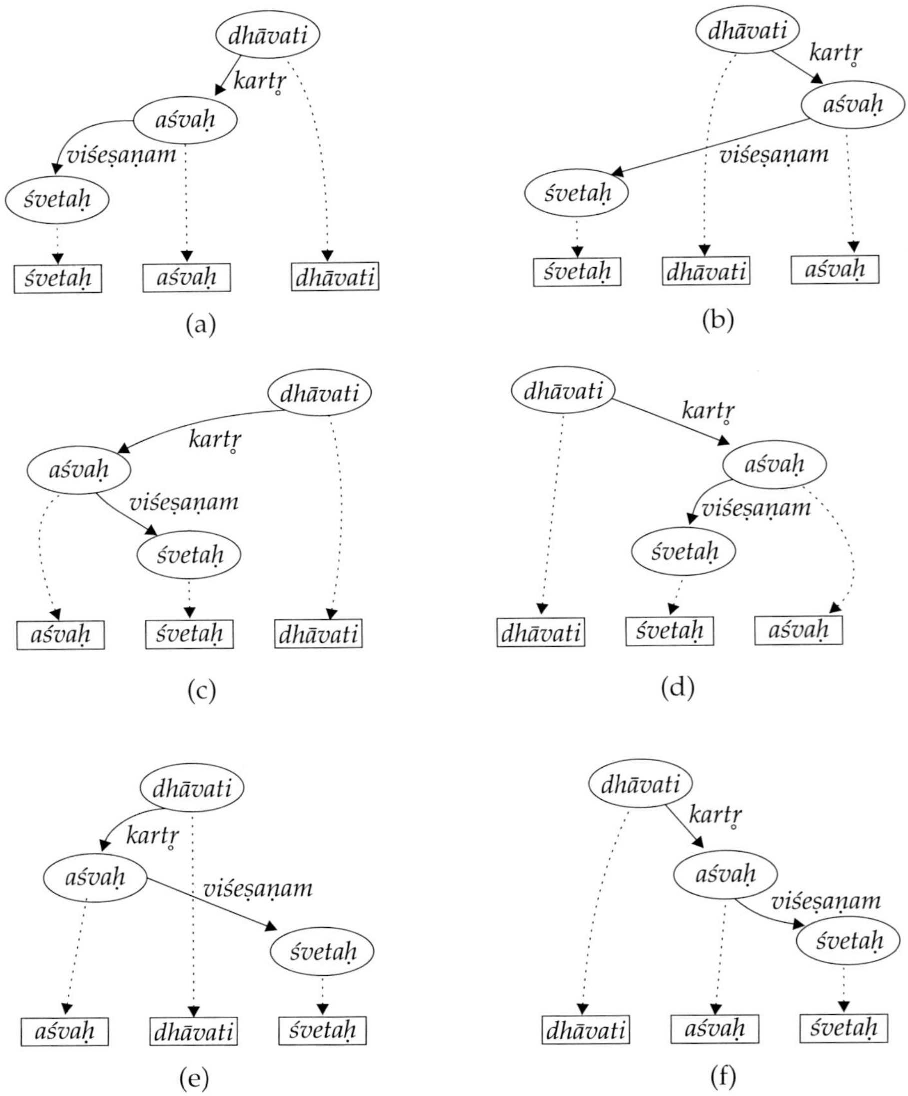

fig. 3.1: Projections for sentences 3.2.1(a)-(f)

(g) Skt: *rāmaḥ dugdham pītvā śālām gacchati* ।
Gloss: Rāma {nom.} milk {acc.} drink {absolutive} school {acc.} go {3p.sg.}.
Eng: Rāma goes to school after drinking milk.

This sentence has five words. Are all the 5! (= 120) combinations meaningful?

(h) Skt: **rāmaḥ śālām dugdham gacchati pītvā* ।
Gloss: *Rāma {nom.} school {acc.} milk {acc.} go {3p. sg.} drink {absolutive}
Eng: *Rāma to school milk goes drinking.

Sentence (h) which is obtained by permuting the words in sentence (g) does not lead to any verbal cognition, and thus it shows that all permutations are not meaningful. Sentence (h) also violates the projectivity principle. *Figure* 3.2 shows the governance relation between *pītvā* and *dugdham* being crossed by the projection of *gacchati*.

Though sentence (h) as well as sentences (b) and (e) show violation of the projectivity principle, there is a difference between the violation in (h) on the one hand and the violation in (b) and (e) on the other. The violation in (h) is an example of *sannidhi* violation of *utthita ākāṅkṣā* while (b) and (e) are examples of *sannidhi* violation of *utthāpya ākāṅkṣā*. Thus there is need to distinguish between these two types of violation; the distinction is not captured by the projectivity principle.

3.2.2 WEAK NON-PROJECTIVITY (PLANARITY)

It is possible to draw the dependency graphs for (b) and (e) by

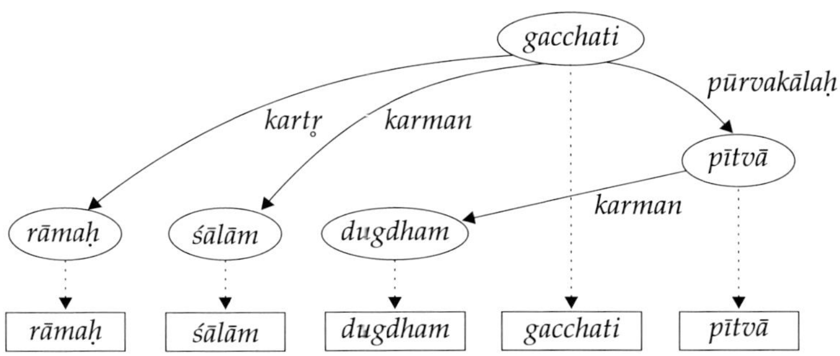

fig. 3.2: Projection for sentence 3.2.1 (h)

rearranging the nodes to avoid the crossing of the projection lines by the dependency relations. *Figure* 3.3 shows possible graphs for (b) and (e) that avoid crossing. However, there is no rearrangement of the nodes of (h) that will avoid crossing. We capture this difference by relaxing the projectivity constraint. Instead of considering the crossing between the two types of relations, viz. projection and dependency, we consider only the crossing between the dependency relations with a further constraint that the nodes of the dependency structure be represented in a linear order that reflects the surface order of the words in the sentence they represent. Such a dependency graph is weakly non-projective if there are no crossing of edges. If all the edges are drawn on the same side of a sentence (either below or above), such a graph results in a planar graph.

> *Definition*: A graph is weakly non-projective or planar, if it does not have two edges $w_i \leftrightarrow w_j$ and $w_k \leftrightarrow w_l$ with $i < k < j < l$.

Thus every projective structure is weakly non-projective, but the reverse is not true.

Let us look at the sentences (b), (e) and (h) above. All these were found to be non-projective. But as we notice in *fig*. 3.4, the sentences (b) and (e) do not have crossing edges in their linear projection. Hence these are weakly non-projective or planar. But *fig*. 3.5 shows

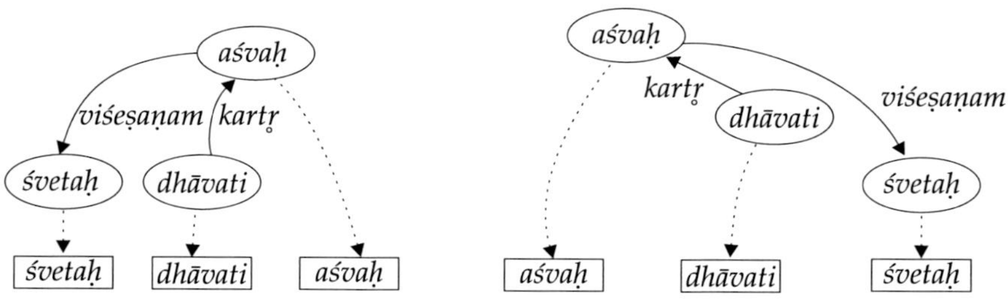

(a) graph for sentence (b) (b) graph for sentence (e)

fig. 3.3: Projection with rearrangement of nodes

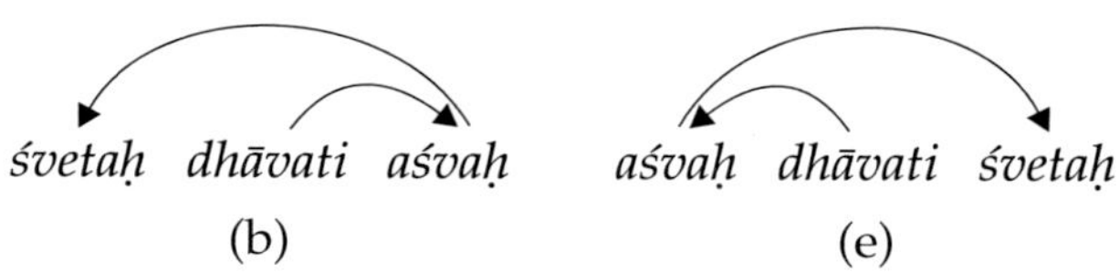

fig. 3.4: Planar dependency graph for sentences (b) and (e)

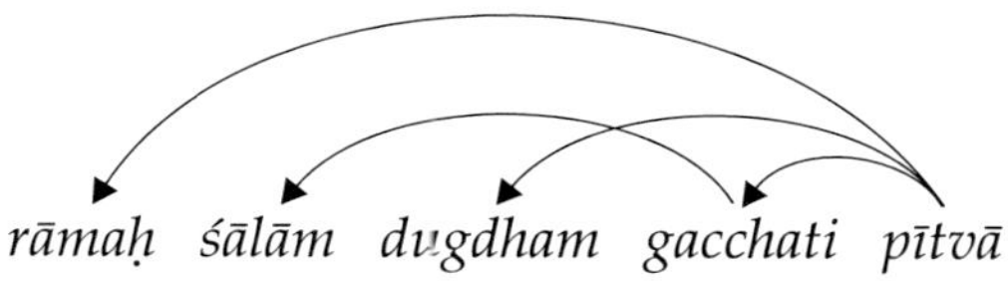

fig. 3.5: Planar dependency graph for sentence (h)

the crossing of edges which makes sentence (h) non-planar.

3.2.3 EMPIRICAL EVALUATION

Now that we have a precise mathematical criterion for evaluating the *sannidhi* violation, we look at a small corpus of prose sentences and verses. Below we discuss some cases where we found a violation of *sannidhi*.

Dislocation of a Genitive

We give below two examples of dislocation of a genitive discussed by Gillon (1996).

(7) Skt: *tayoḥ baddhayoḥ kim-nimittaḥ ayam mokṣaḥ*। – *ASG* 14.1.2
Gloss: of_those of_prisoners what_basis this release?
Eng: What basis does the release of the two prisoners have?

A copulative verb *asti* is supplied in the dependency structure. The two Indian schools Vyākaraṇa (grammar) and Nyāya (logic) differ in the analysis of sentences with missing copulative verbs. The Vyākaraṇa school supplies the missing copulative verb *asti*[10] and then establishes relations between the substantive and its predicative adjective through this verb, while the Nyāya school establishes the relation between the substantive and the predicative adjective directly. We follow the Vyākaraṇa school. The non-planar and planar dependency graphs are shown in *fig.* 3.6. As one can see, the crossing links involve the verb *asti* and the position of this verb is crucial in the planarity of the dependency graph. If the verb *asti* is placed in juxtaposition with the word *kim-nimittaḥ* then there is no crossing. The verb *asti* in this sentence has only two arguments. In example (8) (*fig.* 3.7) below, where there are more than two arguments, the linear

---

[10] *astir bhavantīparaḥ prathamapuruṣo 'prayujyamāno 'pyasti*।
– A 2.3.1, vt. 11

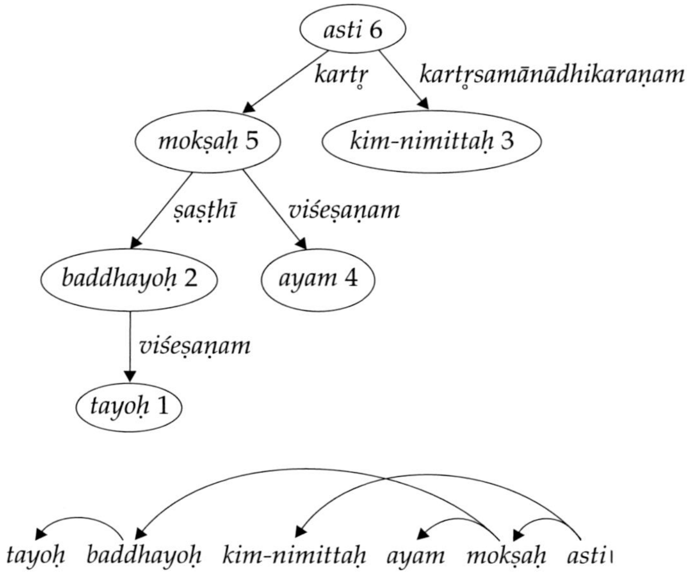

fig. 3.6: Dislocation of a genitive

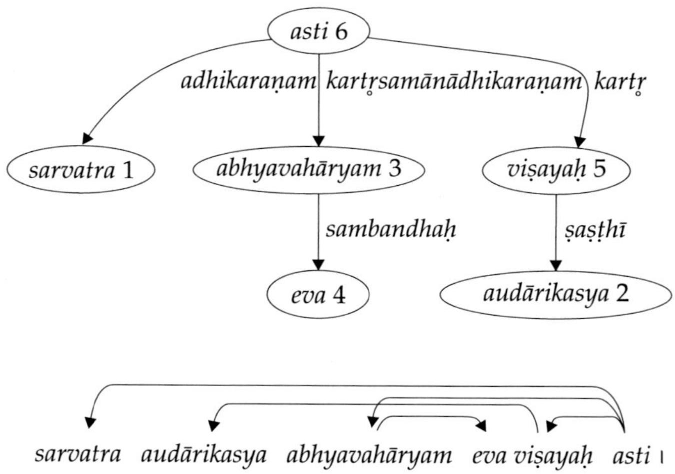

fig. 3.7: Dislocation of a genitive

representation of the sentence has crossing of links no matter where the copulative verb is placed.

(8) *sarvatra audārikasya abhyavahāryam eva viṣayaḥ* । – ASG 1.1.2

In every case, a glutton's object is only food.

Dislocation of a Viśeṣaṇa

Example (9) (*fig.* 3.8) shows the evidence of *sannidhi* violation due to dislocation of an adjective. We supply the missing copulative verb *bhavanti* following the Vyākaraṇa school.

(9) *ete hi hṛdaya-marma-bhidaḥ saṁsāra-bhāvāḥ*। – *ASG* 8.1.3

For, these worldly things are heart breakers.

Here the position of the missing copulative verb *bhavanti* dictates the crossing of links. Certain positions of *bhavanti* lead to crossing of links; others do not.

Dislocation Involving Other Relations

Example (10) is a case where the relations involved in *sannidhi* violation are other than *viśeṣaṇa* and genitive (*fig.* 3.9).

(10) *aham manda-autsukyaḥ asmi nagara-gamanam prati*।
– *ASG* 3.1.3

I am (one who is) little eager about going to the city.

The edge marking the non-*kāraka* relation between the words *manda-autsukyaḥ* and *prati* crosses the edge between the *kartṛ* relation between *aham* and *asmi*.

The word order in verse, though free, is constrained by the metrical considerations. In order to study the effect of metrical considerations on *sannidhi*, we analysed all the verses of the *Bhagavadgītā*. A total of

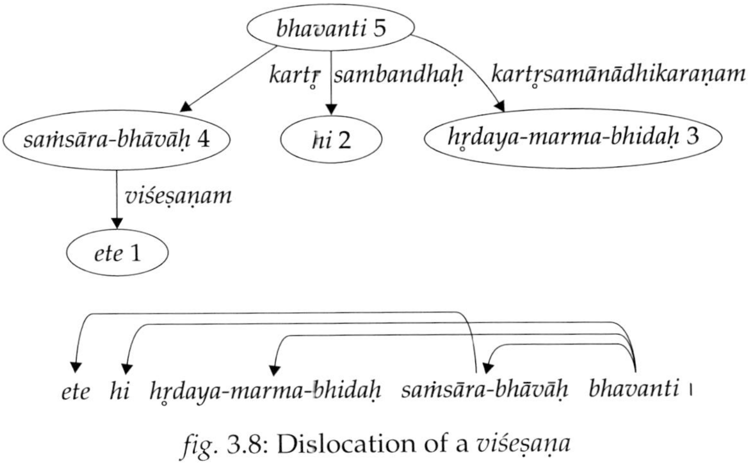

fig. 3.8: Dislocation of a *viśeṣaṇa*

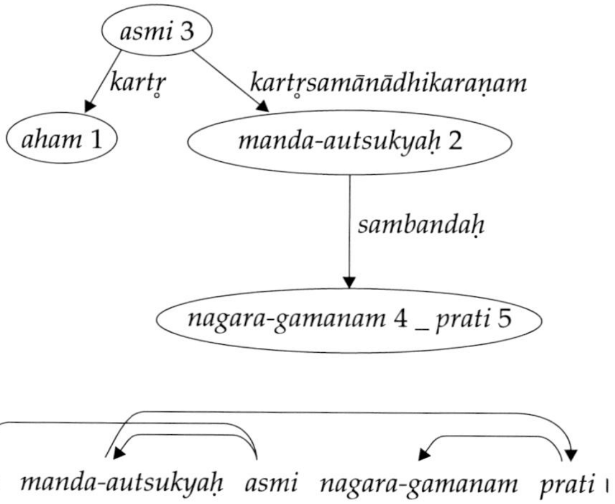

fig. 3.9: Dislocation of an argument

nine cases of anomalous behaviour were found. Of these, in seven cases both of the relations involved in crossing were the *kāraka* relations. In two cases there was crossing of an adverb with a *kāraka* relation. We discuss these cases below.

Sannidhi Violation Involving Kartṛ and Karman

Five among the nine anomalous cases had the *kartṛ* relation of one verb crossing with the *karman* relation of another verb. These instances are examined below:

(11) *cañcalaṁ hi manaḥ kṛṣṇa pramāthi balavaddṛḍham* ।
tasya aham nigraham manye vāyoḥ iva suduṣkaram ॥
– *Bhagavadgīta* VI.34

Oh Kṛṣṇa! the mind is fickle, turbulent, obstinate and strong, hence I think it is as difficult to control the wind.

In the second line of this verse the main verb is *manye* whose *kartṛ* is *aham*. The *karman* of the verbal noun *nigraham* is the pronominal *tasya*, which refers to *manaḥ* in the first sentence. Thus the word sequence *tasya aham nigraham manye* produces two crossing edges involving the relations of *kartṛ* and *karman* (*fig*. 3.10).

(12) *dhūmo rātriḥ tathā kṛṣṇaḥ ṣaṇmāsā dakṣiṇāyanam* ।
tatra cāndramasaṁ jyotiḥ yogī prāpya nivartate ॥
– *Bhagavadgītā* VIII.25

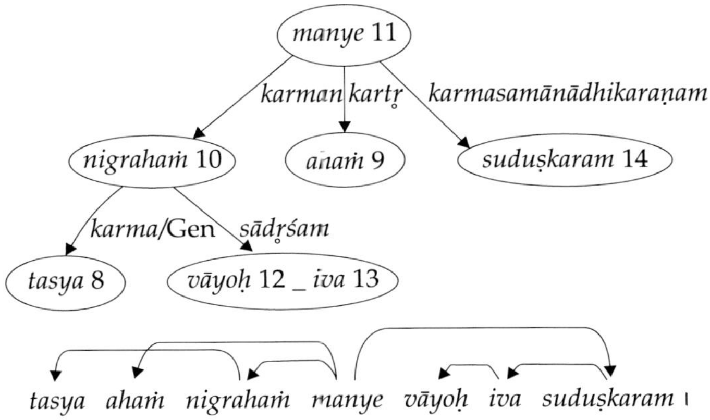

fig. 3.10: Analysis of *Bhagavadgītā* VI.34

> The *yogī* on travelling the path of smoke, night, the dark half of the month and the six months of the southern path (of the sun) after death, obtains the lunar light and returns (to this world).

The second example with similar crossing of *kartṛ* and *karman* was found in verse in the *Bhagavadgītā* VIII.25. In this verse, in the word sequence *jyotiḥ yogī prāpya nivartate*, *jyotiḥ* is the *karman* of the absolutive verb *prāpya* and *yogī* is the *kartṛ* of the verb *nivartate* resulting in the crossing (*fig.* 3.11).

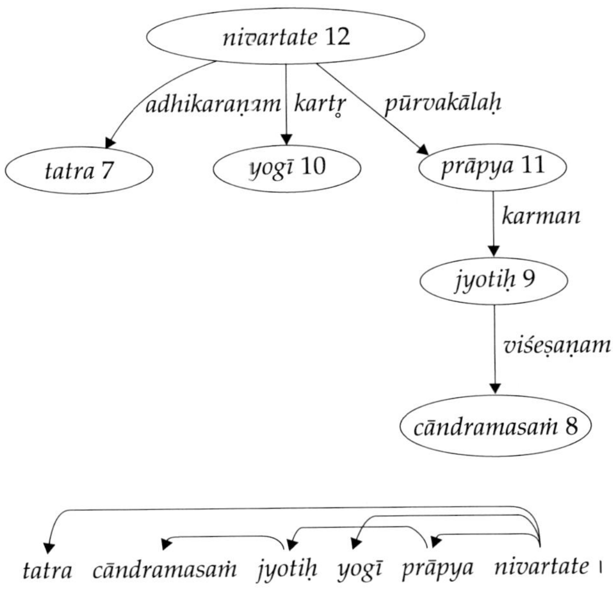

fig. 3.11: Analysis of *Bhagavadgītā* VIII.25

(13) *vaktum arhasy aśeṣeṇa divyāḥ hy ātmavibhūtayaḥ* ।
yābhiḥ vibhūtibhiḥ lokān imān tvam vyāpya tiṣṭhasi ॥
– *Bhagavadgītā* X.16

You could tell me about your divine manifestations by which you exist pervading these worlds.

The third example is from *Bhagavadgītā* X.16. Here the word sequence *lokān imān tvam vyāpya tiṣṭhasi* results in crossing edges with *lokān* being the *karman* of *vyāpya* and *tvam* being the *kartṛ* of *tiṣṭhasi* (*fig*. 3.12).

(14) *aśraddadhānāḥ puruṣāḥ dharmasya asya parantapa* ।
aprāpya māṁ nivartante mṛtyusaṁsāravartmani ॥
– *Bhagavadgītā* IX.3

Oh Parantapa! those who have no faith in this *dharma* return to the circle of death and rebirth without attaining me.

The fourth example is from *Bhagavadgītā* IX.3, where the dependency arrow corresponding to the *karman* of the *kṛdanta a-śraddadhānāḥ* crosses the arrow corresponding to the *kartṛ* of the main verb *nivartante* (*fig*. 3.13).

(15) *tān samīkṣya saḥ kaunteyaḥ sarvān bandhūn avasthitān* ॥
– *Bhagavadgītā* I.27cd

kṛpayā parayā āviṣṭaḥ viṣīdan idam abravīt ।
– Ibid. I.28ab

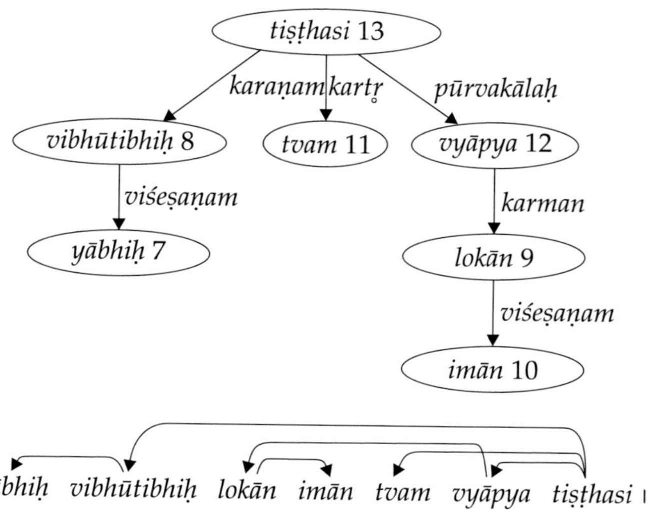

fig. 3.12: Analysis of *Bhagavadgītā* X.16

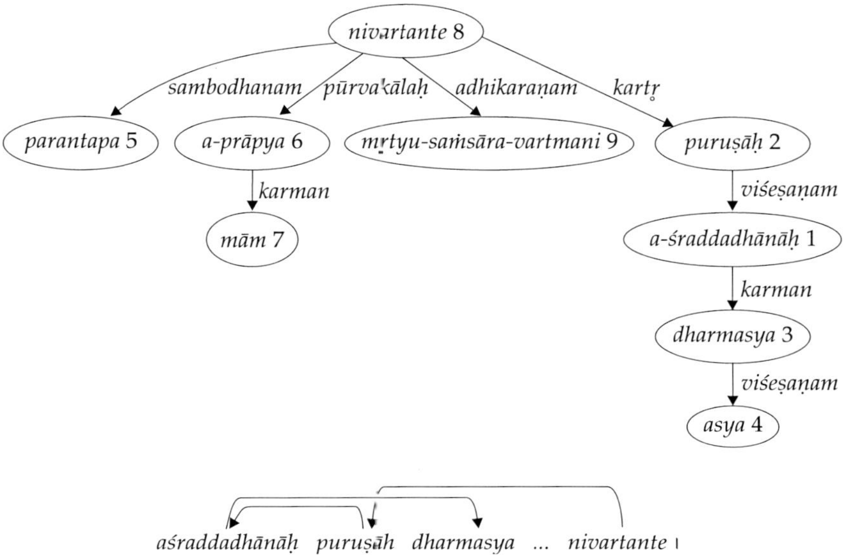

fig. 3.13: Analysis of *Bhagavadgītā* IX.3

Seeing all these relatives present there (on the battlefield) Kaunteya filled with compassion uttered these words in dejection.

In *Bhagavadgītā* I.27-28 also we find the crossing of the dependency arrows pointing to a *kartr̥* and a *karman*. *Bandhūn* is the *karman* of the absolutive *samīkṣya* and *kaunteya* is the *kartr̥* of the verb *abravīt*, and the edges marking these relations cross (*fig*. 3.14). In this example if we choose *tān*, which is an adjective of *bandhūn* as the *karman* of *samīkṣya*, then this crossing vanishes! This, in fact, happens to be an example of cataphora and would be analysed as in *fig*. 3.15.

Sannidhi Violation Involving Karman and Kriyā-viśeṣaṇa

In *Bhagavadgītā* I.37, the relation of *karman* of the absolutive *hatvā* is crossed by the *kriyā-viśeṣaṇa* of the main verb *syāma* (*fig*. 3.16).

(16) *tasmāt na arhāḥ vayaṁ hantuṁ dhārtarāṣṭrān svabāndhavān* ।
sva janaṁ hi kathaṁ hatvā sukhinaḥ syāma mādhava ॥
– *Bhagavadgītā* I.37

Therefore Oh Mādhava! it is not suitable on our part to kill our relatives, for by killing our own kinsmen, the sons of Dhr̥tarāṣṭra, how can we remain happy?

A similar example is found in *Bhagavadgītā* XI.32 where the relation of *kartr̥* crosses with that of an adjective.

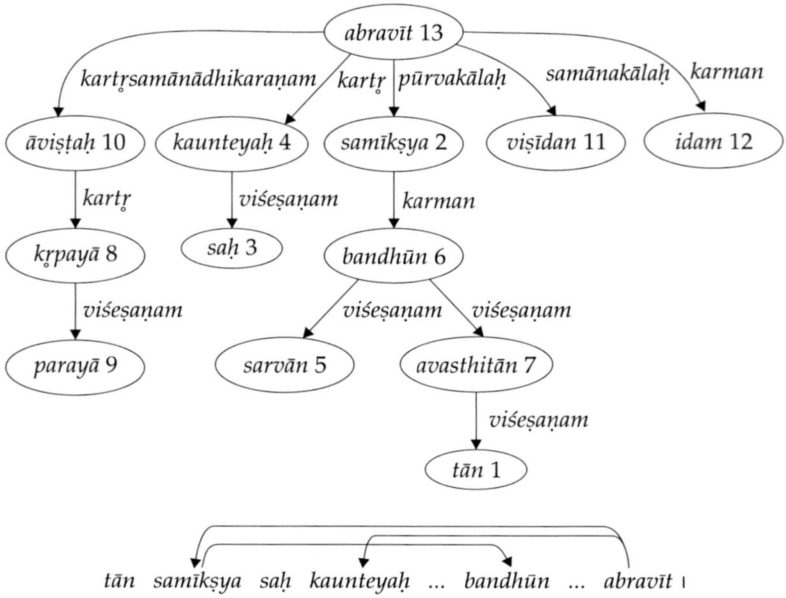

fig. 3.14: Analysis of *Bhagavadgītā* I.27

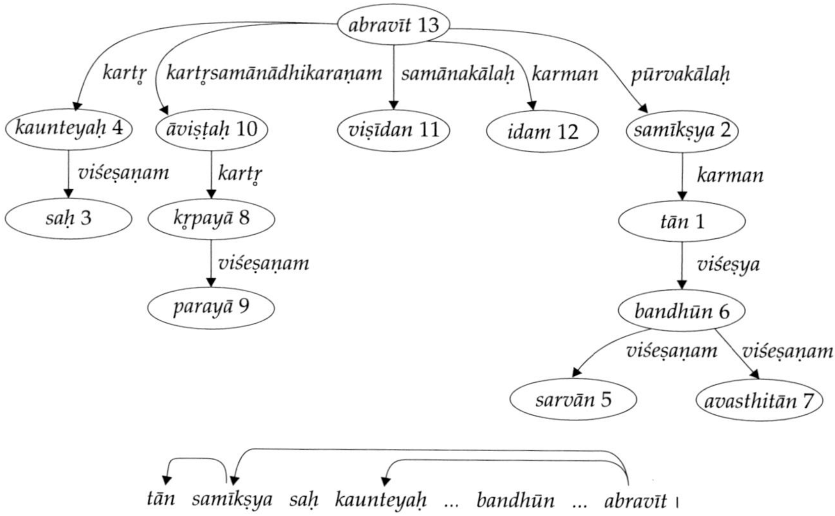

fig. 3.15: Modified analysis of *Bhagavadgītā* I.27

Sannidhi Violation Involving Karman and Apādāna

The last example is from the last chapter of the *Bhagavadgītā*. Here the *karman* of the non-finite verb *kathayataḥ* crosses the relation of *apādāna* between *śrutavān* and *kṛṣṇāt* (*fig*. 3.17).

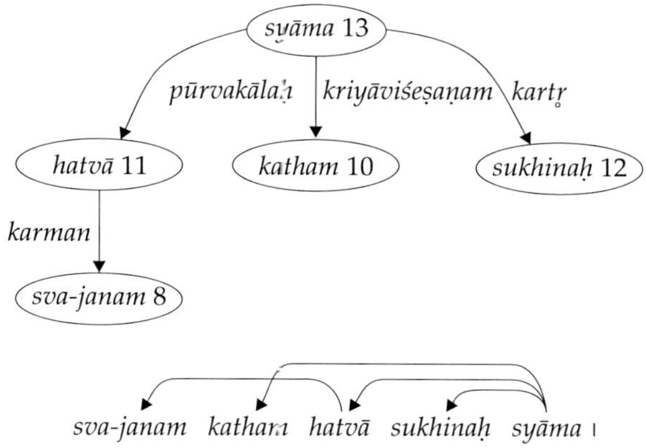

fig. 3.16: Analysis of *Bhagavadgītā* I.37

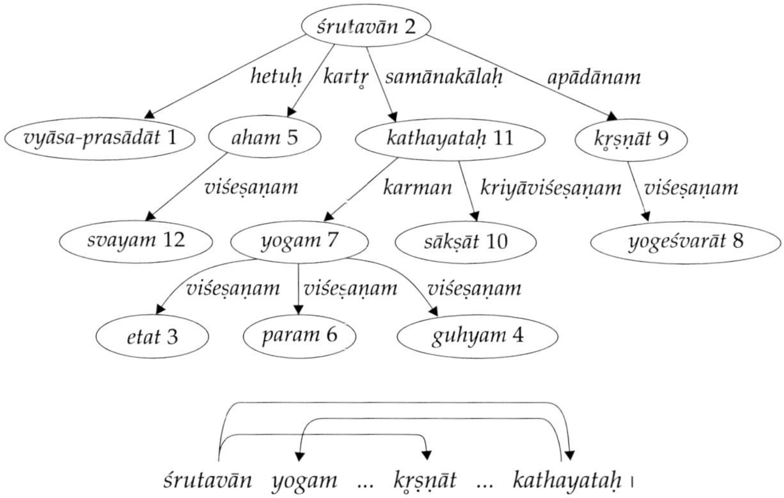

fig. 3.17: Analysis of *Bhagavadgītā* XVIII.75

(17) *vyāsaprasādāt śrutavān etad guhyam aham param* ।
yogam yogeśvarāt kṛṣṇāt sākṣāt kathayataḥ svayam ॥
– *Bhagavadgītā* XVIII.75

By the grace of Vyāsa I have heard this supreme secret *yoga* directly from the Lord of Yoga, Kṛṣṇa.

3.2.4 CONCLUSION

Planarity (or weak non-projectivity) is the precise characterization of the *sannidhi* constraint. *Sannidhi* violation leads to non-planar graphs.

The number of violations is much greater in verse than in prose. This may be attributed to metrical considerations. The behaviour of *utthita* (mutual) and *utthāpya* (unilateral) *ākāṅkṣā*s (expectancies) are different. Mutual expectancies are tightly coupled and the words that have mutual expectancy are always in close proximity (*sannidhi*). In contrast, a word that has unilateral expectancy (*utthāpya ākāṅkṣā*) may be moved away from its relatum and its relational path may be interrupted by one or more words unrelated to them.

Two major relations involved in *sannidhi* violation in both prose and verse are the *viśeṣaṇa* and the genitive. Some of the other relations involved in *sannidhi* violation are *sambodhana* (vocative), negation, precedence and simultaneity. All these relations have unilateral expectancy and thus correspond to *utthāpya ākāṅkṣā*.

3.3 Yogyatā: Semantic Restrictions

As seen above, the concept of *ākāṅkṣā* provides clues for establishing relations and *sannidhi* provides some constraints on the possible combinations of relations. It is not the case that all the relations proposed by *ākāṅkṣā* would be meaningful. In order for a relation between two words to be meaningful, the corresponding word meanings should be mutually compatible (*yogya*) with reference to that relation.

The first attempt to use the concept of *yogyatā* in the field of machine translation was by Bhanumati (1989) in the Telugu–Hindi machine translation system. Selectional restrictions were used in defining the *kāraka* charts that provided a subcategorization frame as well as selection restrictions over the arguments of the verbs. On similar lines noun *lakṣaṇa* charts and verb *lakṣaṇa* charts were also used for disambiguation of noun and verb meanings. These charts expressed selectional restrictions using both ontological concepts as well as semantic properties. An example *kāraka* chart for the Hindi verb *jānā* (to go) is given in Table 3.1.

Here *upādhi* is an imposed property. The first row in Table 3.1 states a constraint that a noun with the case marker *se* has a *kāraka* relation of *apādāna* (source) provided it is not a vehicle. The ontological classification was inspired by the ontology that originated in the Vaiśeṣika school of philosophy. By using such

Table 3.1: Kāraka Chart for the Verb Jānā (to go)

Case Relation	*Degree of Necessity*	*Case Marker*	*Semantic Constraint*
apādāna	desirable	*se*	not (*upādhi*: vehicle)
karaṇa	desirable	*se*	*upādhi*: vehicle
karman	mandatory	0/*ko*	–
kartṛ	mandatory	0	–

ontological classifications, the parsers for Indian languages were further improved. Bharati, Chaitanya and Sangal (1995) mention the importance of two semantic factors in parsing, viz. animacy and humanity, that remove the ambiguity between the *kartṛ* and *karman kāraka*. This hypothesis was further strengthened with experimental verification by Bharati et al. (2008).

3.3.1 SELECTION RESTRICTION

In Western linguistics, a concept similar to *yogyatā* is termed *selection restriction*. A selection restriction imposes a semantic constraint on the arguments that fill the slots in subcategorization frames. These selection restrictions are of two types. The first one is S-selection or semantic selection, and the second one is C-selection or category selection. The C-selection is more syntactic in nature and thus it is synonymous with the concept of subcategorization frames. The S-selection is introduced to block the generation of sentences such as *colourless green ideas sleep furiously*. The S-selection, being semantic in nature, is closed to the concept of *yogyatā* in Indian tradition.

Katz and Fodor (1963) proposed a model of selection restrictions as necessary and sufficient conditions for semantic acceptability of the arguments of a predicate. Identifying a selection restriction that is both necessary and sufficient is a very difficult task. Hence there were attempts to propose alternatives. One such alternative was proposed by Wilks (1975) who viewed these restrictions as preferences rather than necessary and sufficient conditions. After the development of WordNet, Resnik (1993) modelled the problem of induction of selectional preferences using the semantic class hierarchy of WordNet. Since then there is an upsurge in the field of computational models for the automated treatment of selectional preferences with a variety of statistical models and machine-learning techniques. In recent times, an ambitious project to represent world knowledge was taken up under the banner of Cyc. This knowledge base contains over 500,000 terms, including about 17, 000 types of relations and about 7 million assertions relating these terms.[11] In spite of the availability of such a huge knowledge base, we rarely find Cyc being used in NLP applications.

Some computational grammatical frameworks incorporate both subcategorization as well as selection restriction together in the lexicon. They are used to capture the world knowledge or the facts about the world which are generally but not necessarily true. As such, they can't account for metaphoric usages. Nevertheless, they are very much useful in filtering out ill-formed sentences or in word-sense disambiguation, anaphora resolution, syntactic disambiguation, etc.

3.3.2 ŚABDA-ŚAKTI (LEVEL OF SIGNIFICATION)

All the above efforts primarily rely on the primary meaning of words. We saw earlier, in Indian theories of meaning, the relation between a word and its meaning, termed *śakti* (significative power) is classified into three types, viz. *abhidhā* (primary relation), *lakṣaṇā* (implication) and *vyañjanā* (suggestion). In order to use the concept of *yogyatā* (mutual compatibility) in designing a parser, we should know whether there is any hierarchy among word meanings or all the significative powers of a word come into play simultaneously.

Let us see an example to seek the answer to this question. Consider the following sentence:

Skt: *yānam vanam gacchati* ।

Gloss: vehicle {nom./acc.} forest {nom./acc.} goes.

Both the nouns, viz. *yāna* (vehicle) and *vana* (forest), are in neuter gender and can be analysed either as singular nominatives or as singular accusatives. The verb *gam* (to go) is transitive and hence has an expectancy for a *kartṛ* as well as a *karman*. *Gacchati* (goes) being in the active voice (*kartari prayoga*), its *kartṛ* would be in the nominative case and its *karman* would be in the accusative case. Thus both the words *yānam* and *vanam* can potentially satisfy the *ākāṅkṣā* of both

[11] www.cyc.com/kb (accessed on 30 August 2017).

kartṛ and *karman* of *gacchati*. Thus there are two[12] possible analyses that fulfil the *ākāṅkṣās*:

1. *yāna* as the *kartṛ* and *vana* as the *karman* of the action of going, and
2. *vana* as the *kartṛ* and *yāna* as the *karman* of the action of going.

While syntactically both these possibilities arise, are they both also semantically valid? *Vana* in the sense of a forest, which is its *abhidheyārtha* (primary meaning), cannot be the *kartṛ* of *gacchati* owing to the fact that the action of going has an expectancy of a movable object as its *kartṛ*. Thus there is a violation of *yogyatā* (congruity) between the *abhidheyārthas* (primary meanings) of *vana* and *gam*. However, if we extend[13] the meaning of *vana* to the people living in the specific forest under discussion, then *vana* has *yogyatā* to be the *kartṛ* of the action of going. Thus we see that resorting to either *abhidhā* or *lakṣaṇā*, we could make sense of both syntactically possible analyses produced by the parser based on the *ākāṅkṣā*.

However, we also note that these two analyses are not on an equal footing. Let us ask whether a human being gets both these interpretations when he listens to this sentence? In a normal situation, when one listens to this sentence, he gets only one *śābdabodha*, viz. that "A vehicle is going to the forest". But if there is a proper context, say for example, a new vehicle is found near a forest, and all the people living in the forest were anxious to see this vehicle. And thus all of them go to (see) the vehicle. In such a situation, *vana*, in the extended sense, would be the *kartṛ*. Thus we see that the analysis involving *abhidhā* is unmarked and hence becomes the first probable interpretation whereas the second sense is marked by its context. Therefore, provided there is a proper context, even the second reading is possible.

Mīmāṁsakas and rhetoricians discuss the usage of *lakṣaṇā*. The very first condition for the use of *lakṣaṇā* is *mukhyārthabādha* (inapplicability/unsuitability of the primary meaning). If the first

---

[12] There are four more other possibilities with *yāna* as the adjective of *vana* and vice versa, with each *vana* and *yāna* as either *kartṛ* or *karman*. But in order to focus on the aspect of the level of signification, we have ignored these possibilities here.

[13] The Vaiyākaraṇas consider this extended meaning also as an *abhidhā*.

analysis satisfies *abhidhā*, one cannot go for *lakṣaṇā*. And thus the second analysis, which uses *lakṣaṇā*, is blocked.

This constraint is further elaborated in the *barhirnyāya* section of Mīmāṁsā. Devasthali (1959: 53) states:[14]

> Of the senses, viz. *mukhya* and *gauṇa* it is only the *mukhya* which is to be accepted as being conveyed by the *mantra* and it alone has to be connected with the enjoined act, which when applied to similar case, means that words, as far as possible, must be understood as conveying their *mukhyārtha* alone, . . .

Further with regard to the use of the secondary meaning, Mīmāṁsā very clearly observes:[15]

> *Lakṣaṇā* is resorted to only as a means to avoid *ānarthakyadoṣa* and that it can be resorted to only if the literal sense is found to be unsuitable in the context; and that too only as the last resort.
>
> – Devasthali 1959: 59

Thus, according to Mīmāṁsakas, *lakṣaṇā* is a *doṣa* (fault). Only if the *abhidhā* (primary relation) does not make any sense and leaves the sentence *anarthaka* (having no meaning), should one use the *lakṣaṇā*.[16]

Rhetoricians also have the same stand with regard to *lakṣaṇā*. They accept three conditions as necessary for a word to denote the implied/extended/metaphoric sense. These three conditions are the following:[17]

1. Inapplicability/unsuitability of the primary meaning,
2. some relation between the primary meaning and the extended meaning, and
3. definite motive justifying the extension.

Of course, there are exceptions to these rules. These exceptions are those where secondary meaning is included along with the primary meaning, such as *ajahad-lakṣaṇā* and *jahad–ajahad-lakṣaṇā*. In order to

---

14 *tasmānmukhyagauṇayormukhye kāryasampratyaya iti siddham*। – Jha 1936: 751

15 *yadāñjasyena śabdārtho nāvakalpate tadā lakṣaṇayāpi kalpyamānaḥ sādhurbhavati*।
– *Śabarabhāṣya* 2.2.6

16 *saptadaśāratnī nyāya*। – Devasthali 1959: 58

17 *mukhyārthabādhe tadyoge rūḍhito 'tha prayojanāt*।
anyo 'rtho lakṣyate yat sā lakṣaṇāropitā kriyā।। – *Kāvyaprakāśa* II.9

decide whether to use only primary meaning or both the primary and the secondary meaning in a given situation, we need to know the intention of the speaker.

Having decided the hierarchy between the primary and extended meanings, now let us turn to the suggestive meaning. Consider the sentence *gato 'stam arkaḥ* discussed earlier, which literally means "the sun has set". Every listener gets this meaning. But in addition, depending on who is uttering it, and to whom, there are different suggestive meanings and these meanings coexist with the primary meaning. They do not block the primary meaning. Therefore *vyaṅgyārtha* exists in parallel with the primary/secondary meaning.

It is also clear that the suggestive meanings are different for different persons and may also differ in different situations. So it is not possible to objectively process this meaning for a given utterance. It involves subjectivity. And hence it is outside the scope of automatic processing which is constrained by objectivity. This also puts an upper limit on the meaning one can get from a linguistic utterance without the intervention of subjective judgements.

In summary, we observe that these three meanings are not in the same plane. *Lakṣaṇā* comes into play only when *abhidhā* fails to provide a suitable meaning for congruent interpretation. The suggestive meaning, however, can coexist with the *abhidhā* as well as the *lakṣaṇā* and, as such, is outside the scope of automatic processing with the existing tools and resources.

These observations then lead us to the following strategy for mechanical processing. First restrict the meanings to *abhidhā* to get the analysis. In case no analysis produces a congruous interpretation in terms of *abhidhā*, use *lakṣaṇā*. Leave the interpretation of *vyañjanā* to the reader. Let us see in what follows, how easy/difficult it is to mechanically distinguish between *abhidhā* and *lakṣaṇā*.

3.3.3 YOGYATĀ AS A FILTER

The necessary condition for understanding a sentence is that a word having an expectancy for another word should become *nirākāṅkṣā* (having no further expectancy) once a relation is established between the two words. Further, such related words should also have mutual compatibility from the point of view of the proposed relation. If they are not mutually compatible, then the expectancy of such words will not be put to rest and there will not be any verbal cognition. Therefore the role of *yogyatā* in verbal cognition is very important. The purpose of using *yogyatā* in parsing is not to make a computer understand the text, but to rule out incompatible solutions from among the solutions that fulfil the *ākāṅkṣā*s. For example, in the sentence

Skt: *yānam vanam gacchati* ।

Gloss: vehicle {neut., sg., nom./acc.} forest {neut., sg., nom./acc.} goes.

There are six possible analyses, based on the *ākāṅkṣā*. They are:

1. ***yānam*** is the *kartṛ* and ***vanam*** is the *karman*,
2. ***yānam*** is the *karman* and ***vanam*** is the *kartṛ*,
3. ***yānam*** is the *kartṛ* and *vanam* is the *viśeṣaṇa* of ***yānam***,
4. ***yānam*** is the *karman* and ***vanam*** is the *viśeṣaṇa* of ***yānam***,
5. ***yānam*** is the ***viśeṣaṇa*** of ***vanam*** which is the *kartṛ*, and
6. ***yānam*** is the ***viśeṣaṇa*** of ***vanam*** which is the *karman*.

If the machine knows that the *kartṛ* of an action of going should be movable and that the designation of ***yāna*** is movable, but that of ***vana*** is not movable, then mechanically it can rule out the second analysis. The words ***yānam*** and ***vanam*** on account of the agreement between them have the potential to be *viśeṣaṇa*s of each other. But the semantic incompatibility between the meanings of these words rules out the last four possibilities, leaving only the first correct analysis.

As another example, look at the sentence:

Skt: *rāmeṇa bāṇena vālīḥ ahanyata* ।

Gloss: Rāma {instr.} arrow {instr.} Vāli was killed.

Eng: Vāli was killed by Rāma with an arrow.

Either *rāma* or *bāṇa*, since both are in instrumental case, can potentially be a *kartṛ* or a *karaṇa* of the verb *han* (to kill). If the machine knows that *bāṇa* can be used as an instrument in the act of killing, while *rāma* being the name of a person, cannot be a potential instrument in the act of killing, it can then filter out the incompatible solution: *Rāma* as a *karaṇa* and *bāṇa* as a *kartṛ*.

Look at another sentence:

Skt: *payasā siñcati* ।
Gloss: Water {instr.} sprinkles.
Eng: (He) sprinkles with water.

Here *payas* (water) is in the instrumental case, denotes a liquid, and hence is suitable to be the instrument of the action of *siñc* (to sprinkle).

But in the sentence,

Skt: *vahninā siñcati* ।
Gloss: Fire {instr.} sprinkles.
Eng: (He) sprinkles with fire.

vahni (fire) is not fit to be an instrument of the action of sprinkling and as such it fails to satisfy the *yogyatā*. Now in such cases, in spite of the word meanings being incompatible, we know that a listener still understands the sentence, and also knows that there is incompatibility between the meanings. However, the cognition of the listener is not a valid cognition and thus, Naiyāyikas would not agree that there is any verbal cognition, since for them the verbal cognition has to be a valid cognition, *śabda* being one of the means of valid cognition. However, Vaiyākaraṇas, while interpreting a sentence, resort to the "world of words" and not to the real world. And hence for them the cognition does take place with such sentences as well. But then, if the meanings are not mutually compatible, then how does verbal cognition take place? It is because, when the primary meanings are not compatible, the secondary/metaphoric meanings come into effect and the mutual compatibility is established.

We explain this further with the previous example. Imagine the following situation in which *vahninā siñcati* is uttered. Let there be a person in a bad mood, and his friend, without knowing this, starts accusing him further for some fault of his, instead of uttering some soothing words to console him. A third person watching this utters *kim vahninā siñcasi*? (Why are you sprinkling with fire?); a perfect verbalization of the situation. The friend's accusation is like fire to the person who is already in a bad mood. This meaning of *vahni* is its extended meaning. Even a Naiyāyika would accept such an interpretation. Thus, even if a relation between the primary meanings does not make sense, if the relation between extended meanings makes sense, we need to produce the parse. Thus, in addition to the primary meanings, machine also, sometimes, needs access to the secondary/extended meanings of the words.

3.3.4 MODELLING YOGYATĀ

Yogyatā is compatibility between the meanings of related words. This meaning, as we saw above, can be either a primary or a metaphoric one. Absence of any hindrance in the understanding of a sentence implies there is *yogyatā* or congruity among the meanings. There have been different views among scholars about what *yogyatā* is. According to one definition, *yogyatā* is *arthābādhaḥ*[18] (that which is not a hindrance). It is further elaborated as *bādhakapramāvirahaḥ*[19] or *bādhakaniścayābhāvaḥ*[20] (absence of the decisive knowledge of incompatibility). There are other attempts to define it as an existing qualifying property. One such definition is *sambandha-arhatvam*[21] (eligibility for mutual association) and the other one is *paraspara-anvaya-prayojaka-dharmavattvam*[22] (the property of promoting mutual association). The first set of definitions presents *yogyatā* as an absence of incompatibility whereas the second set of definitions present it as the presence of compatibility between the meanings.

Let us see the implications of modelling *yogyatā* through these two lenses:

1. We establish a relation only if the two morphemes are mutually congruous. In this case we need to take care of not only the congruity between primary meanings but even the same between the metaphoric/secondary meanings.
2. We establish a relation if there is no incongruity between the two meanings.

The first possibility ensures that the precision is high and there is less chance of Type-1 error, i.e. of allowing wrong solutions. The second possibility, on the other hand, ensures that the recall is high

---

[18] *arthābādhaḥ yogyatā* – *Tarkasaṁgraha*, p. 30

[19] *Nyāyakośa*, p. 675.

[20] Ibid., p. 676.

[21] *Vākyārthamātṛkāvṛtti*, p. 9.

[22] *Tattvacintāmaṇi*, vol. III.

and there is less chance of Type-2 error, viz. the possibility of missing any correct solution with a possibility that we allow some meaningless solutions as well. If we decide to go for the first possibility, we need to handle both the primary and the secondary meanings, and we need to state precisely under what conditions the meanings are congruous. This means modelling congruity for each verb and for each relation. This is a gigantic task and there is a possibility of missing correct solutions, if we do not take into account all the possible extensions of meanings. Therefore, we decided to go for the second choice allowing a machine to make some mistakes in choosing incongruous solutions but we did not want to throw away correct solutions even by mistake. This decision is in favour of our philosophy of sharing the load between man and machine. Our aim is to provide access to the original text by reducing the language learning load. So we cannot afford to miss a possible solution. Thus at the risk of providing more solutions than the actual possible solutions, we decided to pass on some load to the reader of pruning out irrelevant solutions manually.

In the first step, we decided to use *yogyatā* only in those cases where a case marker is ambiguous between more than one relation. We noticed the following three cases of ambiguities with reference to the relations.

1. *Viśeṣya–viśeṣaṇa-bhāva* (adjectival relation). Here both the *viśeṣya* and the *viśeṣaṇa* agree in gender, number and case, and hence only on the basis of the word form, we cannot tell which one is *viśeṣya* and which one is *viśeṣaṇa*.
2. A *kāraka* and non-*kāraka* relation as in
    a. *karaṇa* (an instrument) and *hetu* (cause), both expressed through an instrument case marker,
    b. *sampradāna* (a beneficiary), *prayojana* (purpose) and *tādarthya* (being intended for), all the three relations encoded with a dative case marker, and
    c. *apādāna* (source) and *hetu* (cause), both being marked by an ablative case marker.
3. *Ṣaṣṭhī sambandha* (genitive relation) and *viśeṣaṇa* (adjective). When two words are in the genitive case, it is not clear whether there is an adjectival relation between them or a genitive relation.

Let us now discuss each of these three cases.

Viśeṣya–Viśeṣaṇa-bhāva

We come across a term *samānādhikaraṇa* (coreference) in Pāṇini to denote an adjective (Joshi and Roodbergen 1998: 6). One of the contexts in which the term *samānādhikaraṇa* is used is the context of an agreement between an adjective and a noun.[23] For example, *dhāvantam mṛgam* (a running deer) or *sundaraḥ aśvaḥ* (a beautiful horse). Pāṇini has not defined the term *samānādhikaraṇa*, either. The term *samānādhikaraṇa* literally means "having the same locus". Patañjali in the Samarthāhnika discusses the term *sāmānādhikaraṇya*. In the example, *sundaraḥ aśvaḥ* (a beautiful horse), both the qualities of *saundarya* (beauty) and *aśvatva* (horseness) reside in an *aśva* (horse), which is the common locus. Similarly, in the case of *ācāryaḥ droṇaḥ* or *agne gṛhapate* (Oh Agni! householder), both the words *ācārya* as well as *droṇa* refer to the same individual, so do *agni* and *gṛhapati*. This is true of various other relation-denoting terms such as *guru*, *śiṣya*, *pitā* and *putra*, and *upādhi*s (imposed/acquired properties) such as *rājā*, *mantrī* and *vaidya*. From all this discussion, we may say *sāmānādhikaraṇya* is the semantic characterization of a *viśeṣaṇa*.

English has a separate morphological category for adjective. Similarly in Hindi, the morphology of adjective is different from that of the substantives (nouns). But in Sanskrit, there is no syntactic/morphological category as a *viśeṣaṇa* (an adjective). Morphologically, in Sanskrit, the adjectives and substantives are indistinguishable. But, gender, number and case of a *viśeṣaṇa* follow that of a *viśeṣya* (the head). From the point of view of analysis this provides a syntactic clue for a possible *viśeṣya–viśeṣaṇa-bhāva* between two words such as in *śuklaḥ paṭaḥ* (a white cloth). This agreement is just a necessary condition, and not sufficient. Because, a *viśeṣaṇa*, in addition to agreeing with the *viśeṣya*, should also be semantically fit to be a qualifier of the *viśeṣya*. For example, there can be two words say *yānam* (a vehicle) and *vanam* (a forest) that match perfectly in gender, number and case, but we cannot imagine a *viśeṣya–viśeṣaṇa-bhāva* between *yāna* and *vana*. Is it only the semantics that rules out such a relation

23 *sāmānādhikaraṇyam ekavibhaktitvam ca। dvayoścaitad bhavati। kayoḥ। viśeṣaṇa-viśeṣyayoḥ vā saṁjñā-saṁjñinorvā।* – *Mahābhāṣya* 1.1.1

or are there any clues, especially syntactic ones, that help us to rule out a *viśeṣya–viśeṣaṇa-bhāva* between such words?

In Search of Clues. Pāṇini has not defined the terms *viśeṣya* and *viśeṣaṇa*. Patañjali uses two terms *dravya* (substance) and *guṇa* (quality) while commenting on the agreement between a *viśeṣya* and a *viśeṣaṇa*.

> *yad asau dravyam śrito bhavati guṇaḥ tasya yat liṅgam vacanam ca tad guṇasya api bhavati* । – *Mahābhāṣya* under A 4.1.3, vārtika VI
>
> A quality assumes the gender and number of the substance in which it resides.

But then What Is This Guṇa? We come across the description of *guṇa* by Kaiyaṭa.

> *sattve niviśate apaiti pr̥thag jātiṣu dr̥śyate* ।
> *ādheyaścākriyājaśca saḥ asattva-prakr̥ti-guṇaḥ* ॥
> – Ibid., A 4.1.44, reference from Kaiyaṭa
>
> *Guṇa* is something which is found in things/substances *sattve niviśate*, which can cease to be there (*apaiti*), which is found in different kinds of substances (*pr̥thag jātiṣu*), which is sometimes an effect of an action and sometimes not so (*ādheyaścākriyājaśca*), and whose nature is not that of a substance (*asattvaprakr̥ti*).

Thus *guṇa* is something which is not a substance, since it resides in other things. It is not a universal, since it is found in different kinds of substance. It is not an action, since *guṇa* is sometimes an effect of an action, as in the case of the colour of a jar and sometimes, not, as in the case of the magnitude of a substance. This characterization of *guṇa* is very close to the Vaiśeṣika's concept of *guṇa* (Kunjunni Raja 1963).

Then, Is This Vaiśeṣika Guṇa a Viśeṣaṇa? Patañjali commenting on the word *guṇa* under *Aṣṭādhyāyī* 2.2.11 provides an example contrasting two types of *guṇa*s. While both *śukla* and *gandha* are qualities (*guṇa*) according to the Vaiśeṣika ontology, the usage *śuklaḥ paṭaḥ* (a white cloth) is possible, while *gandham candanam* (fragrance sandalwood) is not. Thus, only some of the Vaiśeṣika *guṇa*s have the potential to be a *viśeṣaṇa*, and not all.

If Viśeṣaṇa Is not a Vaiśeṣika Guṇa, What Is It? The characterization of *guṇa* by Bhartr̥hari in his Guṇa-Samuddeśa includes *bhedakam* as one of the characteristics of *guṇa*. But, in addition, *guṇa*, according to him, is also capable of expressing the degree of quality in a substance through a suffix. He defines *guṇa* as

> *saṁsargī bhedakam yad yad savyāpāram pratīyate*।
> *guṇatvam paratantratvāt tasya śāstra udāhṛtam*॥
> – *Vākyapadīya* III.5.1

> Whatever rests on something else (*saṁsargī*), differentiates it (*bhedaka*) and is understood in that function (*savyāpāra*) is, being dependent, called quality in the *śāstra*. – Iyer 1971

According to Bhartṛhari, a quality is that which is intimately related (*saṁsargī*) to a substance and differentiates (*bhedaka*) that substance delimiting its scope. Apart from being a differentiator, a *guṇa* has another important characteristic, that such a distinguishing quality can also express the degree of excellence through some suffix (such as a comparative suffix *tarap* or a superlative suffix *tamap*). This concept of *guṇa* of Bhartṛhari, thus, is different from the concept of the *guṇa* of a Vaiśeṣika. This definitely rules out the case of *gandha*, since we cannot have *gandhatara* but we can have *śuklatara* to distinguish the whiteness between two white cloths. Nāgeśa in his *Udyota*, under *Mahābhāṣya* in *sūtra* A2.1.1, explains *savyāpāram* as follows:

> A quality is such that it invariably represents its substratum and by presenting its substratum it enters into the domain of meaning of a word which expressed that quality. Alternatively, a quality is such that it invariably represents all the individuals delimited by that quality. – Matilal 1985: 388

This explanation of a *guṇa* is nothing but the *guṇa-vacana* of Pāṇini.

Guṇa-vacana of Pāṇini. We have another hint from Pāṇini through Patañjali. While in *Aṣṭādhyāyī* 4.1.3, Patañjali has used the terms *dravya* and *guṇa* in connection with agreement, in *Aṣṭādhyāyī* 1.2.52 he has used the term *guṇa-vacana* while describing a *viśeṣaṇa*.

> *guṇavacanānāṁ śabdānāmāśrayataḥ liṅgavacanāni bhavantīti*
> – *Mahābhāṣya* on A 1.2.52

> The words which are *guṇa-vacana*s take the gender and number of the substance in which they reside.

The term *guṇa-vacana* is used for those words which designate a quality and then a substance in which this quality resides (Cardona 2009). In the example, *śuklaḥ paṭaḥ*, since *śukla*, in addition to being a quality (white colour), can also designate the substance, such as a *paṭa* (cloth), which is (white) in colour, it is a *guṇa-vacana*. But *gandha* (fragrance) designates only a quality and cannot be used to designate a substance that has a fragrance, and hence is not a *guṇa-vacana* word.

Is Guṇa-vacana Necessary and Sufficient to Describe a Viśeṣaṇa? Let us look at the examples above. It definitely rules out *yānam* and *vanam* to be qualifiers of each other, since neither of them is a quality. But then what about *dhāvan* (the one who is running) in *dhāvan bālakaḥ* (a running boy)? Is *dhāvan* a *guṇa-vacana*?

Guṇa-vacana is a technical term, used by Pāṇini, to define an operation of elision of *matup* suffix in certain quality denoting words such as *śukla*. So technically, a word such as *dhāvan*, though it designates a *dravya* (substance), is not a *guṇa-vacana*. This is clear from Patañjali's commentary on *Aṣṭādhyāyī* 1.4.1,[24] where he states that compounds (*samāsa*s), primary derivatives (*kṛdanta*s), secondary derivatives (*taddhitānta*s), indeclinables (*avyaya*s), pronouns (*sarvanāma*s), words referring to universals (*jāti*s) and numerals (*saṅkhyā*) cannot get the designation *guṇa-vacana*, since the latter *saṁjñā*s (technical terms) supersede the previous ones.[25]

The very fact, that Kātyāyana had to mention that words belonging to all the latter categories are not *guṇa-vacana*, indicates that all these categories of words have a potential to get the *guṇa-vacana* designation, but Pāṇini did not intend to assign this *saṁjñā* to these words. This list of various categories, in fact, provides us a morphological clue for a word to be a *viśeṣaṇa*. Thus we observe that the notion of *guṇa-vacana* in Pāṇini is very empirical and is useful to formulate the semantics necessary for processing Sanskrit texts.

Here are some examples of *viśeṣaṇa*s belonging to these different grammatical categories:

---

[24] The *vārttika guṇavacanam ca* is followed by several other *vārttika*s, of which the following two are relevant:

samāsakṛttaddhitāvyayasarvanāmāsarvaliṅgā jātiḥ ||
saṅkhyā ca ||

[25] *guṇavacanasaṁjñāyāḥ ca etābhiḥ bādhanam yathā syāt iti* |

1. *Samāsa* (a compound). *Bahuvrīhi* (exocentric) compounds refer to an object different from the components of the compound and thus act as adjectives. For example, *pītāmbaraḥ* is made up of two components *pīta* (yellow) and *ambara* (cloth), but it refers to the "one wearing a yellow-cloth" (and is conventionally restricted to Viṣṇu). An example of a *tat-puruṣa* (endocentric) compound as a *viśeṣaṇa* is *parama-udāraḥ* (extremely noble).
2. *Kṛdanta* (an adjectival participle). Nouns derived from verbs act as qualifiers of a noun. For example, in the expression *dhāvantam mṛgam* (a running deer), *dhāvantam*, a verbal noun, is a *viśeṣaṇa*. Only certain *kṛt* suffixes such as *śatṛ*, *śānac* and *kta* produce nouns that can be *viśeṣaṇa*s, not all.
3. *Taddhitānta* (a secondary derivative). *Taddhitānta*s with certain suffixes derive new nouns such as *bhāratīya* (Indian), *dhanavāna* (wealthy) and *guṇin* (possessing good qualities) that denote a *dravya* (substance), as against certain other *taddhitānta* words such as *manuṣyatā* (humanity) *vārddhakya* (senility) which derive new words designating *guṇa*s (qualities).
4. *Sarvanāma* (a pronoun). Pronouns also act as qualifiers. For example, in an expression *idam pustakam* (this book), *idam* is a *viśeṣaṇa*.
5. *Jāti* (a universal). In the expression *āmraḥ vṛkṣaḥ* (a mango tree), both the words *āmraḥ* and *vṛkṣaḥ* designate common nouns. But one is a special and the other one a general one. So the designation of *āmra* is a subset of the designation of *vṛkṣa*. Only in such cases, where there is a *parājāti–aparājāti* (hyponymy–hypernymy) relation, the one denoting an *aparājāti* (hyponymy) qualifies to be a *viśeṣaṇa* of the other one.
6. *Saṅkhyā* (a numeral). In an expression *ekaḥ puruṣaḥ* (a man), the word *ekaḥ* designates a number, and is a *viśeṣaṇa* of *puruṣa*.

There are still two more classes of words that are not covered in the above list, but which can be *viśeṣaṇa*s. They are: words denoting an acquired property or an imposed property and the relation denoting terms. For example, *ācārya* in *ācāryaḥ droṇaḥ* or *putra* in *daśarathaputraḥ rāmaḥ*.

In summary, *samasta-pada*, certain *kṛdanta*s, certain *taddhitānta*s, *saṅkhyā*, *sarvanāma*, ontological categories such as *parā–aparā jāti*s, semantico-syntactic property such as *guṇa-vacana* and finally semantic properties such as relation denoting terms and *upādhi*s, all these serve as characterizations of a *viśeṣaṇa*. This characterization is only a necessary condition, and not sufficient, since it does not involve any mutual compatibility between the words. However, it brings in more precision in the necessary conditions for two words to be in *viśeṣya–viśeṣaṇa-bhāva*.

Deciding a Viśeṣya. Once we have identified the words that are mutually compatible with regard to an adjectival relation, next thing is to decide the *viśeṣya* (head) among them. The commentary on *Aṣṭādhyāyī* 2.1.57 is useful in deciding the *viśeṣya*. This *sūtra* deals with the compound formation of two words that are in *viśeṣya–viśeṣaṇa-bhāva*. In Sanskrit compound formation, the one which is subordinate gets the designation of *upasarjana*. The *sūtra*s that provide a condition for assigning the technical term *upasarjana* give us clues about which word classes are subordinate to which ones. The words may refer to a *dravya* (substance) through a common noun (*jāti*) such as *utpalam* (a flower), or through an action associated with it (*kriyā-vacana*), as in *dhāvan* (running), or through a *guṇa-vācaka* such as *nīlam*. If there are two words indicating common nouns, one denoting a special noun and the other one denoting a general noun, then the one which denotes a special type of common noun is subordinate.[26] For example, in *āmraḥ vṛkṣaḥ*, *āmra* is a special kind of tree, and hence is a *viśeṣaṇa* and *vṛkṣa* is its *viśeṣya*. If one word designates a common noun and the other one is either a *guṇa-vacana* or a *kriyā-vacana*, then the one denoting the *guṇa-vacana* becomes the *viśeṣya*.[27] Thus in *nīlam utpalam*, *utpalam* is the *viśeṣya*. In *pācakaḥ brāhmaṇaḥ* (cook brāhmaṇa), *brāhmaṇaḥ* is the *viśeṣya*. When one of the words designates a *guṇa-vacana* and the other a *kriyā-vacana*, or both the words designate either *guṇa-vacana*s or *kriyā-vacana*s, then either of them can be a *viśeṣya*, as

---

[26] *sāmānyajāti-viśeṣajātiśabdayoḥ samabhivyāhāre tu viśeṣajātireva viśeṣaṇam* । – under *Aṣṭādhyāyī* 2.1.57, in BM

[27] *jātiśabdo guṇakriyāśabdasamabhivyāhāre viśeṣyasamarpaka eva na tu viśeṣaṇa samarpakaḥ, svabhāvāt* – under *Aṣṭādhyāyī* 2.1.57, in BM

in *khañjaḥ kubjaḥ* (a humpbacked who is limping) or *kubjaḥ khañjaḥ* (a limping person with humpback), similarly as in *khañjaḥ pācakaḥ* (a limping cook) or *pācakaḥ khañjaḥ* (a limping person who is a cook), etc.

On the basis of the above discussion, we have the following preferential order for the *viśeṣya*:

jātivācaka > {*guṇa-vacana, kṛdanta*}.

We saw earlier that a *viśeṣaṇa* can be any one of the following: a pronoun, a numeral, a *kṛdanta*, a *taddhitānta*, a *samasta-pada*, *guṇa-vācaka*, *jāti*, relation-denoting terms and an *upādhi*. So adding all these categories to the above preferential order, we get:

jāti-vācaka > *upādhi* > *taddhitānta* > *guṇa-vacana* > numeral > *kṛdanta* > pronoun.[28]

Flat or Hierarchical Structure? After we identify all the words that have a *samānādhikaraṇa* relation between them and mark the *viśeṣya* (the head) among them, the next task is to know whether a *viśeṣaṇa* is related to this *viśeṣya* directly or through other *viśeṣaṇa*s.

If there are *n* *viśeṣaṇa*s and all of them are related to the *viśeṣya* directly, then it results in a flat structure. But if a *viśeṣaṇa* is related to the *viśeṣya* through other *viśeṣaṇa*s, then there is an exponentially large number of ways in which *n* *viśeṣaṇa*s can relate to the *viśeṣya*. For example, if there are three words say *a*, *b* and *c*, of which *c* is the *viśeṣya*. Then there are three ways in which the other two words can relate to *c*.

1. Both *a* and *b* are the *viśeṣaṇa*s of *c*.
2. *a* is a *viśeṣaṇa* of *b* and *b* that of *c*.
3. *b* is a *viśeṣaṇa* of *a* and *a* that of *c*.

In positional languages like English, only the first two cases are possible. For example, consider the phrase "light red car", which may either mean a car which is red in colour and is light in weight, or a car which is light-red in colour. In the second case, light-red is a compound.

Sanskrit being a free word-order language, one can imagine,

[28] This preferential order is purely based on some observations of the corpus and needs further theoretical support, if there is any.

computationally, a possibility for the third type as well. The relation between the adjectival terms being that of *sāmānādhikaraṇya*, semantically, only a flat structure is possible with adjectives. The other two cases of hierarchical structures result into compound formation in Sanskrit.

This is also supported by Jaimini's *Mīmāṁsāsūtra*:

guṇānām ca parārthatvāt asambandhaḥ samatvāt syāt । – 3.1.22

> Inasmuch as all subsidiaries are subservient to something else and are equal in that respect, there can be no connection among themselves.
> – Jha 1933: 373

Thus, a *viśeṣaṇa* is not connected to another *viśeṣaṇa*. The associated structure is a flat one, with all the *viśeṣaṇa*s being connected to the *viśeṣya*.

Distinguishing a Kāraka from a Non-kāraka

In Sanskrit, some case markers denote both a *kāraka* relation as well as a non-*kāraka* relation, as we saw earlier. In a sentence, if a verb denotes an action, then nouns denote the participants in such an action. These participants, which are classified into six types, viz. *kartṛ*, *karman*, *karaṇa*, *sampradāna*, *apādāna* and *adhikaraṇa*, are collectively called as *kāraka*s. Other nouns in the sentence, which do not participate directly in the action, express non-*kāraka* relations such as *hetu* (cause) and *prayojanam* (purpose). We get a clue to distinguish between the nouns which are related by a *kāraka* relation and those which are related by a non-*kāraka* one in the Aruṇādhikaraṇa of the *Śābara-Bhāṣya*. There it is mentioned:

na ca amūrta-arthaḥ kriyātāḥ sādhanaṁ bhavatīti ।
– *Śābara-Bhāṣya*, p. 654

> No unsubstantial object can ever be the means of accomplishing an act.

Thus anything other than *dravya* cannot be a *kāraka*. As we saw earlier, the *guṇa-vacana*s also can designate a *dravya*. And thus, all the *dravya*s and the *guṇa-vacana*s are qualified to be a *kāraka*. And the rest, that is nouns which denote either a *guṇa*, which is not a *guṇa-vacana* or a *kriyā* (verbal noun), may have a non-*kāraka* relation with a verb.

Let us see some examples.

Skt: *rāmaḥ daśarathasya ājñayā rathena vanam gacchati* ।

Gloss: Rāma {nom.} Daśaratha {gen.} order {ins.} *ratha* {ins.} forest {acc.} goes.

Eng: On Daśaratha's order, Rāma goes to the forest by a chariot.

Skt: *rāmaḥ adhyayanena atra vasati.*

Gloss: Rāma {nom.} study {ins.} here lives.

Eng: Rāma lives here in order to study.

In the first sentence *ājñā* (order) is the cause (*hetu*) for Rāma's going to forest, *ratha* (chariot) is the instrument (or vehicle) for his going and in the second sentence *adhyayana* is the cause (*hetu*) of Rāma's stay.

Since both *hetu* as well as *karaṇa* demand a third case suffix, *ākāṅkṣā* would establish a relation of *karaṇa* between *ājñayā* and *gacchati*,[29] between *rathena* and *gacchati* and also between *adhyayana* and *gacchati*. Now with the above definition of a *kāraka*, *adhyayana*, being a verbal noun (a *kr̥danta*) in the sense of *bhāva*, represents an abstract concept and therefore it does not designate a *dravya* (a substance). Hence *adhyayana* cannot be a *karaṇa*. Similarly *ājñā*, which is a *guṇa* (according to Vaiśeṣika ontology, being a *śabda*), cannot be a *karaṇa*. Thus use of congruity helps in pruning out impossible relations.

On the same grounds, establishment of *apādāna* and *sampradāna* relations between a non-*dravya*[30] denoting noun and a verb can also be prevented.

Congruous Substantive for a Ṣaṣṭhī (Genitive)

Pāṇini has not given any semantic criterion for the use of the genitive case. His rule is *ṣaṣṭhī śeṣe* (A 2.3.50) which means, in all other cases that are not covered so far, the genitive case suffix is to be used. The relations expressed by *ṣaṣṭhī* (genitive) fall under the *utthāpya* (to be raised) *ākāṅkṣā*. This is a case of unidirectional expectancy. Thus, there is no syntactic clue as to with which noun the word in the genitive case would get attached. All other nouns in the sentence are potential

---

[29] To be precise, the relation is between the meaning denoted by the nominal stem *ājñā* and the one denoted by the verbal root *gam*.

[30] To be precise, a non-*dravya* and non-*guṇa-vacana*.

candidates for a genitive relation to join with. The clue is, however, semantic. Patañjali in the *Mahābhāṣya* on *Aṣṭādhyayī* 2.3.50 provides some semantic clues. He says there are hundreds of meanings of *ṣaṣṭhī*. Some of them are *sva–svāmī-bhāva* as in *rājñaḥ puruṣaḥ* (a king's man), *avayava–avayavī-bhāva* as in *vṛkṣasya śākhā* (branch of a tree), etc. So in order to establish a genitive relation, we need the semantic inputs. However, there are certain constraints. They are:

1. A genitive connecting a verbal noun expressing *bhāva*, such as *lyuṭ*, expresses a *kāraka*[31] relation and not the genitive one, as in *rāmasya gamanam*.
2. A genitive always connects with a *viśeṣya* and never with a *viśeṣaṇa*, since there is a *samānādhikaraṇa* relation between the *viśeṣya* and *viśeṣaṇa*. For example, in the expression *rāmasya vīreṇa putreṇa*, the genitive relation of *rāmasya* is with *putreṇa* and not with *vīreṇa*.

Lexical resources such as Sanskrit WordNet[32] and the *Amarakośa*[33] that are marked with the semantic information of part–whole relation, *janya–janaka-bhāva* (child–parent relation), *ājīvikā* relation, etc. help in identifying the genitive relations with confidence. When both the words refer to two *dravya*s (substantives), then also there is a genitive relation. So note that, while for other relations, we look for the absence of non-congruity for ruling out the relations, in the case of genitives, instead, we look for the presence of congruity, to prune out impossible relations. We took this decision, since we found it difficult to describe the non-congruity in the case of genitive relations.

Ambiguity between a Genitive and an Adjectival Relation. We come across an ambiguity in the genitive relation, in the presence of adjectives since an adjective carries the gender number and case of the head it modifies. Look at the following two examples:

Skt: *vīrasya rāmasya bāṇam.*

Gloss: brave {gen.} Rāma {gen.} arrow.

Eng: An arrow of brave Rāma.

---

31 *kartṛkarmaṇoḥ kṛti* । A 2.3.65

32 http://www.cfilt.iit b.ac.in/wordnet/webswn/english_version.php

33 http://scl.samsaadhanii.in/amarakosha/index.html

and

> Skt: *rāmasya putrasya pustakam.*
> Gloss: Rāma {gen.} son {gen.} book.
> Eng: A book of Rāma's son.

In these examples, the relation between Rāma and *bāṇa* in the first example, and between *putra* and *pustaka* in the second example is that of genitive. However, the relation between *vīra* and Rāma in the first example is the adjectival relation, and not the genitive one while the relation between Rāma and *putra* in the second example is a kinship relation.

3.3.5 EVALUATION

As stated earlier, *ākāṅkṣā* states the possibility of relations between two words. The mutual compatibility between the meanings further helps in pruning out the incompatible relations. We classified the content nouns into two classes: *dravya* and *guṇa*. *Guṇa*s being further marked if they are *guṇa-vacana*s. We tested the mutual compatibility only when the suffix is ambiguous. To be precise, the *yogyatā* is used only to disambiguate between a *kāraka* vs non-*kāraka* relation, to establish the *viśeṣya–viśeṣaṇa-bhāva* and to establish a genitive relation. This ensured that we do not miss on the metaphoric meanings. In the case of *kāraka* relations, if the noun denotes a *guṇa-vacana*, then the possible *kāraka* relation, on the basis of expectancy, is pruned out. Similarly, in the case of adjectival relations, the relations with a non-*guṇa-vācaka guṇa* is pruned out.

The performance of the system with and without *yogyatā* was measured to evaluate the impact of *yogyatā*. The corpus for evaluation of sentences consists of around 2,300 sentences. It includes sentences with various grammatical constructions, a few passages from school textbook, the *Bhagavadgītā* and a sample from Māgha's *Śiśupālavadham*. The *śloka*s in the *Bhagavadgītā* as well as in the *Śiśupālavadham* were converted to a canonical form.[34] The sentences with conjunction were not considered for the evaluation, since the nouns in conjunction conflict with the adjectives and the criteria for handling conjunction

[34] All the *śloka*s were presented in their *anvita* form, following the traditional *daṇḍānvaya* method, where the verb typically is at the end, and *viśeṣaṇa*s precede the *viśeṣya*s.

Table 3.2: Corpus Characteristics

Type	*Sentences*	*Words*	*Characters*	*Average Sentences Length*	*Average Word Length*
Textbooks	260	1,295	9,591	4.98	7.40
Syntax	937	3,339	25,410	3.56	7.61
Māgha's *Śiśupālavadham*	66	623	5,851	9.40	9.39
Bhagavadgītā	940	5,698	42,251	6.06	7.41
Total/average	2,203	10,955	83,103	4.96	7.58

are under development. The statistics showing the size of various texts, the average word length and the average sentence length is given in Table 3.2.

All these sentences were run through a parser, first without using the conditions of *yogyatā* and second time using the conditions of *yogyatā*. In both the cases, the parser produced all possible parses. We also ensured that the correct parse is present among the produced solutions. Table 3.3 shows the statistics providing the number of solutions with and without using the filter of *yogyatā*. The number of parses produced was reduced drastically. This improved the precision by 63 per cent in textbook stories, by 67 per cent in the grammatical constructs and by 81 per cent in case of the text from the *Bhagavadgītā* and Māgha's *kāvya*. Better results in the case of these texts pertains to the fact that these texts have more usage of adjectives and non-*kāraka* relations as against the textbook sentences and artificial grammatical constructs.

Table 3.3: Improvement

Corpus Type	*Sentences*	*Average Solutions without Yogyatā*	*Average Solutions with Yogyatā*	*Improvement in Precision %*
Textbooks	260	39.76	14.56	63
Syntax	937	19.5	6.33	67
Literary	66	11,199	2,107	81
Bhagavadgītā	940	2,557	478	81
Total	2,203	1,439.54	271.49	81

3.4 Conclusion

In this chapter, we have seen how the three factors, viz. *ākāṅkṣā*, *yogyatā* and *sannidhi*, are useful in the development of a sentential parser.

Ākāṅkṣā plays an important role in establishing relations between words of a sentence. It provides clues to look for the source of information that expresses an expectancy. Pāṇinian grammar, together with various commentaries and the texts on *śābdabodha*, provides us the repository of relations between the words in a sentence and the associated semantics. It is also important to note what is expressed through the morphemes explicitly and what is coded implicitly by the conventions of the language. In the parse structure, we represent only the explicitly encoded information. The implicitly encoded information is inferred from various other sources and thus needs extra processing. If this implicit information also is coded, then the parse structure ceases to be a tree. However, this information is very much useful for handling divergences among languages.

All the arguments that correspond to the *utthita ākāṅkṣā* (mutual expectancy) always follow weak non-projectivity. But the expressions that correspond to the *utthāpya ākāṅkṣā* (unilateral expectancy) experience more freedom and move around the sentence violating even weak non-projectivity. The genitive relation and adjectival relation are the two important relations that fall under this category. These observations are important for building a parser. This thus helps in pruning out all non-solutions thereby reducing the possible number of parsed trees.

Among the three significative powers of a word, there is a hierarchy. The metaphoric meaning comes into play only when the primary meaning is non-congruous with the meaning of other words. In a given context, only one of these would be relevant and operational. Suggestive meaning, however, can exist in parallel with any of these two. And as such, it is not mechanically processable without extralinguistic information.

It is difficult to provide information of mutual congruity for each word (since this involves handling of both primary and secondary meanings). Among the several definitions of *yogyatā*, we modelled it as an absence of non-congruity. This ensures that the correct solutions are not missed. Due to lack of any syntactic criterion for *viśeṣaṇa* (adjectives) in Sanskrit, parsing Sanskrit texts with adjectives resulted in high number of false positives. Hints from Vyākaraṇa texts helped us in the formulation of a criterion for *viśeṣaṇa* with syntactic and ontological constraints, which provided us a hint to decide the absence of non-congruity between two words with respect to the adjectival relation. A simple two-way classification of nouns into *dravya* (substance) and *guṇa* (quality) with further classifications of *guṇa*s into *guṇa-vacana*s was found to be necessary for handling adjectives. The same criterion was also found useful to handle the ambiguities between *kāraka* and non-*kāraka* relations.

Finally, the fact that there cannot be an adjective of an adjective, having identified a *viśeṣya*, there is only one way all the *viśeṣaṇa*s can connect with the *viśeṣya*. This theoretical input provided much relief from practical point of view, in the absence of which possible solutions would have been exponential.

4

Sanskrit Parsing

4.1 Introduction

In this chapter we describe the parsing algorithms for dependency parsing that are developed based on the theories described in previous chapters. A dependency parser produces a parsed structure showing the dependency relations between the words of a given sentence. Regarding the input to a Sanskrit parser, there are two concerns:

1. The first concern is related to segmentation. Sanskrit being most often written as a continuous string of phonemes, due to the influence of an oral tradition, the question is whether we design a parser to allow a continuous string or should we insist on a segmented text.
2. The second concern is about the genre of the text. Most of the Sanskrit literature is in the form of poetry. Poetry enjoys more freedom with respect to the word order than the prose. So the question is, whether we develop a general parser that can handle both poetry as well as prose or only one of them, preferably prose to start with.

We saw in Chap. 2 that in the commentarial tradition, the sentential analysis is preceded by the segmentation (*padaccheda*), word analysis (*pada-paricaya*) and compound word analysis (*vigraha*), followed by an *anvaya*. *Anvaya* helps in identifying the relations between words. Therefore, it is reasonable for a parser module, which deals with the sentential analysis, to expect a segmented text with word analysis. Regarding the genre of the Sanskrit text, we noticed that the commentators rewrite the original verse as a prose following the canonical word order. This suggests that it is easy to understand a prose in canonical order than the one in non-canonical order or in the form of a verse. From this we infer that it should be comparatively easier to develop a parser that handles sentences in canonical order compared to verses or sentences in non-canonical form.

Ideally, from the user's perspective, the parser should allow both an unsegmented and a segmented text, as well as texts in both canonical and non-canonical order, as an input. When the input is a continuous string, the parser should call a segmenter module to split the given continuous string into words, undoing the *sandhi* at the word junctures. However, there is a practical difficulty with this step. It is possible that there are more than one way of splitting a given string. And the user would be interested in only one or a few of the analyses, and not all possible analyses. This calls for an interface that allows a user to select the segmentation for which a parse is needed. Alternatively it is also possible to weed out the nonsensical segmentations with a feedback from the parser.

We decided to allow both an unsegmented text as well as a segmented text as an input to a parser. If the input is an unsegmented text, then it is passed through the Heritage segmenter[1] which shows all possible morphologically valid segments of a text. The interactive intelligent user interface (Huet and Goyal 2016) allows a user to select correct segments. The interface intelligently prunes out all those segments that are morphologically incongruent during each user selection. It is also possible to call a parser on all possible segmentations, without the requirement of any human intervention. However, since this increases the complexity, the current implementation does not allow this possibility. When a user chooses a desired segmentation, as a next step the words need to be placed in the canonical word order. In order to change the word order to the canonical word order, an interface is provided that allows a user to drag the words and place them in the desired position. Alternately, user may also choose to enter a manually segmented text where the external *sandhi* between the words is split into morphologically valid words and the components in a compound are also separated by hyphens. It is assumed that such a segmented text is in canonical order. The segmented text, along with the analysis of each word, is forwarded to the parser. *Figure* 4.1 shows the flow and interaction between various modules such as segmenter, word analyser, user interfaces and parser.

In the design of a parser, thus, it is assumed that its input is segmented and is in the canonical word order.

[1] http://sanskrit.inria.fr

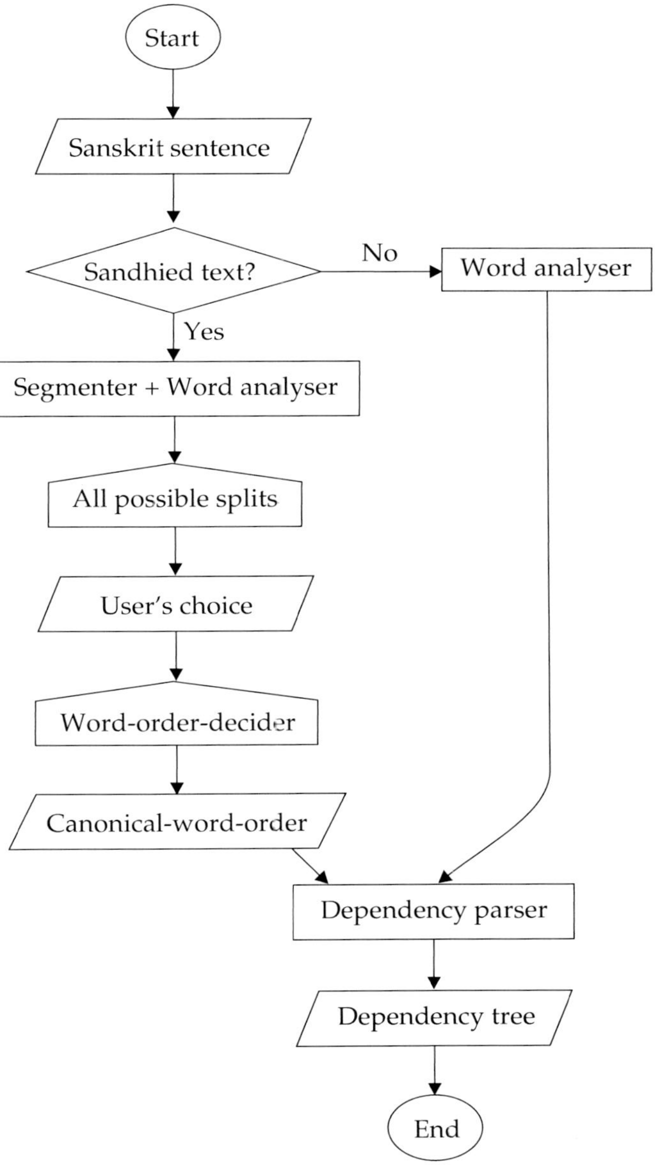

fig. 4.1: Flow and interaction among various modules

4.1.1 DEPENDENCY PARSE STRUCTURE

In Chap. 1 we have seen the *śābdabodha*s of various schools. Theories of *śābdabodha* provide the details of sources of various kinds of information encoded in a language string and how this information collectively produces the verbal import. We also noticed that the schools differ among each other in their *śābdabodha*s. Major difference is with respect to the *mukhya viśeṣya* (the chief qualificand). While for the grammarians the chief qualificand is the activity of the verb, for the logicians the one in the nominative case is the chief qualificand. There are other minor differences as well, such as which morpheme codes what kind of information and how the information flows in a sentence. There is ample literature discussing the merits and limitations of the *śābdabodha*s of each school. But any discussion on these is out of the scope of the present monograph. Interested readers may refer to Subbarao (1969). As far as the *kāraka* and non-*kāraka* relations are concerned, all the schools follow the Pāṇinian model at a gross level.

We decided to follow the *śābdabodha* of Vaiyākaraṇas, since they depend only on the words for their analysis and do not use any extralinguistic information in their analysis. They believe in the "world of words". And this provides us a natural cut for the level of semantics which can be arrived at solely on the basis of the information available in the language string. This is the level of the semantics that is represented in the dependency parse.

Let us relook at the Vaiyākaraṇas' *śābdabodha* reproduced in *fig*. 4.2. In this figure the morphemes are shown in ovals and their denotations are shown in squares connected by dotted lines. The solid lines joining the denotations of various morphemes produce the verbal import.

The *śābdabodha* describes the chief qualificand in terms of its qualifiers and hence the arrows are towards the root node representing the chief qualificand. For example, in *fig*. 4.2 the activity denoted by the main verb is described as qualified by various *kāraka*s participating in that action. And hence the arrows are directed towards the activity denoted by the main verb. In this description, over and above the denotations of various morphemes, what is important are the two indirect relations shown by solid lines, between the denotation of *rāma* and *gam*, and the denotations of *vana* and *gam*. These relations denote the roles of the denotations of *rāma* and *vana* with respect to the activity denoted by *gam*. These roles are termed as *kartṛ* and *karman*, respectively. It is these roles which are important to get the semantics associated with the sentence. All other information shown in *fig*. 4.2 is necessary to infer these roles. And once the role is inferred,

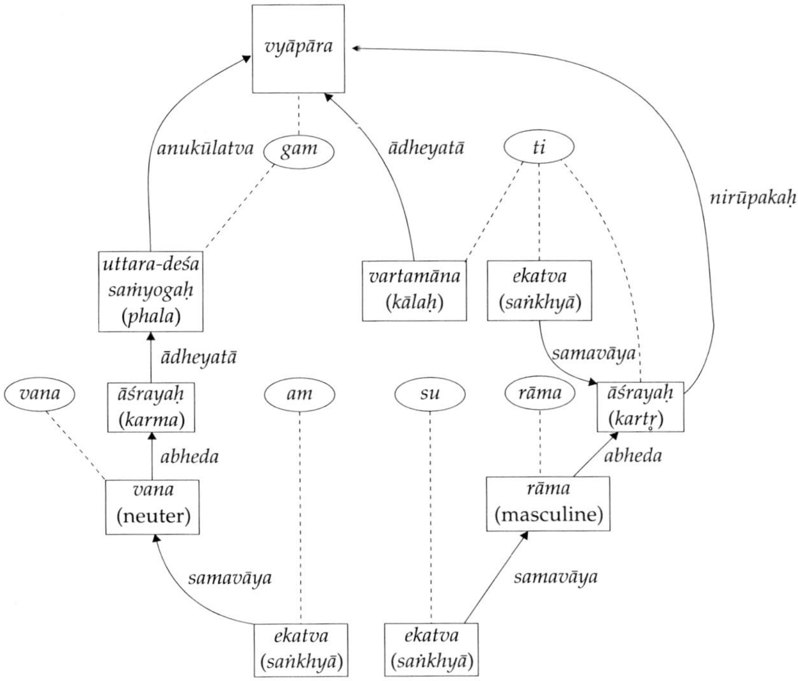

fig. 4.2: Grammarians' verbal import

all the information leading to the inference becomes redundant. Suppressing all these minute details, we represent the dependency parse compactly showing only these roles as in *fig*. 4.3. In this compact representation, the roles are shown between the words themselves rather than the denotations of the involved morphemes. The root node of this dependency tree is the predicate. The directed edge between the nodes is labelled with the role of the word at the head node. Thus all the arrows in this representation are directed away from the root node. This representation exhibits the complete information. It is a better representation than *fig*. 4.2, from the reader's perspective. The label on the directed edge indicates the role of the denotation of the head node with respect to the denotation of the tail node.

This compact dependency parse is a tree structure. Does this tree structure faithfully represent the gist of the content of *śābdabodha*? In order to seek answer to this question, we have the following observations based on the *śābdabodha* structure.

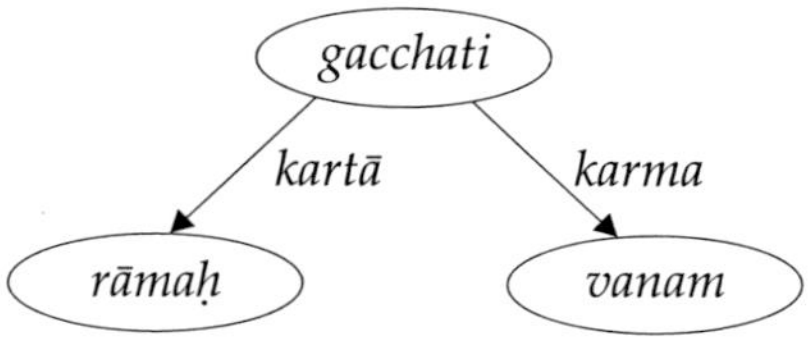

fig. 4.3: Compact dependency parse

1. According to the Mīmāṁsakas, a sentence is an integral unit conveying a single purpose,[2] and when it is split in two parts, some words in one part would have an expectancy for some other words in the other part. This implies that each word in a sentence either satisfies an expectancy of or has an expectancy for some other word in a sentence. That is every word in a sentence should be connected with at least one other word in it. Let us represent the words in a sentence by the nodes and the expectancies between words by edges joining the nodes. Then, the above criterion of a sentence implies that there are at least $n - 1$ edges if there are n words in a sentence.
2. Two nodes connected by an edge do not have the same status. One of them has an expectancy and the other one satisfies the expectancy. Hence we use directed edges to mark this asymmetry. The node at the head of a directed edge satisfies the expectancy of the node at its tail.
3. A word (*pada*[3]) in Sanskrit consists of a *prakṛti* (root) and a *pratyaya* (suffix).[4] Every such suffix marks explicitly only one role[5] (or satisfies only one expectancy) of some other word in the sentence. If these roles are represented by edges between the words, then there can be at the most n edges between n words.

---

[2] *arthaikatvāt ekaṁ vākyaṁ। sākāṅkṣaṁ cet vibhāge syāt ॥* – *Mīmāṁsāsūtra* 2.1.46

[3] *suptiṅantaṁ padaṁ* – A 1.4.14.

[4] Here we deal with only the nominal (*sup*) and verbal suffixes (*tiṅ*), and the derivational suffixes that produce indeclinables. The derivational suffixes producing new nominal and verbal stems mark the word internal structure. We do not show the word internal structure in the dependency parse. We need the word internal structure of compounds, though. However, in the present discussion, we do not deal with the internal structure of compounds.

[5] With an exception of the nominative case marker which does not mark any role.

4. Every finite verbal suffix marks either a *kartṛ* or a *karman* or an action. When it marks a *kartṛ* (*karman*), the noun that satisfies the *kartṛ* (*karman*) expectancy is in the nominative case, which does not mark any semantic role, over and above the role marked by the verbal suffix. When the verbal suffix marks an action, it does not mark any semantic role. Thus there can be at the most $n - 1$ edges between n words.[6]
5. From 1 to 4 above, we conclude that there are exactly $n - 1$ directed edges in the dependency structure.
6. For the parse to be complete, each word has to be connected to at least one other word in a sentence, and there are only $n - 1$ edges. This implies there are no loops in the structure.
7. This structure with n nodes, each node representing a word in a sentence, and $n - 1$ directed edges marking the expectancies between the words, without any loops, thus, represents a Directed Acyclic Graph (DAG).
8. This DAG is a tree since every node satisfies only one expectancy.
9. It is also a rooted tree with the root denoting the sentential head. Since we follow the Vaiyākaraṇa's *śabdabodha*, in which the activity denoted by the main verb is the chief qualificand, in the dependency-parsed structure we posit the main verb as the root node of the tree. In this dependency parse we represent only those relations that are marked explicitly. As discussed in Chap. 3, the information of implicit relations is also important. However, we mark this information in a different way so as to distinguish it from the one that is marked explicitly. This is to ensure that we do not lose the rooted tree structure of the dependency parse.

As an example, the dependency parse of the following sentence is shown in *fig*. 4.4:

Skt: *tapasvī vālmīkiḥ tapas-svādhyāya-niratam vāg-vidām varam munipuṅgavam nāradam paripapṛccha* (1)

---

[6] We assume that every sentence has at least one main verb. In case a sentence does not have a verb, as in the case of *aśvaḥ śvetaḥ* (the horse {is} white), we demand that the sentence be presented as *aśvaḥ śvetaḥ asti* (the horse is white) with an appropriate copula such as *asti*.

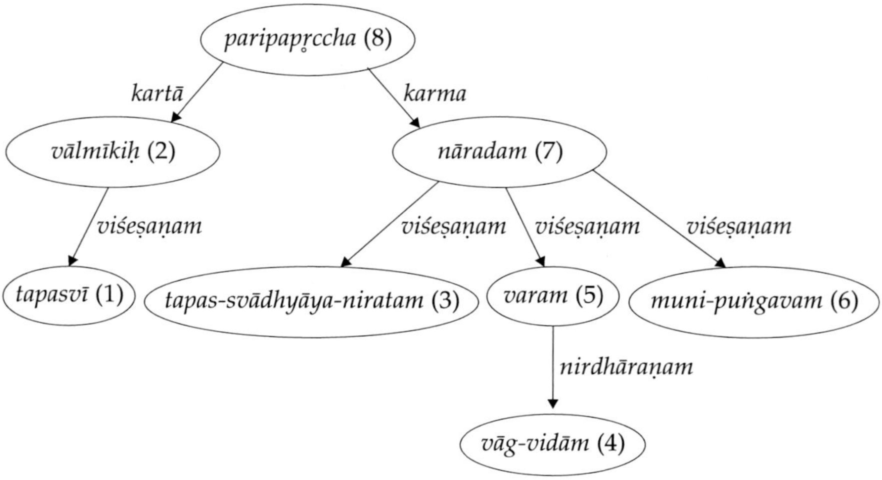

fig. 4.4: Dependency parse of statement (1) above

Gloss: Who_performs_penance Vālmīki constantly_engaged_in_penance and_self_study among_the_wise_men greatest greatest_among_sages to_Nārada asked.

English: Vālmīki, who performs penance, asked Nārada, the greatest among sages, the greatest among the wise men, who is constantly engaged in penance and self-study.

In this dependency structure, the node labels also include the word position. The position is included to distinguish between two occurrences of the same word in a sentence. Note also that the relations are shown between the words. Thus a relation of *kartṛ* is shown between *vālmīkiḥ* and *paripapṛccha*. It would have been more appropriate to mark this relation between the *prātipadikam* (nominal stem) *vālmīki* and the *dhātu* (verbal root) *pari_pṛch*. Since such a representation may hamper the readability, we have marked the relations between the words themselves.

4.2 Design of a Parser

We find two main approaches towards the design of a dependency-based parsing. They are grammar-based and data-driven. The link parser based on link grammar formalism and the minipar based on Chomsky's minimalism are among the grammar-based dependency parsers for English. The data-driven dependency parsers are the state-of-the-art parsers. They use supervised machine learning algorithms to train the machine on the set of annotated corpus. These parsers thus need manually annotated corpus for training, called tree banks. Among these parsers, we come across two dominating approaches. They are graph-based dependency parsing and transition-based dependency parsing. The graph-based approach creates a parser model that assigns scores to all possible dependency graphs and then use maximum spanning tree methods from graph theory for getting the highest-scoring dependency graph. The transition-based approach scores transitions between parser states based on the parse history and then follow a greedy approach and produce a single parse corresponding to the highest-scoring transition sequence that derives a complete dependency graph. For more details refer to Attardi 2006; McDonald and Nivre 2007; McDonald et al. 2005; Nakagawa 2007; Nivre 2006; Yamada and Matsumoto 2003.

Most of the natural language parsers call a Part of Speech (POS) tagger and a chunker before invoking a parser. These two modules reduce the ambiguity due to multiple morphological analyses. A POS tagger selects the best part of speech in the context, and a chunker groups all the auxiliary verbs with the main verbs, the post-positions with the noun and multi-word expressions as one chunk. The head of such chunks is marked which relates to other words/heads of other chunks in a sentence. The POS taggers and chunkers ease the task of a parser, by reducing the ambiguities at the morphological level. However, the disadvantage of calling these modules before a parser is that the errors may get cascaded.

Our parser differs from the state-of-the-art parsers in three ways. First, in the absence of any annotated corpus, we follow the grammar-based approach. Second, our parser is invoked right after the morphological analyser. The main reason behind this decision was, when we looked at various Indian literature, there was no discussion on any kind of POS tagger or chunker. Moreover, use of chunker also presupposes that dependencies relate the whole chunk and do not involve a sub-part of it. But in Sanskrit we come across instances of compounds termed as *asamartha-samāsa* (Joshi and Roodbergen), (Gillon 1993, *asamartha*) where the dependencies relate to the sub-part of a compound which need not necessarily be a head. Use of a chunker module before calling a parser would fail to parse such constructs. On the other hand, the Indian literature on verbal import was found to be useful from parsing point of view since it has discussions on various factors that are instrumental in the process of verbal cognition. We decided to use these factors in the development of our parser. Finally, the state-of-the-art parsers typically produce a single parse. We decided to produce all possible parses. This is to ensure that we do not miss out the correct parse. The onus of choosing the correct parse, from among the parses produced, is on the reader.

Now we describe the basic algorithm for our parser. In the dependency structure described earlier, the nodes correspond to the words in a sentence, and the directed edges correspond to the semantic role of one word with respect to the other. The semantic roles are expressed through the morphemes. If a word is ambiguous between more than one morphological analyses, then different morphological analysis may suggest different roles. Therefore, while designing a parser, we represent each morphological analysis of a word by a node in a graph. Thus, corresponding to each word, there would be as many nodes as there are morphological analyses of it. To make the point clear, let us consider the sentence:

rāmaḥ gacchati । (2)

The word *rāmaḥ* has two possible analyses: one as a noun with a nominative case and the other as a verb *rā* in present tense, third person, singular. Similarly the word *gacchati* also has three possible analyses: one as a verb in present tense and the other two as the locative case of the present participial form *gacchat* in masculine and neuter gender. Now when we say *rāmaḥ* is related to *gacchati* by *kartṛ* relation, it is the nominative analysis of *rāma* which is responsible for this relation and not the verbal analysis. Similarly, it is the verbal analysis of *gacchati* which, due to the expectancy of the underlying verb relates with the noun *rāma*.[7] In order to capture these minute details, the nodes in our graph represent distinct morphological analyses of a word rather than the word itself. And a semantic role of one word[8]

---

[7] To be precise, the expectancy of the verb for a *kartṛ* is expressed by the verbal suffix itself. The relation of *samānādhikaraṇa* between the *kartṛ* of the verb expressed by the verbal suffix and the word *rāmaḥ* in nominative form is further marked by the agreement between the two in number and person.

[8] By word we mean the denotation of a word.

with respect to another due to a specific morphological analysis is represented by a directed labelled edge between corresponding nodes. For example, the *kartṛ* relation between *rāma* and *gacchati* is represented by a directed edge from *gacchati* to *rāma* and is labelled as *kartṛ*.

Let us call this graph G. Then the problem of parsing a sentence may be modelled as the task of finding a sub-graph T of G such that G is a directed tree (or a Directed Acyclic Graph).

The basic algorithm for parsing is given below and is explained in detail afterwards:

1. *Defining the nodes.* Define one node each corresponding to each morphological analysis for every word in a sentence.
2. *Establishing directed edges.* Establish directed edges between the nodes, if there is either a mutual or unilateral expectancy (*ākāṅkṣā*) between the corresponding words and the word meanings are not mutually incongruous (*yogyatā*).
3. *Defining the constraints.* Define constraints, both local on each node as well as global on the graph as a whole. One of these constraints corresponds to *sannidhi*.
4. *Solving the constraints.* Extract all possible trees from this graph that satisfy both local and global constraints. Produce all possible solutions to ensure that in case of sentences with multiple interpretations,[9] machine does not miss any interpretation.
5. *Prioritizing the solutions.* Produce the most probable solution as the first solution by defining an appropriate cost function. The cost C associated with a Solution Tree is defined as

   $C = \sum_e d_e * r_k$, where e is an edge from w_j to w_i with label k,

   $d_e = |j - i|$, r_k is the rank[10] of the role k.

Now we explain the necessary resources for establishing the edges, followed by a list of various constraints. This is followed by three constraint-solving algorithms.

---

[9] As in the case of texts involving pun or multiple meanings (*śleṣa*).

[10] All the roles are ranked, on the basis of heuristics, starting from 1.

4.2.1 ESTABLISHING DIRECTED EDGES

In Chap. 3, we saw various sources that encode the information of expectancies. We also argued how the concept of absence of incongruity helps in pruning out non-sensical relations. In this section, now we describe the organization of various lexical resources as well as sample rules that are used for establishing the edges between the words (Panchal, forthcoming).

Lexical Resources

1. Each verb is associated with the following features:
   a. semantic category:[11] {*gati, buddhi, pratyavasānārtha, śabdakarma, ādikarma*}
   b. transitivity: {*akarmaka, sakarmaka, dvikarmaka* of type 1,[12] *dvikarmaka* of type 2}
   c. expectancy for a *karaṇa-kāraka*: {True, False}
   d. expectancy for a *sampradāna-kāraka*: {True, False}
   e. expectancy for an *apādāna-kāraka*: {True, False}
   f. expectancy for a *kartṛsamānādhikaraṇa*: {True, False}
   g. expectancy for a *karmasamānādhikaraṇa*: {True, False}
   h. expectancy for a *vākyakarma*:[13] {True, False}
2. Each noun in the dictionary is classified into one of the two categories {*dravya, guṇa*}. The relation-denoting terms under *dravya* and the *guṇa-vacana*s under the *guṇa* are further marked.
3. All the words that expect an *upapada vibhakti* are marked with the following two features:
   a. *vibhakti* governed by an *upapada*: {2, 3, 4, 5, 6, 7}
   b. its relation with other words in a sentence: {*adhikaraṇa, apādāna, viśeṣaṇa*, etc.}

---

[11] This category has the basis of Pāṇini's *sūtra*s that assign different *vibhakti*s to different classes of verbs when new verbs are derived with derivational suffixes such as *ṇic*.

[12] This classification is based on the behaviour of *mukhya* and *gauṇa karman* in the causative constructions.

[13] *Vākya-karma* is a *karma* in the form of a sentence.

4. Closed lists of auxiliary verbs[14] and indeclinables such as negative particles and emphatic markers are provided.

Grammatical Rules

A directional edge d from a node A to node B is established provided the nodes A and B satisfy the necessary feature requirements. We denote such an edge as $d : A \rightarrow B$. We give below some sample rules for establishing such edges. These rules are developed following the Pāṇini's grammar. In his *Aṣṭādhyāyī*, Pāṇini has stated rules that provide case markers for different *kāraka* and non-*kāraka* roles. We use these rules in the reverse direction, guessing a *kāraka* and a non-*kāraka* role from the case suffix. While the feature structure used is very elaborate, in the rules given below, we show only those features that are just sufficient to explain the rule.

1. *Kārakas* expressed by a verbal suffix (*abhihita*) are marked by the following rule:

   abhihita_kāraka:

   V (stem: *r*, voice: v, derivational_suffix: *ds*, Number: N_v, Person: P_v)

   $\rightarrow$

   N (stem: *n*, gender: *g*, Number: N_n, Person: P_n, case: 1)

   provided, $N_v = N_n$ and $P_v = P_n$. The name of an expressed *kāraka* (a *kartṛ*, a *karman* or a *prayojaka kartṛ*) is governed by the voice and the derivational suffix.

2. Rule for marking *kārakas* unexpressed by a verbal suffix (*anabihita*) is given below:

   K_i:

   V (stem: *r*, voice: v, derivational_suffix: *ds*, Number: N_v, Person: P_v)

   $\rightarrow$

   N (stem: *n*, gender: *g*, Number: N_n, Person: P_n, case: c_i)

   provided *r* has an expectancy for a *kāraka* k_i, *n* denotes either a *dravya* or a *guṇa-vacana* and c_i = *vibhakti* corresponding to k_i, as

[14] *śaka-dhṛṣa-jñā-glā-ghaṭa-rabha-labha-krama-saha-arha-asti-artheṣu* – A 3.4.65

per the Pāṇini's rules.

3. Non-*kāraka* relations between a noun and a verb. Two relations *hetu* and *prayojana*[15] are identified as below:

   k_i : V (stem: r) $\rightarrow$ N (stem: n, case: c_i)

   provided $c_i = 4$ for k_i to be a *prayojana* and either 3 or 5 for k_i to be a *hetu*.

   Similar conditions have been worked out for other non-*kāraka* relations such as *kriyāviśeṣaṇa* and *sambodhana*.

4. *Genitive relation*. Two nodes with noun analysis, say, N_1 (stem: n, case: 6) and N_2 (stem: m) have a genitive relation from N_1 to N_2, provided, N_2 is not a *viśeṣaṇa*. Some semantic relations that are used are part–whole relation (*avayava–avayavī-bhāva*) and is a kind of (*sāmānya–viśeṣa/parā–aparā jāti*) relation. Other resources that may be of use for exploring the possibility of using other semantic relations are the Sanskrit WordNet developed at IIT Bombay and the Knowledge Network of *Amarakośa* developed at the University of Hyderabad.

The relations established as above, on the basis of *ākāṅkṣā* and *yogyatā* produce a directed graph. This graph represents all possible relations between the words.

An Illustration

For example, consider the following sentence:

Skt: *rāmaḥ vanam gacchati* ।　　　　(3)

Gloss: Rāma {nom.} forest {acc.} go {pres. sg. 3rd person}

Eng: Rāma goes to a forest.

The analyses of the various words are numbered as $[i, j]$, where i is the word index and j is the index of the morphological analysis of ith word.

There are two possible analyses for the word *rāmaḥ*, viz.

[1, 1]: *rāma* {gender = m, case = 1, number = sg},

[1, 2]: *rā* {*gaṇaḥ* = *adādi*, *lakāra* = *laṭ*, person = 1, number = pl, *prayogaḥ* = *kartari*, *parasmaipadī*}.

15 *Tādarthya* has been marked as a *prayojana*. Since it is out of the scope of this monograph, we do not provide the arguments here.

The word *vanam* also has two possible analyses as below:

[2, 1]: *vana* {gender = n, case = 1, number = sg},

[2, 2]: *vana* {gender = n, case = 2, number = sg}.

Gacchati has three possible analyses as below:

[3, 1]: *gam* {*lakāra* = *laṭ*, person = 3, number = sg, voice = active, *parasmaipadī*},

[3, 2]: *gacchat* (*gam śatṛ*) {gender = m, case = 7, number = sg},

[3, 3]: *gacchat* (*gam śatṛ*) {gender = n, case = 7, number = sg}.

In the absence of any grammatical information, the initial graph will be fully connected, with every node connected to every other node in the graph. With the condition that an edge between two nodes is established only if there is an expectancy and semantic compatibility, the number of edges reduce drastically. In the above example, with seven nodes, forty-two bidirectional edges are possible. *Ākāṅkṣā* and *yogyatā* reduce them to 10 as listed below:[16]

[1, 1] is a possible *kartṛ* of [1, 2]
[1, 1] is a possible *kartṛ* of [3, 1]
[2, 1] is a possible *kartṛ* of [1, 2]
[2, 1] is a possible *kartṛ* of [3, 1]
[2, 2] is a possible *karman* of [1, 2]
[2, 2] is a possible *karman* of [3, 1]
[2, 2] is a possible *karman* of [3, 2]
[2, 2] is a possible *karman* of [3, 3]
[3, 2] is a possible *adhikaraṇa* of [1, 2]
[3, 3] is a possible *adhikaraṇa* of [1, 2]

The resulting graph is shown in *fig*. 4.5.

4.2.2 DEFINING THE CONSTRAINTS

We note that certain combinations of relations, in the above example, are not possible. For example, we cannot have *vanam* as a *karman* of *rāmaḥ* and *rāmaḥ* as a *kartṛ* of *gacchati* simultaneously, since these two relations involve two different analyses of the same word *rāmaḥ*.

---

16 For the purpose of illustration, we do not assume the input to be in canonical form. If we assume the input to be in canonical form, some of the relations shown above would not be possible.

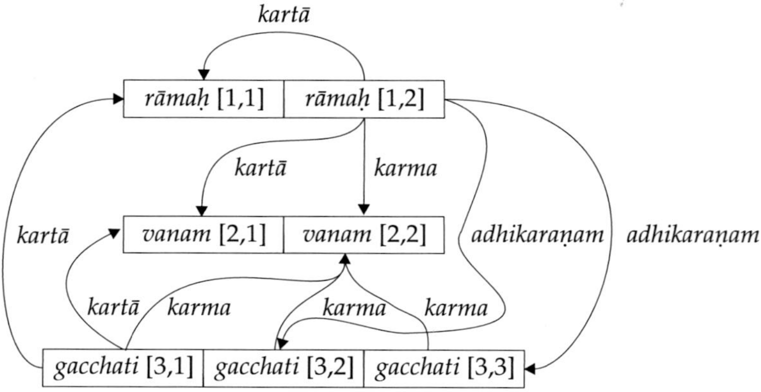

fig. 4.5: Graph showing possible edges satisfying *ākāṅkṣā*

Similarly, it is not possible to have *vanam* as a *karman* of both *rāmaḥ* and *gacchati*, because the *am* suffix in *vanam* can designate only one relation. Some of these constraints are local while some are global. These constraints are given below:

1. Local Constraints:
   a. *A morpheme corresponding to a suffix marks only one relation.* That is, a node can have one and only one incoming edge. For example, in the above example, *vanam* cannot be the *karman* of two verbs.
   b. *Each kāraka relation is marked by a single morpheme.* There cannot be more than one outgoing edges with the same label from the same node, if the relation corresponds to a *kāraka* relation,[17] i.e. there cannot be two words satisfying the same *kāraka* role of the same verb. For example, in the above example, *kartṛ* of *gacchati* can be either *rāmaḥ* or *vanam*, but cannot be both.
   c. *A morpheme does not mark a relation to itself.* A word cannot satisfy its own expectancy, i.e. a word cannot be linked to itself. This means, there cannot be self loops in a graph.
   d. *There can be only one valid analysis of every word per solution.*

[17] *Adhikaraṇa* is treated as an exception since one can have more than one *adhikaraṇa* as in

Skt: *rāmaḥ adya pañca vādane gṛham agacchat* ।
Eng: Today Rāma came home at five o'clock.

Since a word has one node corresponding to each morphological analysis it has, there are further restrictions as below:

i. If a word has both an incoming edge as well as an outgoing edge, it should be through the same node.
ii. If there is more than one outgoing edge for a word, then all of them should be through the same node.
iii. A *viśeṣaṇa* cannot have a *viśeṣaṇa*.[18]

These conditions ensure that only one morphological analysis is chosen per word.

2. Global Constraints:
    a. *Sannidhi*: There are no crossing of edges. If all the nodes are plotted in a straight line, then the edges connecting them when drawn on one side of the line should not intersect each other. There are, however, some cases of *sannidhi* violation, as described in Chap. 3, of relations involving adjectives and genitive case. If we assume the input to be in canonical form, then such cases would not arise.
    b. Certain relations always occur in pairs. For example, a *kartṛsamānādhikaraṇa* (a predicative adjective, literally having same locus as that of *kartṛ*) assumes that there is a relation of *kartṛ* already established.

4.3 Solving the Constraints

In this section, we describe algorithms for extracting trees that satisfy the local and global constraints. Assuming that the words can be partitioned into two classes, viz. the words which have an expectancy called demand words and the words which satisfy the demand called source words, Bharati, Chaitanya and Sangal (1995: 96) reduced the parsing problem to matching a bipartite graph. But in reality, the words cannot be partitioned into two classes. We come across words which can be demand words in some context and source words in some other context, or in the same context a *kṛdanta* (primary derivative), for example, can be both a demand word as well as a source word. Thus these words need to be repeated in both the classes.

---

[18] *guṇānāṁ ca parārthatvāt asambandhaḥ samatvāt syāt* । – *Mīmāṁsāsūtra* 3.1.22

Bharati, Chaitanya and Sangal (1995: 91) also needed the requirement of *kārakas* and their optionality (mandatory, desirable and optional) for each verb. But then, a parser based on such information will fail to parse sentences with ellipsis, or the sentences with incomplete information.

With a robust parser, that produces at least partial solution in case of ellipsis, as an aim, we relax the above conditions. So we give away the constraint that a word can be exclusively either a demand or a source word. Further we treat all *kārakas* at the same level, irrespective of whether they are mandatory or optional, and assign penalty to lower the priority of those solutions which do not satisfy the mandatory expectancies.

The graph-based and transition-based dependency parsing methods assume that there is only one node corresponding to each word. These methods also demand annotated data for initial training. Moreover, all these parsers produce only one parse. In our graphs, we have multiple nodes corresponding to each word. Not enough annotated corpus is available. We insist on all possible parses. And finally, there are certain local and global constraints the dependency parse should satisfy. Owing to all these considerations, we have developed three algorithms for solving the above-stated constraints. The first algorithm was modelled as a constraint satisfaction problem (Kulkarni, Pokar and Shukl 2010). The next two algorithms are graph centric. The second algorithm was implemented as a node-centric traversal with Dynamic Programming (Kulkarni 2013). The third algorithm is implemented as an edge-centric traversal with binary join. Each of these algorithms is an improvement over the previous ones. We describe below each of them in detail.

4.3.1 CONSTRAINT SATISFACTION PROBLEM

A constraint satisfaction problem consists of a set of constraints over a set of decision variables. With each decision variable a domain of potential values is associated. In our case, with each edge of a graph is associated a potential binary value 0/1. And the local and global constraints provide the constraints over these edges. We represent the graph as a matrix, called a constraint matrix C. Thus the address of a typical element of this constraint matrix C is (i, j, R, k, l), where R is the relation from k^{th} word due to its lth morphological analysis to i^{th}

word due to its jth analysis. Thus, the initial graph with all possible relations between various nodes is represented as a 5D matrix C such that $C[i, j, R, k, l] = 1$, if such a relation satisfies the expectancy and semantic compatibility,

$= 0$, otherwise.

Based on the available information in a given sentence in the form of *ākāṅkṣā* and *yogyatā*, the matrix C is populated with 0s and 1s.

The local constraints described earlier are then translated as below:

1. A morpheme corresponding to a suffix marks only one relation. That is there can be at the most only one incoming arrow for every node.
2. Each word can have only one valid morphological analysis per interpretation. That is there can be at the most only one incoming arrow among all the nodes corresponding to a word. This condition is stronger than and includes the previous condition as well.

   I.e. a node can have one and only one incoming edge.

   $\sum_{j, R, k, l} C[i, j, R, k, l] = 1, \forall_i.$
3. Each *kāraka* relation is marked by a single morpheme. There cannot be more than one outgoing edges with the same label from the same cell, if the relation marks a *kāraka* relation,[19] i.e. there cannot be two morphological analyses satisfying the same *kāraka* role of the same verb.

   $\sum_{i, j} C[i, j, R, k, l] = 1$, for each tuple (R, k, l), where R is a *kāraka* relation.
4. A morpheme does not mark a relation to itself. A word cannot satisfy its own expectancy, i.e. a word cannot be linked to itself or there cannot be self loops in a graph.

   $\sum_{j, R, k} C[i, j, R, i, k] = 0, \forall_i.$
5. Only one valid analysis of every word per solution:
   a. If there are both an incoming edge as well as an outgoing edge corresponding to the nodes of a word, they should be through the same node. In other words, if a node has an

[19] With an exception of *adhikaraṇa kāraka*.

incoming (outgoing) edge then no other node corresponding to that word can have an outgoing (incoming) edge.

$\sum_{R,\, l,\, n} C[i,\, j,\, R,\, l,\, n] + \sum_{a,\, b,\, R,\, k \neq j} C[a,\, b,\, R,\, i,\, k] \leq 1,\, \forall_{i,\, j}.$

b. If there are more than one outgoing edge through the nodes of a word, then they should be through the same node.

if, $\exists_{i,\, j,\, R,\, l,\, m}$ such that $C[i,\, j,\, R,\, l,\, m] = 1$,

then $\sum_{a,\, b,\, R,\, k \neq m} C[a,\, b,\, R,\, l,\, k] = 0$.

6. All the words in a sentence should be connected. Each word should have at least one node with an incoming or an outgoing edge.

   $\sum_{a,\, b,\, R}(C[a,\, b,\, R,\, i,\, j] + C[i,\, j,\, R,\, a,\, b]) \geq 1,\, \forall_{i,j}$

7. There are no crossing of links. If all the nodes are plotted in a straight line, then they should not intersect each other, i.e.,

   if $\exists_{i,\, j,\, R,\, k,\, l}$ such that $C[i,\, j,\, R,\, k,\, l] = 1$, then

   $\forall_{x,\, u}$ such that

   $i < x < k$ and $u < i$ or $u > k$, or

   $i < u < k$ and $x < i$ or $x > k$,

   $\sum_{v,\, x,\, w} C[u,\, v,\, w,\, x,\, y] = 0$,

8. There should be exactly $n - 1$ edges.

   $\sum_{a,\, b,\, R,\, i,\, j} C[a, b, R, i, j] = n - 1$.

To solve these constraints, we used off-the-shelf general purpose fast, scalable, constraint solver MINION.[20] MINION provides all possible solutions. We ranked these solutions using the cost C defined earlier.

The main disadvantage of this approach is the space complexity. The size of the 5D matrix is $N * M * K * N * M$, where N is the total number of words in the sentence, M is the maximum number of morph analyses for a word in the given sentence and K is the maximum number of distinct possible relations among the words in a given sentence. Sanskrit words being overloaded with morphological analysis, frequently occurring words tend to have several analyses

[20] http://minion.sourceforge.net

possible.[21] Such words in a sentence determine the size of the matrix. As the number of words in a sentence increases or if a sentence has even a single word with considerable number of morph analyses, the size of the 5D matrix explodes. For example, with approximately ten words in a sentence, assuming maximum number of analyses per word as 15, and maximum possible relations as 35, the total entries in the matrix is almost a million. Most of these cell entries being zero, we get a sparse matrix. And the constraint solver has to choose only $n-1$ entries with value 1 from this matrix satisfying the constraints stated above. Thus we observe that this representation consumes too much space and the use of the parser for parsing long sentences from literary texts becomes unfeasible.

The second disadvantage of this method is that the constraints are applied globally to the matrix. However, we notice that some of the constraints are local to a node. Separating the local constraints from the global and applying the local constraints at an early stage to rule out non-solutions should improve the efficiency of the system. This led us to redesign the parser.

Instead of viewing the problem as a constraint specification problem, we model it as extracting a directed tree from a labelled graph. The problem then is similar to getting a spanning tree of a graph. However, the problem also substantially differs from that of a spanning tree. First, the edges in the graph are both directional and labelled. Thus between any two nodes of a graph, there may be more than one edge. Second, our graph has as many nodes as there are total morphological analyses of all the words put together, and the tree has only as many nodes as there are words in a sentence. Thus in this sense, the extracted tree does not correspond to a spanning tree, since the number of nodes in the tree is not the same as those in the graph. Finally, this tree also should satisfy various constraints – both local applied to a node as well as global. We are also interested in all possible solutions, instead of just the optimal one. This led us to develop our own algorithms instead of trying existing algorithms. We present below two algorithms: the first one is a vertex-centric traversal and the second one is an edge-centric binary join.

---

21 The word *te* has sixteen possible inflectional analyses. If we take into account the derivational information, the possibilities explode further.

4.3.2 VERTEX-CENTRIC TRAVERSAL

We now describe a deterministic parsing algorithm that applies the local constraints locally and also uses dynamic programming for efficient parsing. In the dynamic programming we share the intermediate results in a computation avoiding the recomputation of sub-problems solved earlier. Thus we solve each sub-problem only once and share its results as and when required later.[22]

Let $G_1 = (N_1, E_1)$ be a graph, where N_1 is the set of nodes corresponding to the morphological analyses of the words in a given sentence and E_1 is the set of triplets (i, j, r) representing directed weighted arcs from j^{th} node to the ith node with a label r. With every relation r a weight w is associated, which reflects its preference over other relations. The total number of nodes equals $\sum_i m_i$, where m_i is the number of possible morphological analyses of the ith word.

Let S and F be two special nodes denoting the START node and the FINAL node. We define the adjacency graph $G_2 = (N_2, E_2)$, where $N_2 = N_1 \cup \{S, F\}$ and E_2 is the set of directed edges (i, j) such that i and j correspond to the morphological analyses of adjacent words w_k and w_{k+1}. The direction of the edge is from j to i. S is adjacent to the nodes corresponding to the morphological analyses of the first word of the sentence and F is adjacent to the nodes corresponding to the morphological analyses of the last word of the sentence.

A "path" P of a graph G_2 is a sequence of edges which connects the nodes from S to F. For example, S-1-3-5-F is the leftmost path in *fig.* 4.7.

An edge (i_1, j_1, r_1) is "locally incompatible" with a set of edges E_1, where $E_1 = \{(i, j, r) | (i, j, r) \in E \text{ of } G_1\}$, under the following conditions:

1. The edge is a self loop. That is, $i_1 = j_1$.
2. E_1 contains an outgoing edge from the node j_1 with label r_1 to some node other than i_1. This means two different words satisfy the same expectancy of a word.

---

22 The best example of dynamic programming is to get the nth Fibonacci number, $F(n)$, which is defined as sum of $F(n-1) + F(n-2)$. Since $F(n-2)$ is needed again to calculate $F(n-1)$, it is "memorized" and used again when needed later. Thus each sub-problem, viz. of calculating $F(k)$, for k ranging from n to 1, is solved only once.

$\exists_{i \neq i1} (i, j_1, r_1) \in E_1$.

3. E_1 contains an incoming edge to i_1 which has a different label than r_1 or which originates from a node other than j_1. This means a word satisfies more than one expectancy.

   $\exists_{j \neq j1} (i_1, j, r_1) \in E_1$, or

   $\exists_{r \neq r1} (i_1, j_1, r) \in E_1$, or

   $\exists_{j \neq j1, r \neq r1} (i_1, j, r) \in E_1$.

A set of edges $E_1 = \{(i, j, r) | (i, j, r) \in E \text{ of } G_1\}$ is said to be "locally compatible", if no edge $(i_1, j_1, r_1) \in E_1$ is locally incompatible with the rest of the edges in E_1.

A set of labelled edges $E_1 = \{(i, j, r) | (i, j, r) \in E \text{ of } G_1\}$ is "globally compatible" provided the following conditions are satisfied:

1. The sub-graph of G_1 with edges from E_1 is projective. In other words, if the nodes corresponding to the edges in E_1 are arranged in an increasing order of their index, then the edges do not cross.
2. For certain relations r such as *kartṛsamānādhikaraṇa* (predicative adjective) there is a matching relation *kartṛ* (agent).
3. The edges in E_1 do not form a loop.

A sub-graph T of G_1 is a "parse" if

1. The nodes in T correspond to some path of G_2. This ensures that each node in T corresponds to a distinct word and every word in the sentence is accounted for.
2. T is a Tree. This ensures that every word in a sentence is related directly to one and only one other word.
3. The set of edges in T are both locally as well as globally compatible.

Parsing Algorithm

1. Starting with node S, every path of G_2 is traversed following the Depth-First-Traversal (DFT). Two stacks are maintained. One stack called Path-Stack P keeps track of the path visited so far and the other stack called Tree-Stack T maintains the list of all possible sets of locally compatible edges on the path visited

so far. This list thus provides the current status of the partial solution(s) at any point of time.

2. At each node on a given path, a list of all incoming edges to this node is obtained from G_1. For each of these edges:
   a. If it is locally compatible with any of the partial solutions in T, the edge is added to the partial solution and the node is pushed on to P.
   b. If the edge is incompatible with all partial solutions so far, this path is abandoned.
3. When the final node F is reached, each solution in T is checked for the global compatibility. Each globally compatible set of edges, which is a subset of edges in G_1, forms a Tree and hence is a possible solution.
4. For each such possible solution, cost is computed using the formula $Cost = \sum w * |j - i|$, where w is the weight associated with the relation label of the edge between the nodes corresponding the jth and i^{th} words.

DFT of the graph G_2 from S to F is equivalent to traversing the sentence from left to right for various combinations of morphological analyses. The parser is deterministic and it is guaranteed to terminate after $\prod_i m_i$ paths are traversed, where m_i is the number of morphological analyses of the ith word. At each node of G_2, the number of compatibility checks is equal to the number of incoming edges for that node in graph G_1 multiplied by the partial solutions construed so far. Total compatibility checks equals $\sum_j \prod_i r_{ij}$, where r_{ij} stands for the number of incoming edges on the ith node of the jth path. The total number of paths, as noted above, is $\prod_i m_i$. Stacking of intermediate partial solutions ensures the dynamic programming.

An Example

We illustrate this algorithm with an example. Consider the sentence (3), and all possible relations in it, which we saw earlier. For easy accessibility, we repeat the information below:

Skt: *rāmaḥ vanam gacchati* ।   (3)

Gloss: Rāma forest {acc.} goes.

Eng: Rāma goes to the forest.

In this sentence, each of the two words *rāmaḥ* (Rāma) and *vanam* (forest) has two possible analyses, while the word *gacchati* (goes) has three possible analyses as shown below:

1. *rāmaḥ* = *rāma* {masc.} {sg.} {nom.}
2. *rāmaḥ* = *rā* {pr.} {1p} {pl.}
3. *vanam* = *vana* {neu.} {sg.} {nom.}
4. *vanam* = *vana* {neu.} {sg.} {acc.}
5. *gacchati* = *gam* {pr.} {3p.} {sg.}
6. *gacchati* = *gam* {pr. part.} {masc.} {sg.} {loc.}
7. *gacchati* = *gam* {pr. part.} {neu.} {sg.} {loc.}

Thus, G_1 has seven nodes (see *fig*. 4.6, which is the same as *fig*. 4.5, redrawn with node numbers). These nodes are numbered sequentially as shown above. Edges marking the relations are listed in Table 4.1. The relations compatible with each relation are also shown in this table. The information of adjacency is shown in Table 4.2 and as a graph G_2 in *fig*. 4.7. Note that we have not assumed the input to be in canonical order.

We now illustrate the stages in computation. The process starts with a visit to the START node S of G_2. Then its first left-most child, viz. node 1 is visited. Among all the incoming edges of node 1 of graph G_1, only those edges that are locally compatible are selected. There are two incoming edges, viz. *a* and *b*. Of these, *a* does not satisfy the local compatibility. This leaves us with only one incoming edge *b*. It forms the initial partial solution. This solution is pushed onto the T and the depth first traversal of G_2 is continued. Next node 3 of

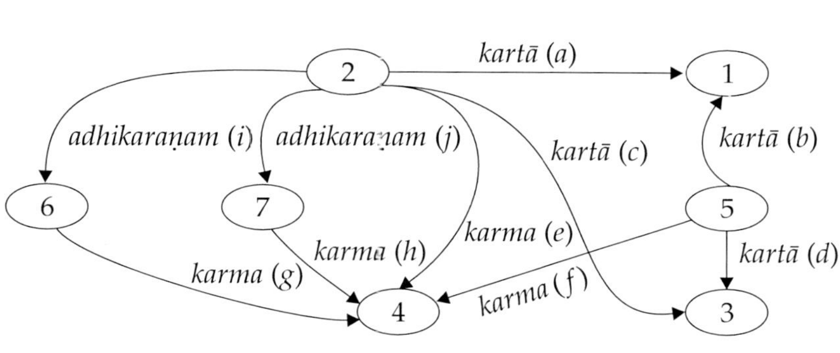

fig. 4.6: Possible relations; graph G_1

Table 4.1: All Possible Relations with Their Compatible Relations

Relation id	*From Node (j)*	*To Node (i)*	*Relation Name (r)*	*Compatible Relations*
a	2	1	*kartṛ*	–
b	5	1	*kartṛ*	*f*
c	2	3	*kartṛ*	*i, j*
d	5	3	*kartṛ*	–
e	2	4	*karman*	*i, j*
f	5	4	*karman*	*b*
g	6	4	*karman*	*i*
h	7	4	*karman*	*j*
i	2	6	*adhikaraṇa*	*c, e, g*
j	2	7	*adhikaraṇa*	*c, e, h*

Table 4.2: Adjacency

Node No.	*Left Word Nodes*	*Right Word Nodes*
1	S	3, 4
2	S	3, 4
3	1, 2	5, 6, 7
4	1, 2	5, 6, 7
5	3, 4	F
6	3, 4	F
7	3, 4	F

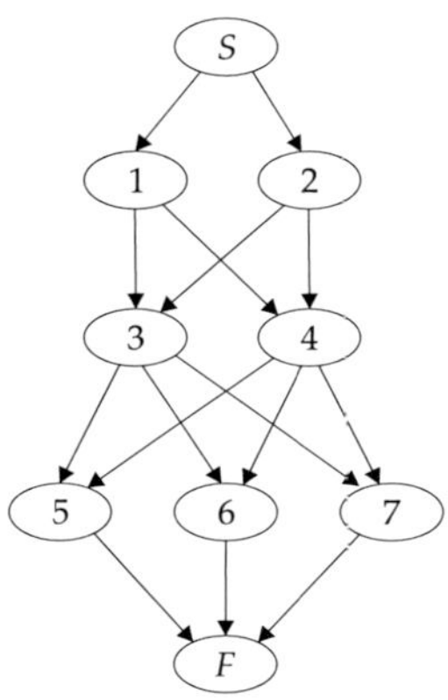

fig. 4.7: Adjacency and possible paths; graph G_2

G_2 is visited. Here there are two incoming edges, viz. *c* and *d*. The compatibility check of these edges with the earlier partial solution on T shows that both these edges are incompatible with the earlier partial solution. Hence the further traversal of this path is stopped. The traversal is continued with node 4, the sibling of node 3. There are four incoming edges *e*, *f*, *g* and *h* with node 4. Of these, only *f* is compatible with *b*. So *f* is added to the partial solution *b*. The traversal is continued further with a visit to node 5. There are no incoming edges. Next node is the finial node *F*, marking the completion of the path with a Solution Tree *f*, *b*. This solution is accepted. The traversal is continued till all the paths are traversed. Table 4.3 shows the complete summary of various paths traversed and the partial solutions formed at each stage. The "accept" state corresponds to the complete paths with compatible solutions.

Thus there are seven solutions possible, corresponding to the accept states shown in *fig*. 4.8. Of these seven solutions, except the first one, all other solutions involve the *kr̥danta* analysis of the verb *gam*, with present participle suffix *śatr̥* in the locative case. Now there is a global requirement for this suffix that there should be at least one another noun in the locative case which can act as a *kartr̥* of this verb. And in the above example, in each of the solutions involving the locative case marker analysis of *gam* in *śatr̥* suffix, another noun in locative case suffix is missing. Hence these solutions do not satisfy the global compatibility, and therefore these are filtered out, leaving only the first solution.

The advantages of this method over the previous method are:

1. It is deterministic.
2. Dynamic programming ensures reduction in processing time when there are overlapping transitions.
3. In addition to the dependency tree, the left–right traversal also produces the trace of the path depicting the word order.

The major disadvantage of this method is, being node-centric traversal, if the initial words have several incoming arrows, then the partial solutions in the beginning are many and as we traverse various paths, the possibilities grow exponentially. We also check the compatibility of each new edge with all the edges on the path

Table 4.3: An Illustration of Various Paths Traversed and Partial Solutions

<table>
<tr><th>Path-Stack</th><th>Tree-Stack</th><th>Action</th></tr>
<tr><td>S</td><td>–</td><td></td></tr>
<tr><td>S-1</td><td>b</td><td></td></tr>
<tr><td>S-1-3</td><td>–</td><td>Abandon</td></tr>
<tr><td>S-1</td><td>b</td><td></td></tr>
<tr><td>S-1-4</td><td>b, f</td><td></td></tr>
<tr><td>S-1-4-5</td><td>b, f</td><td></td></tr>
<tr><td>S-1-4-5-F</td><td>b, f</td><td>Accept</td></tr>
<tr><td>S-1-4-6</td><td>–</td><td>Abandon</td></tr>
<tr><td>S-1-4-7</td><td>–</td><td>Abandon</td></tr>
<tr><td>S-2</td><td>–</td><td></td></tr>
<tr><td>S-2-3</td><td>c | d</td><td></td></tr>
<tr><td>S-2-3-5</td><td>c | d</td><td></td></tr>
<tr><td>S-2-3-5-F</td><td>c | d</td><td>Reject</td></tr>
<tr><td>S-2-3-6</td><td>c, i | d</td><td></td></tr>
<tr><td>S-2-3-6-F</td><td>c, i | d</td><td></td></tr>
<tr><td>S-2-3-6-F</td><td>c, i</td><td>Accept</td></tr>
<tr><td>S-2-3-6-F</td><td>d</td><td>Reject</td></tr>
<tr><td>S-2-3</td><td>c | d</td><td></td></tr>
<tr><td>S-2-3-7</td><td>c, j | d</td><td></td></tr>
<tr><td>S-2-3-7-F</td><td>c, j | d</td><td></td></tr>
<tr><td>S-2-3-7-F</td><td>c, j</td><td>Accept</td></tr>
<tr><td>S-2-3-7-F</td><td>d</td><td>Reject</td></tr>
<tr><td>S-2-4</td><td>e | f | g | h</td><td></td></tr>
<tr><td>S-2-4-5</td><td>e | f | g | h</td><td></td></tr>
<tr><td>S-2-4-5-F</td><td>e | f | g | h</td><td>Reject</td></tr>
<tr><td>S-2-4</td><td>e | f | g | h</td><td></td></tr>
<tr><td>S-2-4-6</td><td>e, i | g, i</td><td></td></tr>
<tr><td>S-2-4-6-F</td><td>e, i | g, i</td><td>Accept</td></tr>
<tr><td>S-2-4</td><td>e | f | g | h</td><td></td></tr>
<tr><td>S-2-4-7</td><td>e, j | h, j</td><td></td></tr>
<tr><td>S-2-4-7-F</td><td>e, j | h, j</td><td>Accept</td></tr>
</table>

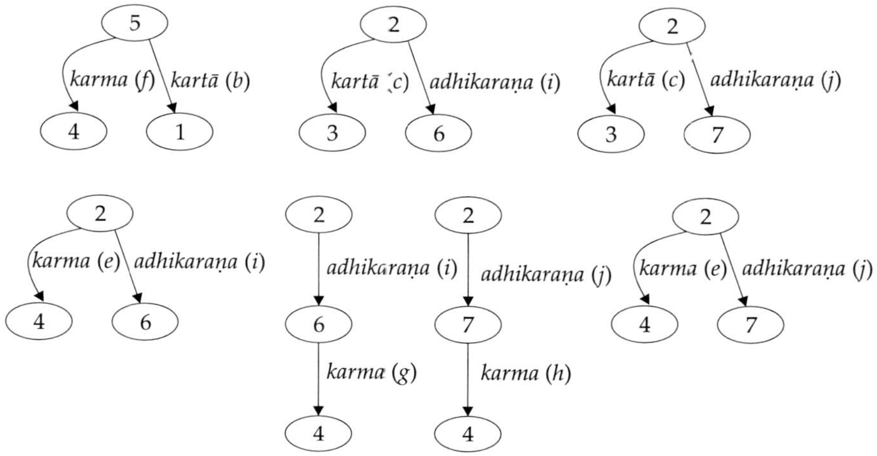

fig. 4.8: Seven possible solutions of sentence (3)

explored so far. This leads to some redundancy, because if a node falls on more than one path, it would be visited more than once, and during each such visit all the incoming edges are checked for compatibility with all other edges on the path traversed so far. In the worst case scenario, the incompatibility between the nodes would be noticed only at the final node.

We discuss the modified version of this algorithm in the next section which avoids the redundancy in compatibility checking, and also removes some of the incompatible edges at the start of the algorithm.

4.3.3 EDGE-CENTRIC BINARY JOIN

We modify the previous algorithm at three levels:

1. Any edge that is a part of the solution should be compatible with remaining $n - 2$ edges in the solution Tree, where n is the number of words in the sentence. Hence, we throw away all those edges that are not compatible with at least $n - 2$ other edges.
2. We define the compatibility of two sets of edges as a simple operation of set intersection.
3. We build the solutions recursively starting with the individual words bottom-up, each time joining two sets of compatible edges. In $n - 1$ joins we get all possible DAGs, where n is the

number of words in a sentence. Join operation is defined as a set union.

This algorithm is edge-centric. Before giving the detailed algorithm, we define a few terms:

Compatible Edge: An edge e_1 is said to be "compatible" with another edge e_2 iff they are locally compatible and we set *Compatible* $(e_1, e_2) = 1$.

Compatible Set of Edges: Let R be a set with edges $\{r_1, r_2, \ldots, r_n\}$. And let C be a set with edges $\{c_1, c_2, \ldots, \mathrm{c}_m\}$. C is "compatible" with R iff $\forall_i\ \forall_j$ *Compatible* $(c_i, r_j) = 1$.

Joinable Sets: Let R_1 and R_2 be two sets of edges. Let C_1 and C_2 be the sets of edges that are compatible, respectively, with R_1 and R_2. R_1 and R_2 are "joinable" provided $R_1 \subseteq C_2$ and $R_2 \subseteq C_1$. For such joinable sets, the edges compatible with $R_1 \cup R_2$ are equal to $(C_1 \cap C_2) - (R_1 \cup R_2)$.

Now we give the detailed algorithm:

1. Let there be N edges.
2. For each edge list down all other edges it is locally compatible with.
3. Construct all possible DAGs, by calling Construct Dags $0N$, where ConstructDags is defined as

   ConstructDags initial final =

   if (final – initial > 0)

   then

   dags = RemoveSmallDags size (JoinDags dag1 dag2)

   where

   size = final – initial – 1

   dag1 = ConstructDags init mid, and

   dag2 = ConstructDags (mid + 1) final,

   where mid = (initial + final)/2

   else

   dags = GetInitialDags init,

   (which returns as many initial DAGs as there are incoming arrows at the node with index initial. Each such initial DAG contains a single incoming arrow.)

RemoveSmallDags N dags

(removes all the DAGs from dags that have less than N edges).

JoinDags D_1 D_2

(joins two dags D_1 and D_2, if they are joinable sets, and for the combined dag D, computes the edges compatible with D.)

4. Remove all those solutions that do not satisfy the global compatibility condition.
5. Each possible solution is then checked for global compatibility. Only those solutions that satisfy the global compatibility condition are retained.
6. For each globally compatible solution, compute the $Cost = \sum w * |j - i|$, where w is the weight of the relation from j^{th} word to i^{th} word and prioritize the solutions on this Cost.

An Example

We illustrate the algorithm with the sentence (3) discussed earlier. For easy accessibility, we repeat the information below.

Skt: *rāmaḥ vanam gacchati* ׀ (3)

Gloss: Rāma forest {acc.} goes.

Eng: Rāma goes to the forest.

In this sentence, as we have seen earlier, each of the two words *rāmaḥ* (Rāma) and *vanam* (forest) has two possible analyses, and the word *gacchati* (goes) has three possible analyses as shown below.

1. *rāmaḥ* = *rāma* {masc.} {sg.} {nom.}
2. *rāmaḥ* = *rā* {pr.} {1p} {pl.}
3. *vanam* = *vana* {neu.} {sg.} {nom.}
4. *vanam* = *vana* {neu.} {sg.} {acc.}
5. *gacchati* = *gam* {pr.} {3p.} {sg.}
6. *gacchati* = *gam* {pr. part.} {masc.} {sg.} {loc.}
7. *gacchati* = *gam* {pr. part.} {neu.} {sg.} {loc.}

All possible relations are shown in Table 4.4. First we filter out the edge *a*, since it maps the relation between two analyses of the same

Table 4.4: All Possible Edges and Their Compatible Edges

Edge id	*From (j)*	*To (i)*	*Relation Name (r)*	*Compatible Edges*
a	2	1	*kartṛ*	–
b	5	1	*kartṛ*	*f*
c	2	3	*kartṛ*	*i,j*
d	5	3	*kartṛ*	–
e	2	4	*karman*	*i,j*
f	5	4	*karman*	*b*
g	6	4	*karman*	*d,i*
h	7	4	*karman*	*e,j*
i	2	6	*adhikaraṇa*	*c,e,g*
j	2	7	*adhikaraṇa*	*c,e,h*

word, thereby violating local compatibility. Similarly, we filter out edge *d*, since it is not compatible with any of other edges. We retain all other edges as they are compatible with at least 1 (= $n - 2$) other edge. Next we start building the solutions recursively. We start with the incoming edges of the first word. There is only one incoming edge, marked as *b*. This forms our first set of edges R_1. The set of compatible edges with R_1, denoted by C_1 has only one edge *f*. For the second word there are five incoming edges, marked as *c, e, f, g* and *h*. Each of these starts a new partial solution. We call them R_2, R_3, R_4, R_5 and R_6. For each of these edges, the compatible edges are shown in Table 4.4. We call them C_2, C_3, C_4, C_5 and C_6, respectively. Now we check which of these partial solutions is joinable with R_1. We notice that only R_4 is joinable with R_1. Joining these two partial solution sets results in {*b*, *f*}. The set of edges compatible with this partial solution is given by $(C_1 \cap C_4) - (R_1 \cap R_4) = \phi$. We carry earlier partial solutions, viz. R_2, R_3, R_4, R_5 and R_6 as well, being potential partial solutions, since each of them has one edge, and we still have one more word to visit. Now we get the edges of the third word and join them with the current partial solutions. Corresponding to the third word, we have *i* and *j* as two incoming edges. Checking compatibility with all the partial solutions in the previous stage, we get seven possible solutions as shown in *fig*. 4.8.

Table 4.5: Trace of Algorithm on Sentence 3

Instructions	*Result*
ConstructDags 0 2	12. {*b,f* ǀ *c,i* ǀ *c,j* ǀ *e,i* ǀ *e,j* ǀ*g,i*ǀ *h,j*}
ConstructDags 0 1	7. {*b* , *f* ǀ *b* ǀ *c* ǀ *e* ǀ *f* ǀ *g* ǀ *h*}
ConstructDags 0 0	2. {*b*}
GetInitDags 0	1. {*b*}
ConstructDags 1 1	4. {*c* ǀ *e* ǀ *f* ǀ *g* ǀ *h*}
GetInitDags 1	3. {*c* ǀ *e* ǀ *f* ǀ *g* ǀ *h*}
JoinDags {*b*}, { *c* ǀ *e* ǀ *f* ǀ *g* ǀ *h*}	5. {*b*, *f* ǀ *b* ǀ *c* ǀ *e* ǀ *f* ǀ *g* ǀ *h*}
RemoveSmallDags	6. {*b*, *f* ǀ *b* ǀ *c* ǀ *e* ǀ *f* ǀ *g* ǀ *h*}
ConstructDags 2 2	9. {*i* ǀ *j*}
GetInitDags 2	8. {*i* ǀ *j*}
JoinDags {*b*, *f* ǀ *b* ǀ *c* ǀ *e* ǀ *f* ǀ *g* ǀ *h*}, {*i* ǀ *j*}	10. {*b*, *f* ǀ *c*, *i* ǀ *e*, *i* ǀ *g*, *i* ǀ *c*, *j* ǀ*e,j* ǀ *h,j*ǀ *b* ǀ *c* ǀ *e*ǀ *f* ǀ *g* ǀ *h* ǀ *i* ǀ *j* }
RemoveSmallDags	11. {*b*, *f* ǀ *c*, *i* ǀ *c*, *j* ǀ *e*, *i* ǀ *e*, *j* ǀ*g,i* ǀ *h,j*}
GlobalCompatibilityCheck	13. {*b*, *f*}

In Table 4.5, we show the invocation of the algorithm for this sentence. The result shows the step number followed by the list of possible relations at that step. In this trace, we have not shown the compatible edges at each stage for each partial dag.

Finally, as in the previous case, we check all these solutions for global compatibility. In this example only {*b,f*} satisfies the global compatibility. And thus we get a unique solution. This corresponds to the top-left tree in *fig*. 4.8. If there are more than one globally compatible solutions, we rank them with the same cost function defined earlier.

In this algorithm, JoinDags is called $n - 1$ times. If there are r_i incoming edges for i^{th} word, then in the worst case, there are $\prod_i r_i$ set union and set intersection operations.

4.4 Compact Display of Multiple Solutions

Sanskrit being a classical language demands certain special features with respect to its computational tools. Being an old classical language, most of the important texts in Sanskrit have been translated manually into several modern languages. So naturally, machine translation takes a back seat for Sanskrit. What a user needs is an access to the original text with the help of various online linguistic tools and resources so that he can himself interpret and understand the texts in original. From this aspect, displaying only the first parse does not serve the purpose. User might like to go through various possibilities and choose his own interpretation. It is also possible that the text is ambiguous with two or more readings, and user would like to go through each of them. Displaying all the parse trees would not serve any purpose, since the trees look almost similar with either a change in one or two branches, or with a change in the label.

In what follows we present a compact way of presenting all the solutions. This was inspired by the slim interface of Heritage segmenter Huet and Goyal (2016).

Let $T_i = (N_i, E_i)$, where $i = 1$ to n be n parses of a given sentence. Let $N = \cup N_i$ and $E = \cup E_i$. The display consists of three rows. The top row lists the words with their positions. The second row consists of morphological analyses corresponding to all the nodes in N. Analyses are written in n columns corresponding to each word. The third row consists of incoming edges into the corresponding word/node.

The user can now choose either a node from the second row or an edge from the third row. Each choice calls the compatibility checker to remove the incompatible nodes and edges corresponding to the user's choice. Each choice results in the reduction of possible parses. At any point in time, a user can choose to display the graphs of current possible parses.

Here is an illustration of the interface. The input sentence is an *anvaya* of *śloka* IV.8 from the *Bhagavadgītā*. The original *śloka* is

> *paritrāṇāya sādhūnāṁ vināśāya ca duṣkṛtām* ।
> *dharma-saṁsthāpanārthāya sambhavāmi yuge yuge* ॥

The *anvaya*, an input to the parser, is: *sādhūnām paritrāṇāya duṣkṛtām vināśāya dharma-saṁsthāpanāya*[23] *ca yuge yuge sambhavāmi* ।

Figure 4.9 shows the summary of parses as a compact display.[24]

[23] The original word is *dharma-saṁsthāpanārthāya*, which we changed to *dharma-saṁsthāpanāya*, since the former was still not recognized by the morphological analyser.

[24] The display shows only first five columns.

The union of relations from all parses for each word is shown. User can choose either the correct morphological analysis or correct relation corresponding to the node. When he chooses the correct morphological analysis, all the relations in the relations row that are incompatible with this choice are removed from the display. Similarly, if a user chooses a relation in the relation row, all the relations that are incompatible with this relation, and all the morphological analyses that are incompatible with this choice of a relation are removed from the display. Thus, for example, the word *sādhūnām* has two morphological analyses in *fig.* 4.9. But, after selecting the appropriate analysis, in *fig.* 4.10, we notice that the relations under this word are also reduced. All those relations which have *sādhūnām* as one of the relata are removed from the display. Similarly, selecting the role of this word as *karman, 2, 2* (*karman* of the second analysis of the second word), not only removes all other relations below this word, but also removes the first morph analysis of the second word, and all the relations having this analysis as one of the relata. The result of this is shown in *fig.* 4.11. Finally when we make all the choices, a unique parse is obtained (see *fig.* 4.12). Clicking on the check sign of unique parse, we get the rendering of the relations in the form of a dependency graph (see *fig.* 4.13).

The parse of a sentence with n words has $n - 1$ edges corresponding to the relations. Hence one can choose the correct parse from this compact display in maximum $n - 1$ choices. This interface thus can also be used for developing a tree bank for Sanskrit semi-automatically. Due to the limitations on space, we do not give the technical details of this interface here.

4.5 Conclusion

The main purpose behind the development of indigenous parsers was to evaluate the usefulness of theories of *śābdabodha* for the mechanical parsing of Sanskrit sentences. The theories of *śābdabodha* discuss in minute detail the flow of information, various means of encoding the information, the amount of information encoded and so on. These theories were further supported by providing various conditions such as *ākāṅkṣā*, *yogyatā* and *sannidhi* that help in the process of verbal cognition. So we decided to model these conditions computationally. The modelling of *ākāṅkṣā* provided us a filter for pruning out impossible edges. *Sannidhi* turned out to be a weak non-projectivity. Modelling *yogyatā* was the most difficult task, since it involved a huge lexicon and compatibility between various lexical items. But various definitions of *yogyatā* provided us clue to model it in terms of absence of non-congruity in order to increase the recall. The use of *yogyatā* further filtered out a few more edges in the graph.

From the theories of *śābdabodha*, we could also conclude that the tree-data structure is the best for representing the dependency parse. Thus, the task of parsing was to extract a tree from the graph that satisfies some local and global constraints. We discussed here three algorithms, each one an improvement over the other. The first one was modelled as a constraint solver. We observed that the constraints are of two types: local and global. Applying the local constraints earlier would reduce the complexity of the problem. Hence next we modelled the problem as extracting a directed tree from a labelled graph. The first algorithm followed the vertex-centric traversal and the second one an edge-centric traversal. Both the algorithms used the dynamic programming for efficiency. The edge-centric algorithm is more efficient than the node-centric, since in the edge-centric algorithm, the incompatibility between the edges is noticed at an early stage. All these parsers assume the input to be in a canonical word order, and unsegmented. However, from the user's perspective, it is undesirable to impose such restriction. An interface between the Heritage Sanskrit Reader and this parser algorithm is developed that allows a user to input even an unsegmented verse. The user interfaces allow the user to select the best-suited segmentation and provide the canonical word order of such segmented text.

The algorithms described above are tested on Sanskrit. However, all these algorithms are general one and should work well for the modern Indian languages as well.

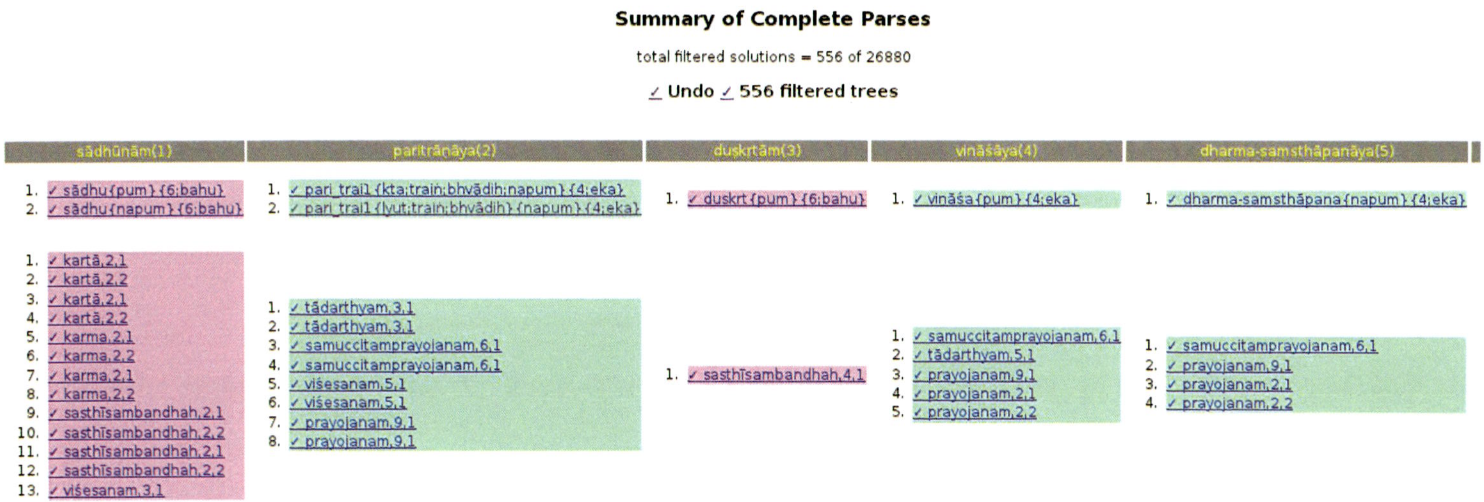

fig. 4.9: Compact display of solutions

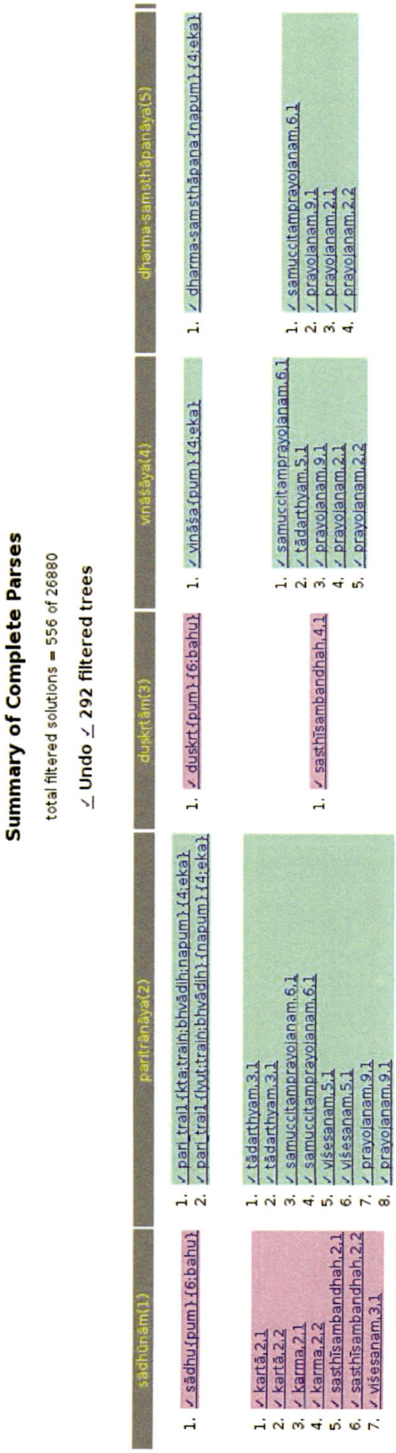

fig. 4.10: Selection of a morphological analysis

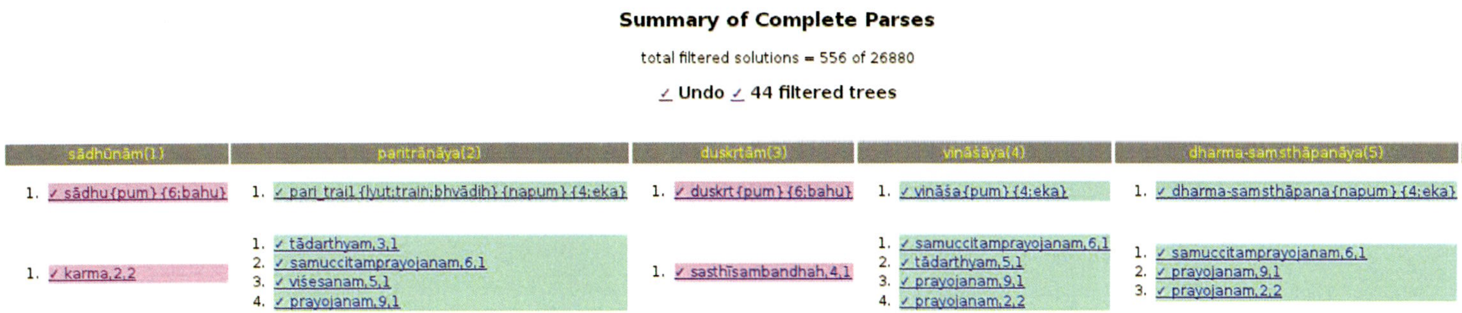

fig. 4.11: Selection of a relation

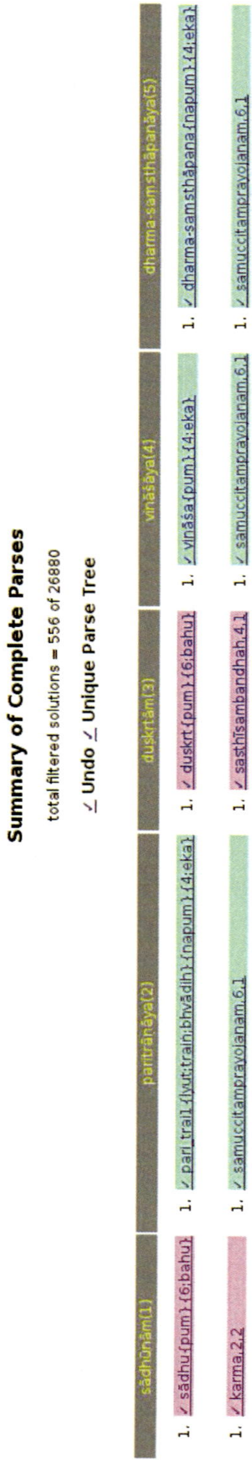

fig. 4.12: Unique solution

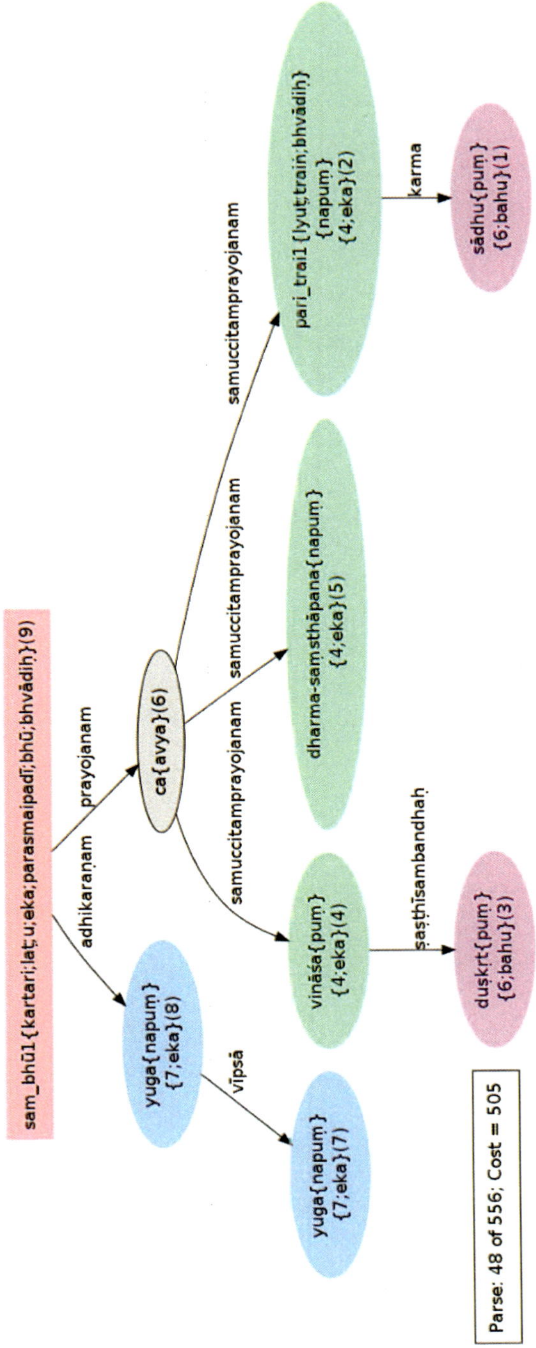

fig. 4.13: Dependency graph

5

Conclusion

PĀṆINI'S grammar has two aspects: one is the *prakriyā-pakṣa* – an aspect that deals with the derivation process of word forms from their stems and the second one the *ārthī-pakṣa* – an aspect that deals with the concepts needed for language analysis. This second part mainly deals with the bridge connecting the syntax to the semantics. This aspect was pursued further by Patañjali, Bhartṛhari, Kauṇḍa Bhaṭṭa and Nāgeśa Bhaṭṭa who have written pioneering works on this branch of Sanskrit grammar. The Naiyāyikas and the Mīmāṁsakas used the concepts described in Pāṇini and developed theories further from the listener's point of view. These theories then led to the theories of *śābdabodha*, which discuss the complete process of verbal understanding describing the sources of information encoding, what kind of information is encoded, the manner in which such information is encoded, the conditions under which such an information encoding can lead to a proper verbal understanding and constraints on word order such as weak non-projectivity, and so on.

Indian theories also discuss various levels of meaning a word conveys and how the sentential meaning is arrived at from all these various meaningful units. Three prominent schools – Vyākaraṇa Nyāya and Mīmāṁsā – developed their own process of sentential verbal import. Among the three schools, we found the *śābdabodha* process of Vyākaraṇa delink the meaning from the real world. For them the meaning of a word is conceptual and resides in the mind and not in the referents in the real world. This grounding of Vaiyākaraṇas to the "world of words" marks a level of semantics that can be extracted purely from the linguistic expression without appealing to the extralinguistic information. We followed Vaiyākaraṇas' treatment of language analysis. Barring a minor difference of chief qualificand, the Mīmāṁsakas' treatment is also similar to that of Vaiyākaraṇas. The Vaiyākaraṇas' main concern is the word and as such the Vyākaraṇa-śāstra is also called as a Padaśāstra, while the Mīmāṁsakas' main concern is interpretation of Vedic sentences, hence it is called Vākyaśāstra. Both the Padaśāstra and Vākyaśāstra provided us important clues for sentential analysis.

We found the complete treatment of the sentential understanding so formal that it was quite natural to model the process automatically. In this monograph we discussed the modelling of three essential conditions – *ākāṅkṣā*, *yogyatā* and *sannidhi* – and discussed parsing algorithms centred around them. There is still scope for improving these algorithms further, especially taking into account the linguistic clues for efficient traversing of the graphs.

Ākāṅkṣā and *sannidhi* deal with the relation between words and possible word orders. *Yogyatā* concerns with the word meanings. In modelling *yogyatā*, instead of modelling it as a presence of compatibility, we modelled it as an absence of non-congruity. This helped us to reduce the probable solutions from millions to hundreds thereby improving the precision. Modelling the non-congruity was much easier since it just involved access to a special semantic category of words termed *guṇa-vacana*. Modelling the congruity on the other hand would have required a huge knowledge base of the compatibility of substantives to be a specific *kāraka* for every verb, compatibility of a substantive to be in a genitive relation with another one and so on. And this compatibility can be either with respect to the primary meaning or the extended or metaphoric meaning. This would have exploded the knowledge base further. The limited success of the Cyc project (that handles only the primary meanings) suggests us the difficulties involved in organizing such a knowledge base. In a limited in-house experiment at IIT Kanpur, the possibility of using *yogyatā* for word sense disambiguation was tried. But that experiment confined only to the primary meanings and did not cover the extended meanings. Based on the experience, I am of the opinion that it would be appropriate to use the state-of-the-art machine-learning algorithms along with the insights from the Indian theories of meaning for handling meaning compatibilities.

It is worth exploring the concept of *tātparya* further for word sense disambiguation. The comparative study between various classifications of *lakṣaṇā* (see Appendix B) may provide new insights into the possible extensions of word meanings that may help further in their mechanical treatment. The theories developed by rhetoricians provide a sound basis for the treatment of *vyaṅgyārtha* (suggestion). Though the suggestion is subjective, and also depends on the context, the theories tell us the possible dimensions the meaning can be extended to account for the suggestion.

The current algorithms perform poorly if the input is not in canonical word order. In order to make the parser more user friendly it is appropriate that the parser operates on the verse directly without having any requirement for canonical word order. All the existing commentaries on various Sanskrit *kāvya*s provide the prose order of the verses. Machine-learning algorithms on such parallel corpus could provide a mechanical way to generate the canonical word order of any verse.

In this monograph, we confined ourselves to Sanskrit processing and have not discussed the possibilities of use of these theories for processing other languages. As has been mentioned briefly in Chap. 4, there are ongoing efforts to exploit them for modern Indian languages. Tree banks for various modern Indian languages such as Hindi, Urdu, Marathi, Telugu and Kannada are being developed following the Pāṇinian dependency framework. There also have been efforts to look at English grammar from Pāṇinian perspective. Modules for mapping the output of dependency parsers for English such as Minipar based on the theory of Minimalism, Stanford Parser, Link parser, etc. have been developed and are being used in the Anusaaraka[1] system.

In conclusion, we find that the treatment of language analysis in Indian grammatical tradition is devoid of any subjective judgements and is purely mechanical. This makes it a natural candidate for use in computational processing of not only Sanskrit but of other languages as well.

---

[1] http://anusaaraka.iiit.ac.in

Appendices

Appendix A

Evaluation of Parsers : Various Parameters

Two important considerations for the evaluation of parsers are (a) measure of correctness of a parse, and (b) the speed. In the following we define various measures of correctness of a parse. We have already discussed the time complexity of each of the above algorithms, and hence we skip any discussion on the speed here.

Measure of Correctness of Parse

To test the correctness of the parser output, we need manually annotated sentences, called the GOLD data. There are various metrics for the evaluation of a parser.

1. *Exact Match or Matching Dependency Trees.* Exact match is the obvious metric. Here we run all the sentences in the GOLD data through the parser and compare the outputs. All those outputs that match with the GOLD data pass the test. Thus this is a 0–1 metric. Either the output matches completely or does not match.

   This metric is not much useful. It was observed that only one statement out of three sentences produce Exact Match. Further, since this metric just produces a binary value, no information about where exactly the parse has failed is available. Such an information would be of immense help to the developers of the parser. This led to other metrics for evaluation of the parser.

2. *Unlabelled Dependency Tree.* This metric matches the two dependency trees ignoring the labels. This metric also produces 0–1 score. If the dependency tree produced by the parser matches exactly with the GOLD data ignoring the labels, then the score is 1, else it is 0.

   This score is useful when there is no agreement with regard to the edges' labels or when the granularity of the edges do not match. In such cases, one may ignore the labels and check at least whether the two structures agree with respect to the dependency structure.

3. *Attachment Scores*. Attachment scores are of two types: labelled accuracy and unlabelled accuracy. Labelled Attachment Score (LAS) checks for each dependency edge whether the two relata and the edge label match. The Unlabelled Attachment Score (UAS) ignores the edge label and checks whether the two relata match exactly. In these two scores, we count the matched edges against the total number of edges in a tree. Sentences with One Wrong Attachment (OWAS) is another score that calculates the percentage of sentences that went wrong in only one attachment.
4. *Precision and Recall*. Since our parser produces all parses, in addition to the above scores, we would also like to measure the precision and recall. Precision tells us how many of the parses produced are valid. And recall tells us in how many cases machine failed to produce the correct parse(s).
5. *Ranking the Correct Parse*. In addition to these two scores, a score to test the effectiveness of ranking module is also needed. This score marks the rank of the correct parse(s) among the parses produced.
6. *Relation-wise Performance Index*. The relation-wise performance index computes the performance score for each relation. This helps in finding out which relations perform poorly and improve them further.
7. *Confusion Matrix*. When the same case marker marks more than one relation in different contexts, in the absence of a necessary and sufficient condition for mutual compatibility, there are chances that machine confuses between the labels. This confusion is captured in the confusion matrix.

A.1 Precision and Recall

Precision tells us about how precise are the results produced by machine, or how much among the produced results is relevant and how much is irrelevant. Recall tells how many results machine could produce out of all possible results, or among all the relevant answers, how many relevant answers machine could produce.

Suppose in a given sentence there are twenty-one words. So there are twenty relations in the parsed structure. If machine can parse this sentence, then it would also produce twenty relations between these words. This parse will be correct only if all the twenty relations match with those in the correct parse. In such a case, the precision and recall are both 1, since machine has precisely produced all the relations. Now suppose, machine produces only eighteen relations. Among these eighteen relations produced by the machine, only eight relations match with those of the correct parse. That means, machine is $\frac{8}{18}$ per cent precise. Further, since machine could produce only eight relations correctly among the twenty relations, its recall rate is $\frac{8}{20}$ per cent.

Let us now see the general formula. Suppose, in *fig.* A1.1, the left circle stands for all relations in the correct parse and the right circle stands for all relations in the machine produced parse. Let A be the number of correct relations missed by the machine, B be the number of relations correctly predicted by the machine and C be the number of relations predicted by machine that are wrong. Then the precision (P) and recall (R) are defined as below:

$$P = \frac{B}{B + C}$$

$$R = \frac{B}{A + B}.$$

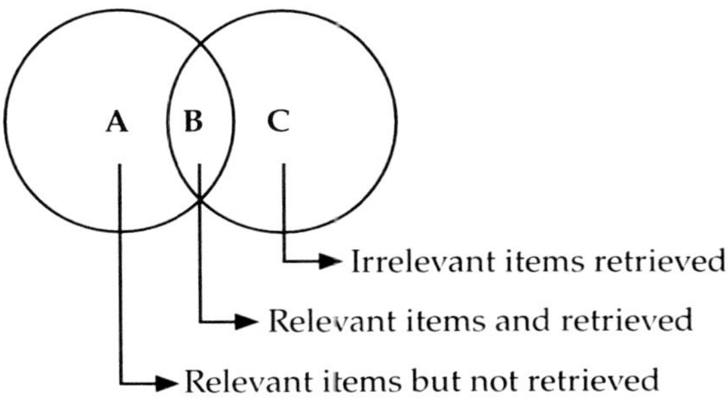

fig. A1.1: Precision and recall

Appendix B

Classification of Lakṣaṇā

THERE is no unanimity among various schools regarding the classification of metaphoric meaning. Below we list some of them:

- Gautama in the *Nyāyasūtra*. According to Gautama the transfer of meaning from primary to secondary is possible only if the secondary meaning is closely related to the primary referent. He enumerates ten such relations with an example for each.

  sahacaraṇa-sthāna-tādarthya-vṛtta-mānadhāraṇa-sāmīpya-yoga-sādhanā-'dhipatyebhyo brāhmaṇa-mañca-kaṭa-rāja-saktu-candana-gaṅgā-śāṭaka-anna-purveṣv atabhāve 'pi tadupacāraḥ ।

  – *Nyāyasūtra* II.2.62

  [In this *sūtra*, *upacāra* is the term used for the secondary or extended meaning.]

  1. *Association* (*sahacaraṇa*). In the example, *yaṣṭikām bhojaya* (feed a stick), a brāhmaṇa, who always carries a stick, is referred to as a *yaṣṭika*.
  2. *Location* (*sthāna*). In the example *mañcāḥ krośanti* (the cots cry), the term *mañca* is being used for "the children on the cot".
  3. *Purpose* (*tādarthya*). To a person who is collecting reeds for the purpose of making a mat, if somebody asks what is he doing, he may reply with *kaṭam karomi* (I am making a mat). In reality, he is just collecting the raw material. But since the purpose for this collection is to make a mat, and collection is an essential part of the process of mat creation, we see the use of the term for aimed activity for which the current activity is a purpose.
  4. *Behaviour* (*vṛtta*). Based on the behaviour of a person, sometimes, one may use a term that stands for the

characteristic behaviour. For example, a king who behaves like a *yama* may be described as *yamo rājā* (a king who is *yama*).

5. *Measure* (*māna*). Sometimes a word is used in the sense of measure of volume. For example "one cup tea", which means "tea whose volume is one cup". The standard Sanskrit example is *āḍhakasaktavaḥ* which means "one *āḍhaka* of flour".
6. *Weighing* (*dhāraṇa*). The measure can be in terms of weight as well. For example, *tūlācandanam* means "sandalwood weighed in the balance".
7. *Proximity* (*sāmīpya*). A word may sometimes refer to a place that is in proximity. For example *gaṅgāyām gāvaścaranti* (cows are grazing in the Ganges), actually means "the cows are grazing on the banks of Ganges".
8. *Inherent connection* (*yoga*). A quality is used to refer to the substance it belongs to. For example *kr̥ṣṇaḥ paṭaḥ* (a black cloth). Here, the word *kr̥ṣṇaḥ* (black) does not stand for the black colour but the thing that is black. "Beauty is praised", here the word beauty stands for the thing that is beautiful.
9. *Cause* (*sādhana*). A substance that is the cause of something may be equated with it. For example, *annam prāṇāḥ* (food is life). Here food, which is the cause of life, is referred to as life itself.
10. *Prominence* (*adhipati*). A prominent person, because of his achievements or hold over an institution or a family, may be referred to as the institution or the family. For example, *ayam kulam* (he is the family).

- Patañjali in his *Mahābhāṣya* also discusses four types of transfers of meanings:[1]

  1. *Location* (*tat-stha*). The examples quoted here are *mañcaḥ hasanti* (the cots laugh) and *girir dahyate* (the hill is burning). Here "the cots" refers to the "children sitting/sleeping on

---

[1] *caturbhiḥ prakārair atasmin sa ity etad bhavanti, tātsthyāt, tāddharmyāt, tatsāmīpyāt, tatsāhacaryād iti* ।
– *Mahābhāṣya* under *A* 4.1.48

the cot" and "the hill" refers to the "trees on the hill". This is similar to the location as described by Gautama.

2. *Quality* (*tad-dharma*). This is similar to the behaviour (*vṛtta*) of Gautama. The word refers to the quality in the referent rather than the referent. For example, *jaṭi brahmadatta* (the man with matted hair is Brahmadatta). When a man with matted hair has the same quality as that of Brahmadatta, the man is referred to as Brahmadatta. Another popular example is *siṁho māṇavakaḥ* (the boy is a lion) to mean the boy is as brave as a lion.
3. *Proximity* (*tat-samīpa*). This is similar to the proximity as used by Gautama. The example Patañjali quotes here is *gaṅgāyām ghoṣaḥ* (the village on the River Ganges) or *kūpe gargakulam* (Garga's house is on the well).
4. *Association* (*tat-sahacara*). This is similar to the *sahacara* of Gautama. Patañjali's example is *kuntān praveśaya* (fetch the lances), *yaṣṭīḥ praveśaya* (fetch the sticks) where the words "lances" and "sticks" are used to indicate the people who carry them.

- Jaimini in the *Mīmāṁsāsūtra* has listed six usages showing the metaphoric or extended usages. They are:
  1. *Accomplishment of the purpose* (*tatsiddhi*). The one who is responsible for accomplishment of the purpose is sometimes termed as the doer of the action. For example, in a sacrifice, the grass bundle accomplish the purpose served by the sacrificer and hence sometimes the grass bundle itself is called the sacrificer as in *yajamānaḥ prastaraḥ*.
  2. *Same origin* (*jāti*) (**Check the following). *X* is related to *Y* if they are siblings. For example, *āgneyo vai brāhmaṇaḥ* (the brāhmaṇa is related to Agni), since both are originated from Prajāpati.
  3. *Similarity* (*sārūpya*). *X* is called *Y* due to the similarity. This similarity may be in the appearance, function, etc. For example, *ādityo yūpah* (the sacrificial post is the sun). Here the similarity is due to the similarity in brightness of both the objects.

4. *Praise* (*praśaṁsā*). The examples discussed under this category are *apaśavo vā anye go-aśvebhaḥ* (those other than cow and horse are not animals) and *yad aghṛtam abhojanam tat* (that without ghee is not food). In the first case, the implied meaning is: cow and horse are the best animals. In the second case, ghee is considered to be the best food.
5. *Preponderance* (*bhūma*). When *X* is related to *Y*, even in the absence of *Y*, *X* is termed *Y*-related *X*. For example there are certain hymns which have the word *sṛṣṭi* in them. The bricks used to construct an alter while chanting these hymns are termed *sṛṣṭi* bricks. Note here that the hymn may or may not have a word *sṛṣṭi* in it.
6. *Presence of a marker* (*liṅgasamavāya*). People who generally carry umbrella are termed *chatriṇaḥ*. Similarly people typically carrying a stick are termed *daṇḍinaḥ*. While referring to such people one may say *chatriṇo yānti* (people with umbrellas are going), or *daṇḍino yānti* (people with sticks are going). The *chatrī* or *daṇḍa* acts as a *liṅga* (marker) to refer to such people. It is not necessary again that at the moment of utterance, all the persons carry an umbrella or a stick.

- Mukula Bhaṭṭa in his *Abhidhāvṛttimātṛkā* mentions five types of metaphoric usages:

abhidheyena sambandhāt sādṛśyāt samavāyataḥ ।
vaiparityāt kriyāyogāl lakṣaṇa pañcadhā matā ॥

Some kind of literal meaning (*abhidheya sambandha*), similarity (*sādṛśya*), association (*samavāya*), contrariety (*vaiparītya*) and association with some action (*kriyā-yoga*) are the five indications (of metaphoric meaning).

We illustrate them with an example each.

1. *Abhidheya sambandha* (*some relation with literal meaning*). The example discussed here is *dvirepha*, literally meaning two *r*s. The word *bhramara* has two *r*s, and hence sometimes it is referred to as *dvirepha*. Such an extension will make sense only if such usages are in vogue. Else the communication will break down.

2. *Sādṛśya* (*Similarity*). This is similar to the ones discussed earlier by other scholars. The example is *siṁho māṇavakaḥ* (the boy is a lion).
3. *Samavāya* (*association, such as proximity*). The illustrative example is *gaṅgāyām ghoṣaḥ*.
4. *Vaiparītya* (*contrariety*). Ironical sentences such as *bṛhaspatir ayam mūrkhaḥ* (this fool is a *bṛhaspati* – the teacher of gods) come under this category.
5. *Kriyā-yoga* (*association with some action*). Proper nouns with etymological meanings are used to describe persons with similar characteristics. For example, one who is very firm or steady in a battle is called *yudhiṣṭhira*.

- Nāgeśa in his *Paramalaghumañjūṣā* adds *tādarthya* also to the list given by Patañjali.

> *tātsthyāt tathaiva tāddharmyāt tatsāmīpyāt tathaiva ca* ।
> *tatsāhacaryāt tādarthyāt jñeyā vai lakṣaṇā budhaiḥ* ॥

The meaning of tādarthya is purpose. During the prize distribution function, the organizer after wrapping the gift, tags it with the name of the receiver. Though the tag is for the gift, in reality the tag refers to a person whom the gift is meant for. But we refer to the gift tagged Y as Y and not as "for Y".

The example discussed in the literature is: the pillar which is for Indra is called Indra (*sthāṇuḥ indraḥ*).

Appendix C

List of Relations in Pāṇinian Grammar

Compiled by K.V. Ramakrishnamacharyulu

These relations are first published in (Ramakrishnamacharyulu, 2009).

1 Proposed Tagset

1.1 *Inter-sentential relations*

1. *pūrvakālīnatvam*
2. *prayojanam* (purpose of the main activity)
3. *samakālīnatvam* (simultaneity)
4. *bhāvalakṣaṇa saptamī*
    - *anantarakālikatvam* (time of the completion of preceding activity)
    - *samakālīnatvam* (simultaneous events)
    - *pūrvakālīnatvam* (time of the main activity before the starting of the subordinate activity)

1.1.1 Relations denoted by words

1. *samānakālīnatvam*
2. *pratibandhaḥ* (conditional relation)
3. *kāraṇasatve'pi kāryābhāvaḥ, kāraṇābhāve'pi kāryotpattiḥ* (non-productive effort (or) product without cause)
4. *hetuhetumadbhāvaḥ* (cause and effect)
5. *anantarakālīnatvam* (following action)
6. *samānādhikaraṇatvam* (co-location)
7. *asāphalyam* (non-fulfilment of expected activity)

2 Sentence Internal Relations

2.1 *Relations related to the activity-denoting words*

- *kāraka* relations
  - *kartā*
    - *anubhavī kartā* (experiencer)
    - *amūrta-kartā* (abstract)
    - *prayojaka-kartā*
    - *prayojya-kartā*
    - *madhyastha-kartā*
    - *abhipreraka-kartā / utpreraka-kartā* (cause for temptation)
    - *karma-kartā*
    - *karaṇa-kartā*
    - *ṣaṣṭhī-kartā*
  - *karma*
    - *utpādyam* (created)
    - *vikāryam* (raw meterial)
    - *prayojya-kartā*
    - *ādhāra-karma* (location)
    - *deśa* (village, town, state, country, etc.)
    - *kāla* (time)
    - *bhāva* (activity)
    - *mārga* (road measurement)
    - *sampradānam* (recipient)
    - *anīpsitam* (not intended)
    - *akathitam* (not expected)
    - *gati-karma*
    - *karaṇam* (instruments of playing)
    - *yaṁ prati kopaḥ*
    - *manya-karma* (in disrespect)
    - *ṣaṣṭhī-karma*

- *karaṇam* (instrument)
  - *karma*
  - *parikrayaṇam* (money in bonded labour)
- *sampradānam* (recipient)
  - *satvāśrayaḥ* (recipient with ownership)
  - *svīkartā* (recipient without ownership)
  - *kriyayā abhipreta-sampradānam* (intended to relate with activity)
  - *jñīpsyamāna-sampradānam* (addressed through praise, etc.)
  - *uttamarṇa* (a creditor)
  - *īpsitam* (desired)
  - *yaṁprati kopaḥ saḥ* (point of anger)
  - *prīyamāṇa* (location of desire)
  - *yasya vipraśna* (enquiry about)
  - *parikrayaṇam* (money in bonded labour)
- *apādānam*
  - *bhaya-hetu* (cause of fear)
  - *ākhyāta-upayoge* (teacher)
  - *yasmāt vāraṇam* (point for obstruction)
  - *yasya/yasy adarśanam iṣṭam saḥ/sā* (person intended not to be seen)
  - *prakṛti* (raw material)
  - *prabhava* (place of first appearance)
  - *parājaya* (defeat from activity)
- *adhikaraṇam* (location)
  - *kāla* (time)
  - *deśa* (place)
  - *viṣaya*
  - *samayasya avadhi* (time duration)
  - *antarāla-deśa* (place in between)

- *a-kārakasambandhaḥ sākṣāt kriyayā* (non-*kāraka* relations, but direct relations with the activity)
  - *sambodhanam* (addressed)
  - *prasajyapratiṣedhaḥ* (uncompounded negation)
  - *sāmyam* (similarity)
  - *kriyā-āvr̥ttyantarālasamayaḥ* (time duration between the repetition of the same activity)
  - *tādarthya* (purpose)
  - *hetu* (cause)
  - *vīpsā* (repetition)
  - *kriyā-āvr̥tti-gaṇanā* (counting of repetition)
  - *kriyāviśeṣaṇam* (manner adverb)
  - *atyanta-sambaddhaḥ kālaḥ* (complete relation with time)
  - *atyanta-sambaddhaḥ mārgaḥ* (complete relation with road)
  - *atyanta-sambaddhaḥ kālaḥ* (complete relation with time and with result)
- Other Relations
  - *ṣaṣṭhī* relation
  - *ārambhasamayaḥ māpane* (starting point of time)
  - *ārambhadeśaḥ māpane* (starting point of place)
  - *lakṣaṇam* (point of direction)
  - *tādarthya* (purpose)
  - *hetu*
  - *saha* (associative)
  - *vinā* (non-associative)
  - *vibhakta* (comparison between two)
  - *nirdhāraṇam* (isolating one from a group – in the superlative degree context)

Appendix D

List of Relations Used in the Sanskrit Parser

- *sambandhaḥ*
  - **Kāraka sambandhāḥ**
  - *kartā*
    * *prayojaka-kartā*
    * *prayojya-kartā*
  - *karma*
    * *mukhya-karma*
    * *gauṇa-karma*
    * *vākya-karma*
  - *karaṇaṁ*
  - *sampradānaṁ*
  - *apādānaṁ*
  - *adhikaraṇaṁ*
    * *kāla-adhikaraṇaṁ*
    * *deśa-adhikaraṇaṁ*
    * *viṣaya-adhikaraṇaṁ*
    * *lyapkarma-adhikaraṇaṁ*
  - **Kāraketara sambandhāḥ**
    * **Kriyā-kriyā-sambandhāḥ**
      · *pūrva-kālaḥ*
      · *vartamāna-samāna-kālaḥ*
      · *bhaviṣyat-kālaḥ*
      · *bhāvalakṣaṇa-pūrva-kālaḥ*

        - *bhāvalakṣaṇa-vartamāna-kālaḥ*
        - *bhāvalakṣaṇa-anantara-kālaḥ*
        - *sahāyaka-kriyā*
    * **Kriyā-sambandhāḥ**
        - *sambodhyaḥ*
        - *hetuḥ*
        - *prayojanam*
        - *kartṛ-samānādhikaraṇam*
        - *karma-samānādhikaraṇam*
        - *kriyāviśeṣaṇam*
        - *pratiṣedhaḥ*
    * **Nāma-nāma-sambandhāḥ**
        - *ṣaṣṭhī-sambandhaḥ*
        - *vākyakarmadyotaka*
        - *udgāravācakaḥ*
        - *aṅgavikāraḥ*
        - *vīpsā*
        - *viśeṣaṇam*
        - *sambodhana-sūcakam*
        - *vibhaktam*
        - *avadhiḥ*
        - *abhedaḥ*
        - *nirdhāraṇam*
        - *atyanta-saṁyogaḥ*
        - *apavarga-sambandhaḥ*
        - *srota*
        - *ābhimukhya*
- **Upapada-sambandhāḥ**
    * *svāmī*
    * *saha-arthaḥ*

    * *vinā-arthaḥ*
    * *ittambhūtaḥ*
    * *sandarbha-binduḥ*
    * *tulanā-binduḥ*
  - **Inter-sentential relations**
    * *anuyogī*
    * *pratiyogī*
    * *nitya-sambandhaḥ*
  - **Conjuncts and disjuncts**
    * *samuccitaḥ*
    * *samuccaya-dyotakaḥ*
    * *anyataraḥ*
    * *anyatara-dyotakaḥ*

Note: The bold entries are the headings and do not indicate relation labels.

Glossary

abhidhā	primary meaning
adhikaraṇa	locus
adhyāya	chapter
ajahad-lakṣaṇā	inclusive implication
akarmaka	intransitive
Ālaṁkārikas	rhetoricians
anvaya	the natural order of words in a sentence
apādāna	source
ākāṅkṣā	expectancy
bhedaka	differentiator
bhramātmaka-jñāna	false cognition
dhātu	verbal root
dravya	substance
gauṇa-artha	secondary meaning
gauṇī	qualitative implication
guṇa	property
hetu	cause
jahad–ajahad-lakṣaṇā	implication with partial inclusion
jahad-lakṣaṇā	exclusive implication
karaṇa	instrument
karman	goal/patient
kartṛ	doer of the action (agent)
kartṛsamānādhikaraṇa	a predicative adjective
kāraka	semantic role
khaṇḍa-pakṣa	analytic approach

kṛdanta	verbal noun
lakṣaṇā	secondary/metaphoric meaning/ implication
liṅga	gender
Mīmāṁsā	exegesis
Mīmāṁsaka	exegesist
mukhya-viśeṣya	chief qualificand
mukhyārtha	primary meaning
Naiyāyika	logician
Navya-Nyāya	Neo-logic
nirūḍha-lakṣaṇā	natural/unintentional implication
Nyāya	Indian school of logic
padārtha	word meaning
prakṛti	stem/root
pramātmaka-jñāna	true cognition
pratyaya	suffix
prayojana	purpose
prayojanavatī-lakṣaṇā	intentional implication
prātipadika	nominal root
pāda	a quarter/a fourth part
rūḍha	conventional
śakti	relation between a word and its meaning
śābdabodha	verbal import
śloka	verse
śleṣa	pun
ṣaṣṭhī	genitive
sakarmaka	transitive
samasta-pada	a compound word
samāsa	compound
sambandha	relation
sampradāna	beneficiary
saṁhitāpāṭha	continuous rendition

sandhi	euphonic combination of adjacent phonemes
sannidhi	proximity
sūtra	a concise formula
taddhita	secondary derivative
tātparya	purport
utthāpya	to be raised
utthita	aroused
Vaiyākaraṇa	grammarian
vākyārtha	sentential meaning
vibhakti	case
vibhakti-pratyaya	case suffix
viśeṣaṇa	modifier/qualifier
viśeṣya	head/modified/qualified
vṛtti	relation between a word and its meaning
vyañjanā	suggestive meaning
vyākaraṇa	grammar
yaugika	etymological
yaugikarūḍha	both etymological and conventional
yogarūḍha	etymological but restricted by convention
yogyatā	mutual compatibility/congruity

Bibliography

Abney, Steven P., 1989, "A Computational Model of Human Parsing", *Journal of Psycholinguistic Research*, 18: 129-44.

Ādyāprasādamiśraḥ, 1988, *Kauṇḍabhaṭṭaviracitaḥ Vaiyākaraṇabhūṣaṇasāraḥ*, Vārāṇasī: Sampūrṇānanda Saṁskṛta Viśvavidyālayaḥ.

Aiyar, V. T. Viswanatha, 1969, *Śabdataraṅgiṇī*, Madras: Sanskrit Education Society.

Anantpur, Amba P., 2009, "Anusaaraka: An Approach for MT Taking Insights from the Indian Grammatical Tradition", PhD thesis, University of Hyderabad.

Anil Kumar, 2012, "An Automatic Sanskrit Compound Processing", PhD thesis, University of Hyderabad.

Anil Kumar, Vipul Mittal and Amba Kulkarni, 2010, "Sanskrit Compound Processor", in *Proceedings of the International Sanskrit Computational Linguistics Symposium*, ed. G.N. Jha, Berlin: Heidelberg, Springer-Verlag LNAI 6465.

Apte, V.S., 1885 [1925], *The Student's Guide to Sanskrit Composition: A Treatise on Sanskrit Syntax for Use of Schools and Colleges*, 9th edn, Bombay: The Standard Publishing Company.

Aralikatti, R.N., 1991, "A Note on Word Order in Modern Spoken Sanskrit and Some Positive Constraints", in *Studies in Sanskrit Syntax: A Volume in Honour of the Centennial of Speijer's Sanskrit Syntax (1886–1986)*, ed. Hans Henrich Hock, pp. 13-18, Delhi: Motilal Banarsidass.

Attardi, Giuseppe, 2006, "Experiments with a Multilanguage Non-projective Dependency Parser", in *Proceedings of CoNLL*, ed. Luis Marquez and Dan Klein, pp. 166-70, New York: Association for Computational Linguistics.

Bhagirath, Hariprasad, 1901, *Samāsacakra*, Bombay: Jagadishwar Press.

Bhanumati, B., 1989, *An Approach to Machine Translation among Indian Languages*, Technical Report, Dept. of CSE, IIT Kanpur.

Bharati, Akshar, Vineet Chaitanya and Rajeev Sangal, 1995, *Natural Language Processing: A Paninian Perspective*, New Delhi: Prentice-Hall.

Bharati, Akshar, Ashok Gupta and Rajeev Sangal, 1995, "Parsing Paninian Grammar with Nesting Constraints", in *Proceedings of 3rd NLP Pacific Rim Symposium*, pp. 1-6, Seoul.

Bharati, Akshar, Samar Husain, Bharat Ambati, Sambhav Jain, Dipti M. Sharma and Rajeev Sangal, 2008, "Two Semantic Features Make All the Difference in Parsing Accuracy", in *Proceedings of the Sixth International Conference on Natural*

Language Processing (ICON-08), Pune: C-DAC.

Bharati, Akshar and Amba Kulkarni, 2010, "Information Coding in a Language: Some Insights from Paninian Grammar", *Dhīmahi, Journal of Chinmaya International Foundation Shodha Sansthan*, I.1: 77-91.

Bharati, Akshar and Rajeev Sangal, 1990, "A Karaka Based Approach to Parsing of Indian Languages", in *Proceedings of International Conference on Computational Linguistics* (vol. 3), Helsinki: Association for Computational Linguistics.

———, 1993, "Parsing Free Word Order Languages in the Paninian Framework", in *Proceedings of the Conference*, 31st Annual Meeting of the Association for Computational Linguistics, pp. 105-11, Morristown, NJ: Association of Computational Linguistics.

Bhate, Saroja and Johannes Bronkhorst, 1993, *Bhartṛhari: Philosopher and Grammarian*, Delhi: Motilal Banarsidass.

Bhatt, V.P., 1994, *Gadādhara's Śaktivāda*, Delhi: Eastern Book Linkers.

Bhattacharyya, Pushpak, 1986, "A System for Sanskrit to Hindi Translation", MTech, dissertation, IIT Kanpur.

Bodirsky, M., M. Kuhlmann and M. Möhl, 2005, "Well-nested Drawings as Models of Syntactic Structure", in *Proceedings of the Tenth Conference on Formal Grammar and Ninth Meeting on Mathematics of Language*, ed. James Rogers, pp. 195–203, Edinburgh: University of Edinburgh.

Brahmadatta, Jijñāsu, 1979, *Aṣṭādhyāyī (Bhāṣya) Prathamāvṛtti*, vol. I, Sonepat: Ramlal Kapoor Trust Bahalgadh.

Cardona, George, 1988, *Pāṇini: His Work and Its Traditions*, Delhi: Motilal Banarsidass.

———, 2007, *Pāṇini and Pāṇinīyas on Śeṣa Relations*, Kochi: Kunjunni Raja Academy of Indological Research.

———, 2009, "On the Structure of Pāṇini's System", in *Sanskrit Computational Linguistics*, 1 & 2, ed. Gérard Huet, Amba Kulkarni and Peter Scharf, Springer-Verlag LNAI 5402.

Caturvedī, Mithileśa, 1992, *Śabdārthamīmāṁsā*, Varanasi: Sampurnananda Samskrit Visvavidyalaya.

Convington, Michael A., 2001, "A Fundamental Algorithm for Dependency Parsing", in *Proceedings of 39th Annual ACM Southwest Conference*, ed. John A. Miller and Jeffrey W. Smith, pp. 95-102, Association for Computing Machinery.

Coward, Harold G., 1983, *Studies in Indian Thought*, Delhi: Motilal Banarsidass.

Dash, Achyutanand, 1991, "The Syntactic Role of Adhi in the Pāṇinian Kāraka System", in *Pāṇinian Studies: S.D. Joshi Falicitation Volume*, ed. Madhav M. Deshpande and Saroja Bhate, pp. 135-60, Michigan: University of Michigan.

Dekang Lin, 2003, "Dependency-Based evaluation of MINIPAR", in *Treebanks: Building and Using Parsed Corpora*, ed. Abeillè Anne, pp. 317-29, Dordrecht:

Springer Netherlands.

Deshpande, Madhav M., 2007, *The Meaning of Nouns*, New Delhi: D.K. Printworld.

Devasthali, G.V., 1959, *Mīmāṁsā: The Vākyaśāstra of Ancient India*, Bombay: Booksellers' Publishing Co.; reprint 2011, *Mīmāṁsā: The Ancient Indian Science of Sentence Interpretation*, ed. with Introduction by V.N. Jha, Delhi: Sri Satguru Publications.

Gent, Ian P., Jefferson Chris and Miguel Ian, 2006, "Minion: A Fast, Scalable Constraint Solver", in *The Proceedings of 17th European Conference on Artificial Intelligence*, pp. 98-102.

Gillon, Brendan S., 1993, "Bhartṛhari's solution to the problem of asamartha compounds", E'tudes Asiatiques Studien, 47(1): 117-33.

———, 1995, "Autonomy of Word Formation: Evidence from Classical Sanskrit", *Indian Linguistics*, 56 (1-4): 15-52.

———, 1996, "Word Order in Classical Sanskrit", *Indian Linguistics*, 57(1): 1-35.

———, 2002, "Bartṛhari's Rule for Unexpressed Kārakas: The Problem of Control in Classical Sanskrit", in *Indian Linguistic Studies: Festschrift in Honor of George Cardona*, ed. Madhav M. Despande and Peter E. Hook, Delhi: Motilal Banarsidass.

———, 2005, "Subject-Predicate Order in Classical Sanskrit", in *Language and Grammar: Studies in Mathematical Linguistics and Natural Language*, ed. Philip Scott, Claudia Casadio and Robert Seely, pp. 211-25, Stanford, CA: Center for the Study of Language and Information.

———, 2007, "Pāṇini's Aṣṭādhyāyī and Linguistic Theory", *J. Indian Philos.*, 35: 445-68.

———, 2009, "Tagging Classical Sanskrit Compounds", in *Sanskrit Computational Linguistics* 3rd, edn. Amba Kulkarni and Gérard Huet, pp. 98-105, Springer-Verlag LNAI 5406.

Goyal, Pawan, Vipul Arora and Laxmidhar Behera, 2009, "Analysis of Sanskrit Text: Parsing and Semantic Relations", in *Sanskrit Computational Linguistics*, 1 & 2, ed. Gérard Huet, Amba Kulkarni and Peter Scharf, pp. 200-18, Springer-Verlag LNAI 5402.

Goyal, Pawan and Gérard Huet, 2013, "Completeness Analysis of a Sanskrit Reader", in *Proceedings of 5th International Symposium on Sanskrit Computational Linguistics*, New Delhi: D.K. Printworld.

Goyal, Pawan, Gérard Huet, Amba Kulkarni, Peter Scharf and Ralph Bunker, 2012, "A Distributed Platform for Sanskrit Processing", in *Proceedings of 24th COLING*, Mumbai. URL: https://www.aclweb.org/anthology/C/C12/C12-1062.pdf.

Goyal, Pawan, Amba Kulkarni and Laxmidhar Behera, 2009, "Computer Simulation of Aṣṭādhyāyī: Some Insights", in *Sanskrit Computational Linguistics*, 1 & 2, ed. Gérard Huet, Amba Kulkarni and Peter Scharf, pp. 139-61, Springer-Verlag LNAI 5402.

Havelka, J., 2005, "Projectivity in Totally Ordered Rooted Trees", *Prague Bulletin of*

Mathematical Linguistics, 84: 13-30.

Hellwig, Oliver, 2009a, "Extracting Dependency Trees from Sanskrit Texts", in *Third International Sanskrit Computational Linguistics Symposium*, ed. Amba Kulkarni and Gérard Huet, pp. 106-15, Springer-Verlag LNAI 5406.

———, 2009b, "Sanskrit Tagger a Stochastic Lexical and POS Tagger for Sanskrit", in *Sanskrit Computational Linguistics*, 1 & 2, ed. Gérard Huet, Amba Kulkarni and Peter Scharf, pp. 266-77, Springer-Verlag LNAI 5402.

———, 2010, "Performance of a Lexical and POS Tagger for Sanskrit", in *Proceedings of the 4th International Sanskrit Computational Linguistics Symposium*, Springer-Verlag.

Hock, H.H. (ed.), 2009, *Studies in Sanskrit Syntax*, Delhi: Motilal Banarsidass.

Hudson, R., 1984, *Word Grammar*, Oxford: Basil Blackwell.

Huet, Gérard, 2002, "The Zen Computational Linguistics Toolkit: Lexicon Structures and Morphology Computations Using a Modular Functional Programming Language", in *Tutorial Language Engineering Conference LEC'2002*, Hyderabad.

———, 2006, "Lexicon-directed Segmentation and Tagging of Sanskrit", in *Themes and Tasks in Old and Middle Indo-Aryan Linguistics*, ed. Bertil Tikkanen and Heinrich Hettrich, pp. 307-25, Delhi: Motilal Banarsidass.

———, 2007, "Shallow Syntax Analysis in Sanskrit Guided by Semantic Nets Constraints", in *Proceedings of the 2006 International Workshop on Research Issues in Digital Libraries*, ed. Prasenjit Majumdar, Mandar Mitra and Swapan K. Parul, pp. 46-52, Kolkata: ACM Digital Library. doi: http://doi.acm.org/10.1145/1364742.1364750. url: yquem.inria.fr/~huet/PUBLIC/IWRIDL.pdf.

———, 2009, "Formal Structure of Sanskrit Text: Requirements Analysis for a Mechanical Sanskrit Processor", in *Sanskrit Computational Linguistics*, 1 & 2, ed. Gérard Huet, Amba Kulkarni and Peter Scharf, Springer-Verlag pp. 162-99, LNAI 5402.

———, 2016, "Sanskrit Signs and Pāṇinian Scripts", in *Sanskrit and Computational Linguistics: Proceedings of the "Sanskrit and the IT World" Section of 16th World Sanskrit Conference*, ed. Amba Kulkarni, pp. 53-76, New Delhi: D.K. Publishers' Distributors.

Huet, Gérard and Pawan Goyal, 2016, "Design and Analysis of a Lean Interface for Sanskrit Corpus Annotation", *Journal of Linguistic Modeling*, 4(2): 145-82.

Huet, Gérard, Amba Kulkarni and Peter Scharf (eds), 2009, *Sanskrit Computational Linguistics*, 1 & 2, Springer-Verlag, LNAI 5402.

Hyman, Malcolm D., 2009, "From Paninian Sandhi to Finite State Calculus", in *Sanskrit Computational Linguistics*, 1 & 2, ed. Gérard Huet, Amba Kulkarni and Peter Scharf, pp. 253-65, Springer-Verlag, LNAI 5402.

Iyer, K.A. Subramania, 1969, *Bhartṛhari: A Study of Vākyapadīya in the Light of Ancient Commentaries*, Poona: Deccan College.

——— (tr.), 1971, *The Vākyapadīya of Bhartṛhari: Chapter III, Pt I*, Poona: Deccan College.

Jere, Atmaram Narayan, 2002, *Kārikāvalī*, Varanasi: Chowkhamba Krishnadas Academy.

Jha, Gaṅgānātha (tr.), 1933, *Śābara Bhāṣya*, vol. 1, Baroda: Oriental Institute.

——— (tr.), 1936, *Śābara Bhāṣya*, vol. 3, Baroda: Oriental Institute.

Jha, Girish Nath (ed.), 2010, *Sanskrit Computational Linguistics 4*, Springer-Verlag LNAI 6465.

Jha, V.N., 1997, *The Vaiyākaraṇabhūṣaṇa of Kauṇḍabhaṭṭa; English Translation*; vol. I, Delhi: Sri Satguru Publications.

Jhalakikar, V.R., 1920, *Kāvyaprakāśa of Mammaṭa with the Bālabodhinī*, 7th edn, Baroda: Bhandarkar Oriental Research Institute.

———, 1928, *Nyāyakośa*, Poona: Bombay Sanskrit and Prakrit Series, 49.

Joshi, K.R., 1985, *Nyāyasiddhāntamuktāvalī*, Bhandarkar Oriental Series, 21, Pune: Bhandarkar Oriental Research Institute.

Joshi, S.D., 1968, *Patañjali's Vyākaraṇa Mahābhāṣya Samarthāhnika (P 2.1.1)*, ed. with tr. and Explanatory Notes, Pune: Centre of Advanced Study in Sanskrit.

———, 1981, *Patañjali's Vyākaraṇa Mahābhāṣya Prātipadikārthaśeṣāhnikam (P2.3.46–2.3.71)*, Pune: Centre of Advanced Study in Sanskrit.

———, 1986, *Patañjali's Vyākaraṇa Mahābhāṣya Paspaśāhnikam*, Pune: Centre of Advanced Study in Sanskrit.

———, 1990, *Patañjali's Vyākaraṇa-Mahābhāṣya Sthānivadbhāvāhnika: Introduction, Text Translation and Notes*, Research Unit Series v. 1, Pune: Bhandarkar Oriental Research Institute.

———, 1998, *The Aṣṭādhyāyī of Pāṇini with Translation and Explanatory Notes*, vol. 7, New Delhi: Sahitya Akademi.

———, 2004, *The Aṣṭādhyāyī of Pāṇini with Translation and Explanatory Notes*, vol. 11, New Delhi: Sahitya Akademi.

Joshi, S.D. and J.A.F. Roodbergen, 1975, *Patañjali's Vyākaraṇa Mahābhāṣya Kārakāhnikam* (*P* 1.4.23–1.4.55), Poona: Centre of Advanced Study in Sanskrit.

Kamboj, J.L., 1986, *Semantic Change in Sanskrit*, Delhi: Nirman Prakashan.

Katz, J.J. and J.A. Fodor, 1963, "The Structure of a Semantic Theory", *Language*, 39: 170-210.

King, Tracy H., Richard Crouch, Stefan Riezler, Mary Dalrymple and Ronald Kaplan, 2003, *The PARC 700 Dependency Bank*.

Kiparsky, Paul, 2009, "On the Architecture of Panini's Grammar", in *Sanskrit Computational Linguistics*, 1 & 2, ed. Gérard Huet, Amba Kulkarni and Peter Scharf, pp. 33-94, Springer-Verlag LNAI 5402.

Kiparsky, Paul and J.F. Staal, 1968, "Syntactic and Semantic Relations in Pāṇini", *Foundations of Language*, 5: 83-117.

Krishna, Amrith and Pawan Goyal, 2016, "Generation of Derivative Nouns by Simulating Pāṇini", in *Sanskrit and Computational Linguistics: Proceedings of the "Sanskrit and the IT World" Section of 16th World Sanskrit Conference*, ed. Amba Kulkarni, pp. 157-92, New Delhi: D.K. Publishers' Distributors.

Krishna, Amrith, Pavankumar Satuluri and Pawan Goyal, 2017, "A Dataset for Sanskrit Word Segmentation", in *Proceedings of the Joint SIGHUM Workshop on Computational Linguistics for Cultural Heritage, Social Sciences, Humanities and Literature*, pp. 105-14, Vancouver: Association for Computational Linguistics.

Kulkarni, Amba, 2013, "A Deterministic Dependency Parser with Dynamic Programming for Sanskrit", in *Proceedings of the Second International Conference on Dependency Linguistics (DepLing 2013)*, pp. 157-66, Prague, Charles University in Prague Matfyzpress, URL: http://www.aclweb.org/anthology/W13-3718.

Kulkarni, Amba and Devanand Shukl, 2009, "Sanskrit Morphological Analyser: Some Issues, Festschrift Volume of Bh. Krishnamoorty", *Indian Linguistics*, 70.1-4: 169-77.

Kulkarni, Amba and Gérard Huet (eds), 2009, *Sanskrit Computational Linguistics 3*, Springer-Verlag LNAI 5406.

Kulkarni, Amba and Anil Kumar, 2011, "Statistical Constituency Parser for Sanskrit Compounds", in *Proceedings of ICON 2011*, Macmillan Advanced Research Series, Delhi: Macmillan.

Kulkarni, Amba and Anil Kumar, 2013, "Clues from Aṣṭādhyāyī for Compound Type Identification", in *Recent Researches in Sanskrit Computational Linguistics*, ed. Malhar Kulkarni and Chaitali Dangarikar, New Delhi: D.K. Printworld.

Kulkarni, Amba and K.V. Ramakrishnamacharyulu, 2013, "Parsing Sanskrit Texts: Some Relation-specific Issues", in *Recent Researches in Sanskrit Computational Linguistics*, ed. Malhar Kulkarni and Chaitali Dangarikar, pp. 191-212, New Delhi: D.K. Printworld.

Kulkarni, Amba P., Preeti Shukla, Pavankumar Satuluri and Devanand Shukl, 2015, "How Free Is the 'Free' Word Order in Sanskrit", in *Sanskrit Syntax*, ed. Peter Scharf, pp. 269-304, Sanskrit Library.

Kulkarni, Amba, Sheetal Pokar and Devanand Shukl, 2010, "Designing a Constraint Based Parser for Sanskrit", in *Fourth International Sanskrit Computational Linguistics Symposium*, ed. G.N. Jha, pp. 70-90, Springer-Verlag, LNAI 6465.

Kulkarni, Malhar, Chaitali Dangarikar, Irawati Kulkarni, Abhishek Nanda and Pushpak Bhattacharyya, 2010, "Introducing Sanskrit Wordnet", in *Principles Construction and Application of Multilingual Wordnets*, ed. Pushpak Bhattacharyya, Christiane Felbaum and Piek Vossen, New Delhi: Narosa Publishing House.

Kulkarni, Malhar and Chaitali Dangarikar, 2013, "Recent Researches in Sanskrit Computational Linguistics", in *Recent Researches in Sanskrit Computational Linguistics*, ed. Malhar Kulkarni and Chaitali Dangarikar, New Delhi: D.K. Printworld.

Kumar, Aravind, 1992, *Bhavānanda kṛt Kārakacakra: Eka Adhyayana*, Calcutta: Nirmal Book Agency.

Kumārasvāmin, 1909, *Pratāparūdrīya of Vidyānātha*, Bombay Sanskrit and Prakrit Series, 65.

Kumārila Bhaṭṭa, 1929, *Tantravārtika*, 97th edn, Poona: Anandasrama Sanskrit Series.

Kunjunni Raja, K., 1963, *Indian Theories of Meaning*, Madras: Adayar Library and Research Centre.

Kuppuswami Shastrigal, M.A., 1908, *Adhvara Mīmāṁsā Kutūhalavṛttiḥ*, Srirangam: Sri Vani Vilas Press.

Maṅgalārāma, 1995, *Saṁskṛta Vyākaraṇa kī Dārśanika Mīmāṁsā*, Jodhpur: Rajasthani Granthagar.

Marcus, S., 1967, *Algebraic Linguistics: Analytical Models, Mathematics in Science and Engineering*, 29, New York: Academic Press.

Marneffe, M., B. MacCartney and C.D. Manning, 2006, "Generating Typed Dependency Parses from Phrase Structure Parses", in *The Fifth International Conference on Language Resources and Evaluation, LREC 2006*, Italy.

Masson, J. Moussaieff, 1979, "Truth or Falsity in Poetry", *Annals of the Bhandarkar Oriental Research Institute*, 60 (1/4): 225-28.

Matilal, B.K., 1985, *Logic, Language and Reality: An Introduction to Indian Philosophical Studies*, Delhi: Motilal Banarsidass.

McDonald, Ryan and Joakim Nivre, 2007, "Characterizing the Errors of Data-Driven Dependency Parsing Models", in *Proceedings of EMNLP-CoNLL*, pp. 122-31.

McDonald, Ryan, Fernando Pereira, Kiril Ribarov and Jan Hajiç, 2005, "Non-projective Dependency Parsing Using Spanning Tree Algorithms", in *Proceedings of HLT/EMNLP*, pp. 523-30.

Mīmāṁsakaḥ, Yudhiṣṭhira, 1990, *Mīmāṁsā Śābarabhāṣya*, Sonepat: Ramlal Kapoor Trust.

———, 1993, *Mahābhāṣyam, Patañjalimuniviracitam*, Sonepat: Ramlal Kapoor Trust.

Mishra, Sri Narayana, 1985, *Kāśikāvṛttiḥ along with Commentaries Nyāsa of Jinendrabuddhi and Padamañjarī of Haradattamisra*, Varanasi: Ratna Publications.

Misra, Anand, 2009, "Simulating the Paninian System of Sanskrit Grammar", in *Sanskrit Computational Linguistics Symposium*, 1 & 2, ed. Gérard Huet, Amba Kulkarni and Peter Scharf, pp. 127-38, Springer-Verlag LNAI 5402.

Mittal, Vipul, 2010, "Automatic Sanskrit Segmentizer Using Finite State Transducers", in *Proceedings of the ACL 2010 Student Research Workshop*, pp. 85-90, Uppsala Sweden: Association for Computational Linguistics, URL: http://www.aclweb.org/anthology/P10-3015.

Munśī, O.K., E.V.P. Unithiri and N.V.P. Unithiri, 2004, *Dhātūrūpaprapañca* (A Dictionary of All the Forms of All the Roots in Sanskrit), Calicut University

Sanskrit Series, pt 2, Calicut: University of Calicut.

Nair, Sivaja, 2011, "The Knowledge Structure in Amarakośa", PhD thesis, University of Hyderabad.

Nair, Sivaja and Amba Kulkarni, 2010, "The Knowledge Structure in Amarakośa", in *Proceedings of the 4th International Sanskrit Computational Linguistics Symposium*, ed. G.N. Jha, Springer-Verlag, pp. 173-89, LNAI 6465.

Nakagawa, Tetsuji, 2007, "Multilingual Dependency Parsing Using Global Features", in *Proceedings of the Joint Conference on EMNLP-CoNLL*, pp. 952-56, Prague: Association for Computational Linguistics.

Natarajan, Abhiram and Eugene Charniak, 2011, "S3-Statistical Sandhi Splitting", in *Proceedings of IJCNLP*, pp. 301-08, Chiang Mai Thailand: Asian Federation of Natural Language Processing.

Nivre, J., 2006, "Constraints on Non-projective Dependency Parsing", in *Proceedings of the Eleventh Conference of the European Chapter of the Association for Computational Linguistics (EACL)*, pp. 73-80, Trento, Italy.

Panchal, Sanjeev, (forthcoming), "Modelling Ākāṁkṣā Following Pāṇinian Grammar for Sentential Parsing", PhD thesis, Hyderabad: University of Hyderabad.

Panchal, Sanjeev and Amba Kulkarni, 2018, "Yogyatā as an Absence of Non-congruity", in *Proceedings of Computational Sanskrit and Digital Humanities, 17th World Sanskrit Conference*, ed. Gérard Huet and Amba Kulkarni, pp. 59-82, New Delhi: D.K. Publishers' Distributors.

Pande, Gopal Dutt, 2000, *Vaiyākaraṇa Siddhāntakaumudī of Bhattojidikshita* (text only), repr. edn, Varanasi: Chowkhamba Vidyabhavan.

———, 2004, *Aṣṭādhyāyī of Pāṇini Elaborated by M.M. Panditraj Dr. Gopal Shastri*, Varanasi: Chowkhamba Surabharati Prakashan.

———, 2012, *Vaiyākaraṇa Siddhāntakaumudī of Bhattojidikshita Containing Bālamanoramā of Śrī Vāsudevadīkshita*, repr. edn, Varanasi: Chowkhamba Surabharati Prakashan.

Pande, Gopaladatta, 2012, *Vaiyyākaraṇasiddhāntakaumudī*, Vārāṇasī: Chowkhambā Surabhāratī Prakāśan.

Pataskar, Bhagyalata A., 2006, "Semantic Analysis of the Technical Terms in the 'Aṣṭādhyāyī', meaning 'Adjective'", *Annals of Bhandarkar Oriental Research Institute*, 87: 59-70.

Patel, Dhaval and Shivakumari Katuri, 2016, "Prakriyāpradarśinī: An Open Source Subanta Generator", in *Sanskrit and Computational Linguistics: Proceedings of the "Sanskrit and the IT World" Section of 16th World Sanskrit Conference*, ed. Amba Kulkarni, pp. 193-220, New Delhi: D.K. Publishers' Distributors.

Patnaik, Tandra, 1994, *Śabda: A Study of Bhartṛhari's Philosophy of Language*, New Delhi: D.K. Printworld.

Prasad, K.S., 2002, *The Philosophy of Language in Classical Indian Tradition*, New Delhi: Decent Books.

Ramakrishnamacharyulu, K.V., 2009, "Annotating Sanskrit Texts Based on Śābdabodha Systems", in *Proceedings of Third International Sanskrit Computational Linguistics Symposium*, ed. Amba Kulkarni and Gérard Huet, pp. 26-39, Hyderabad: Springer-Verlag LNAI 5406.

Ramanujatatacharya, N.S., 2005, *Śābdabodha Mīmāṁsā*, Pondicherry: Institut Français de Pondichéry.

Rāmapriya, Bhā. Va. and V. Saumyanārāyaṇa, 2001, "Saṅgaṇakayantre Nyāyaśāstrīyaśābdabodhaḥ", *Journal of Foundation Research*, VI.1-2: 61-68.

Reddy, Vikas, Amrith Krishna, Vishnu Dutt Sharma, Prateek Gupta, M.R. Vineeth and Pawan Goyal, 2018, "Building a Word Segmenter for Sanskrit Overnight", in *LREC*, pp. 1666-1671, Miyazaki, Japan: European Language Resource Association.

Resnik, Phillip, 1993, "Semantic Classes and Syntactic Ambiguity", in *Proceedings of ARPA Workshop on Human Language Technology*, pp. 278-83, Princeton, NJ: Association for Computational Linguistics.

Sanfillip, A. et al., 1996, *Subcategorization Standards: Report of the EAGLES Lexicon/ Syntax Group*, SHARP Laboratories of Europe.

Sangal, Rajeev, Vineet Chaitanya and Amba Kulkarni, 2000, "Anusaaraka: Overcoming the Language Barrier in India", in *Anuvad*, ed. Rukmini Bhaya Nair, pp. 224-50, New Delhi: Sage Publishers.

Sanka, Usharani, 2015, "A Study of Kāraka-demand of Some Dhātus, Based on Meaning, Following Śābdabodha for Machine Translation", PhD thesis, Rashtriya Sanskrit Vidyapeetha, Tirupati.

Sastri, Gangadhara, 1903, *Tantravārtikam*, Benares: Chowkamba Sanskrit Book Depot.

Sastry, Vempaty Kutumba, 2002, *Saṅkṣepa Rāmāyaṇam*, Delhi: Rashtriya Sanskrit Sansthan.

Satuluri, Pavankumar, 2016, "Sanskrit Compound Generation: With a Focus on the Order of Operations", PhD thesis, University of Hyderabad.

Scharf, Peter, 1990, "The Denotation of Generic Terms in Ancient Indian Philosophy: Grammar, Nyāya, and Mīmāṁsā", PhD thesis, University of Pennsylvania.

———, 2009a, "Levels in Pāṇini's Aṣṭādyāyī", in *Proceedings of Third International Symposium on Sanskrit Computational Linguistics*, ed. Amba Kulkarni and Gérard Huet, pp. 66-77, LNAI 5406, Hyderabad: Springer.

———, 2009b, *Madhaviyadhatuvrittisaidhantikanukramani Providence*, The Sanskrit Library.

———, 2016, "An XML Formalisation of the Aṣṭādhyāyī", in *Sanskrit and Computational Linguistics: Proceedings of the "Sanskrit and the IT World" Section of 16th World Sanskrit Conference*, ed. Amba Kulkarni, pp. 77-102, New Delhi: D.K. Publishers.

Scharf, Peter, Anuja Ajotikar, Sampada Savardekar, and Pawan Goyal, 2015, "Distinctive Features of Poetic Syntax Preliminary Results", *Sanskrit Syntax*, ed. Peter Scharf, pp. 305-24, Sanskrit Library, USA.

Scharf, Peter, Pawan Goyal, Anuja Ajotikar and Tanuja Ajotikar, 2015, "Voice, Preverb and Transitivity Restrictions in Sanskrit Verb Use", in *Sanskrit Syntax*, ed. Peter Scharf, pp. 157-202, Sanskrit Library, USA.

Shailaja, N., 2014, "Comparison of Pāṇinian Dhātuvṛttis", PhD thesis, University of Hyderabad.

Shailaja, N. and Amba Kulkarni, 2013, "Comparison of Pāṇinīya Dhātuvṛttis", in *Recent Researches in Computational Linguistics: Proceedings of the 5th International Sanskrit Computational Linguistics Symposium*, ed. Malhar Kulkarni and Chaitali Dangarikar, pp. 103-14, New Delhi: D.K. Printworld.

Shailaja, N. and Amba Kulkarni, 2019, "Pāṇinīyadhātuvṛttīnām Tulanātamaka-madhyanam", *Dhīmahi, Research Journal of Chinmaya International Foundation*, vol. X: 22-38.

Sharma, Pandit Shivadatta, 2007, *Vyākaraṇamahābhāṣyam*, Delhi: Chaukhamba Sanskrit Pratishtan.

Sharma, Rama Nath, 1987, *The Aṣṭādhyāyī of Pāṇini: English Translation of Adhyāyas Two and Three with Sanskrit Text*, Delhi: Munshiram Manoharlal.

———, 2003, *The Aṣṭādhyāyī of Pāṇini: English Translation of Adhyāyas Seven and Eight with Sanskrit Text*, Delhi: Munshiram Manoharlal.

Sharma, Raghunath, 1974, *Vākyapadīyam, Part III with Commentary Prakāśa by Helaraja and Ambakartri*, Varanasi: Varanaseya Sanskrit Visvavidyalaya.

Sharmā, Ramaṇakumāra, 2001, *Śabdaśaktivimarśa*, Delhi: Vidyanidhi Prakashan.

Shastri, Gaurinath, 1959, *The Philosophy of Word and Meaning*, Calcutta: Sanskrit College.

Shastri, Swami Dwarikadas and Pt. Kalika Prasad Shukla, 1965, *Kāśikāvṛttiḥ with the Nyāsa Commentary and Padamañjarī*, Varanasi: Chaukhamba Sanskrit Pratishthan.

Shukla, Preeti, Amba Kulkarni and Devanand Shukl, 2013, "Geeta: Gold Standard Annotated Data, Analysis and Its Application", in *Proceedings of ICON 2013, the 10th International Conference on NLP*, Macmillon Advanced Research Series, pp. 134-44, Delhi: Macmillon.

Shukla, Rajaram, 2015, *Viśvanātha-pañcānanakṛta Nyāyasiddhāntamuktāvalī dinakarī sahita*, Shimla: Indian Institute of Advanced Study.

———, 2017, *Viśvanātha-pañcānanakṛta Nyāyasiddhāntamuktāvalī dinakarī sahitā (anumānakhaṇḍamārabhya)*, Varanasi: Sampoornanda Sanskrit Vishwavidyalaya,

Sohoni, Samir J. and Malhar A. Kulkarni, 2018, "A Functional Core for the Computational Aṣṭādhyāyī", in *Computational Sanskrit and Digital Humanities, 17th World Sanskrit Conference Proceedings*, ed. Gérard Huet and Amba Kulkarni, pp. 1-30, New Delhi: D.K. Publishers' Distributors.

Somayājulu, K.V., 2002, *Vākyapadīyasthasādhanasamuddeśavimarśaḥ: A Critical Study on the Sādhanasamuddeśa of Vākyapadīya*, Delhi: Amara Grantha Publications.

Speijer, J.S., 1886, *Sanskrit Syntax*, repr. 2009, Delhi: Motilal Banarsidass.

Staal, J. Fritz, 1967, *Word Order in Sanskrit and Universal Grammar*, Foundations of Language Supplementary Series v. 5, Dordrecht: D. Reidel.

Staal, J.F., 1988, *Universals: Studies in Indian Logic and Linguistics*, Chicago, IL: The University of Chicago Press.

Subbanna, Sridhar and Shrinivasa Varakhedi, 2009, "Computational Structure of the Aṣṭādhyāyī and Conflict Resolution Techniques", in *Sanskrit Computational Linguistics, 3rd International Symposium, Hyderabad, Proceedings*, ed. Amba Kulkarni and Gérard Huet, pp. 56-65, Springer-Verlag LNAI 5406.

———, 2010, "Asiddhatva Principle in Computational Model of Aṣṭādhyāyī", in *Sanskrit Computational Linguistics, 4th International Symposium, New Delhi, India, December 2010, Proceedings*, ed. Girish Nath Jha, pp. 231-38, LNAI 6465, Berlin–Heidelberg: Springer-Verlag.

Subbarao, Veluri, 1969, *The Philosophy of a Sentence and Its Parts*, Delhi: Munshiram Manoharlal.

Subrahmanyam, Korada, 2001, *Four Vṛttis in Pāṇini*, Hyderabad: Korada Subrahmanyam.

———, 2012, *Mahāvākyavicāraḥ*, Bhāgyanagaram: Śrīlakṣmaṇarāya Bhavyasmṛti Granthamālā.

Susarla, Sarada, Tilak M. Rao and Sai Susarla, 2018, "PAIAS: Pāṇini Aṣṭādhyāyī Interpreter as a Service", in *Computational Sanskrit and Digital Humanities, 17th World Sanskrit Conference Proceedings*, ed. Gérard Huet and Amba Kulkarni, pp. 31-58, New Delhi: D.K. Publishers' Distributors.

Tesnière, Lucie (ed.), 1959, *Éléments de Syntaxe Structurale*, Paris: Librairie C. Klincksieck.

Tripāṭhī, Dāmodararāma, 2002a, *Vākyatattvavimarśaḥ*, Delhi: S.S. Publishers.

———, 2002b, *Ātmatattvavimarśaḥ*, Delhi: S.S. Publishers.

Tripāṭhī, Rāmasureśa, 1972, *Saṁskṛta Vyākaraṇa Darśana*, New Delhi: Rajakamal Prakashan.

Tubb, Gary A. and Emery R. Boose, 2007, *Scholastic Sanskrit: A Handbook for Students*, New York: The American Institute of Buddhist Studies at Columbia University.

Varmā, Satyakāma, 1964, *Bhāṣātattva aura Vākyapadīya*, New Delhi: Bharatiya Prakashan.

Vijayapāla, Vidyavaridhi, 2001, *Kāśikā*, Sonepat: Ramlal Kapoor Trust.

Wilks, Yorick, 1975, "A Preferential, Pattern-seeking, Semantics for Natural Language Interface", *Artificial Intelligence*, 6: 53-74.

Yamada, H. and Y. Matsumoto, 2003, "Statistical Dependency Analysis with Support Vector Machines", in *Proceedings of IWPT*, pp. 195-206, Nancy, France: Association for Computational Linguistics. https://www.cs.cmu.edu/usigparse/previousmeetings/iwpt2003/index.html.

Index

abhidhā xv, 13, 18, 40, 70-73
abhihita 43, 105
abhihitānvayavāda 31-32
ablative 45, 77
absolutive 57, 63
accusative 18, 25, 35, 45, 50, 52, 70
acyclic 99, 103
adhikaraṇa 44, 49-50, 85, 104, 107-08, 111, 118, 124
adjective 5, 25, 38-39, 41, 45-46, 59, 61, 65, 71, 77-78, 82, 87-89, 91, 109, 115
agent 13-14
ajahad-lakṣaṇā 21, 72
ākāṅkṣā xiii, xv, xxii, 13, 24-25, 32, 40-41, 57, 68, 70-71, 74, 86, 88, 90, 103, 106-08, 111, 127, 136
akhaṇḍa-pakṣa 31
ālaṁkārikas 30
Amarakośa 6, 87, 106
anabihita 105
Anusaaraka 137
anvayamukhī 38
anvaya-vyatireka 32
anvitābhidhānavāda 31
apādāna 44, 66, 68-69, 77, 85-86, 104
argument-sharing 54
ārthī-bhāvanā 14
ārthī-pakṣa 135
aruṇādhikaraṇa 85
asamartha-samāsa 101
Aṣṭādhyāyī viii, 3, 6, 15, 51, 53-54, 79-81, 83, 87, 105
avadhāraṇa 46
āvāpaudvāpa 32
avayava–avayavī-bhāva 49, 51, 87, 106

bahuvrīhi 82
barhirnyāya 72
beneficiary 11
Bhartṛhari 17, 52, 79, 80, 135
bhāvanā 13-14, 20
bhramātmaka-jñāna 26
bipartite graph 109
bi-transitive 41

canonical-word-order 93-95, 107, 109, 117, 128
case suffix 5, 42, 44-45, 49, 52, 54, 86, 105, 119
chief qualificand 14, 34, 36
chunker x, 101
CLIPS x, xii
confusion matrix 142
congruent 73
congruity ix, xv, 24, 28, 35, 71, 76-77, 86-87, 90
congruous 28, 32, 35, 73, 76-77, 86
constituency
  analysis 7
  parse 8
  parser 7, 11
  structure 7-10
  tree 9-11
constraint solver xii, 112-13
coreferentiality 52

CPG ix
C-selection 69
Cyc 70

DAG 99, 121-23
daṇḍa-anvaya 38-39, 88
data-driven xv, 100
deep-learning 1
DeitY x
dependency
  analysis 11,
  grammar 10, 13, 41
  graph 57-59, 101, 127
  parse 96-99, 128
  parser xiv, 10, 12, 93, 97-102, 110, 127-28
  parsing xiv, 93, 100-101,110
  relation 10, 58, 93
  structure 7, 10-11, 55, 59, 99-100
  tree xii, 10-11, 55, 97, 119
Depth-First-Traversal 115
derivational suffix 43-44, 98, 104-05
deterministic parsing 114
DFT 115, 116
dhātupāṭha 6, 42
dhātuvṛttis 42
dravya 79, 80-83, 85-88, 91, 104-05
dvikarmaka 104
dvirepha 148
dynamic programming 110, 114, 116, 119, 128

edge-centric xii, 110, 113, 121-22, 128
exegesists 13
expectancy ix, 13, 24-27, 32, 35, 39, 41-43, 68, 70-71, 73-74, 86, 88, 90, 98-99, 102-05, 107-09, 111, 115
extended meaning 20, 22, 71-73, 76
extra-linguistic 5, 51, 90, 96, 135

free word order 10, 36

Gaṅgeśopādhyāya 28
gauṇī 18-19, 21
Gautama 145, 147
generative grammar viii
genitive 44, 49, 51, 59-61, 68, 77, 86-88, 90
global
  compatibility 116, 119, 123, 125
  constraint 103, 108-10, 113, 128
Grammarians vii, ix, xiv, 13, 50-51, 96-97
graph 10, 55, 58, 59, 67, 101-03, 106-11, 113-14, 116-18, 126, 130, 127-28
guṇa-vacana 80-81, 83-85, 88, 91, 104-105, 136

Haskell 3
hetu 106
homonymous 15, 29
HPSG 41
hypernymy 82
hyponymy 82

implied meaning 19
imposed property 50, 68, 78, 82
inconceivable 28
incongruent 94
incongruity 28, 104
incongruous 103
inconsistent 28
indeclinables 42, 46, 81, 98, 105
Indo-Aryan xiii
inflectional suffix 43
instrument 43, 47-49, 74-75, 77, 86
intentional implication 19
interger-programming 12

jahad–ajahad-lakṣaṇā 19, 21, 72
jahad-lakṣaṇā 21
Jaimini 24, 85, 147

janya–janaka-bhāva 49, 87
jāti-vācaka 84
JSON 3
kāraka viii, 5, 20, 25-26, 42-45, 47, 50-51, 62, 68-69, 77, 85-86, 88, 91, 96, 105, 108, 110-11
kāraka chart 68
karaṇa(m) 5, 34, 43-44, 49, 69, 74, 77, 85-86, 104
karma(n) 11, 13-14, 20, 25-26, 34-35, 39, 43-44, 50-52, 62-66, 69-71, 74, 85, 96, 99, 104-05, 107-08, 117-18, 124, 127
karmapravacanīya 45
karma-samānādhikaraṇa 104
karmatva 50
kartṛ(ā) 11, 13-14, 20, 26, 35, 38-39, 43-44, 47-54, 61-65, 69-71, 74, 85, 96, 99-100, 102-03, 105, 107-09, 115, 118-19, 124
kartṛsamānādhikaraṇa 104, 109, 115
kartṛtva 49, 52
katham-bhūtinī 39
Kātyāyana 81
Kauṇḍabhaṭṭa 135
khaṇḍa-anvaya 39
khaṇḍa-pakṣa 31-32
kriyā-vacana 83
kriyāviśeṣaṇa(m) 45-46, 65, 106
Kumārila Bhaṭṭa 23, 28, 31-32, 148

lakṣaṇāropitā 72
lakṣaṇā xv, 13, 18-19, 70-73
local constraint 103, 108-10, 111, 113-14, 128
locative 102, 119
logician ix, 13, 34, 36-37, 96

machine-learning x, 1, 2, 7, 70, 136-37
machine translation 1, 11
Mahābhāṣya xiv, 33, 78-80, 87, 146
Mammaṭa 22
matrix 110-11, 113
meaning congruity 13
metaphoric 70, 72, 75-76, 88, 90
Mīmāṁsaka 13, 20, 23, 28, 30-31, 71-72, 98, 135
Mīmāṁsā xiii, xiv, 31-32, 34, 72, 135
minimalism 100, 137
MINION 112
minipar 100, 137
modifier–modified 34, 36, 45
morpheme vii, 18, 34-36, 49, 51, 76, 90, 96-97, 102, 108, 111
morphological x, xii, 38, 78, 81, 101-03, 106, 109-10, 111-14, 116, 126-27
morphology xii, 78
mukhyārtha 72
mukhyārthabādha 71-72
mukhya-viśeṣya 10, 14, 36, 96, 104
Mukula Bhaṭṭa 148
mutual expectancy 24-27, 35, 68, 70, 73, 75-76, 83, 88, 90

Nāgeśa 30, 80, 135, 149
Naiyāyika ix, 14, 18, 23-25, 27, 29, 30, 34-35, 50, 75, 135
natural implication 19
Navya-Naiyāyika 13
Navya-Nyāya 13
neo-logicians 13
n-gram 7, 11
nirākāṅkṣā 73
nirdhāraṇa 45
nirūḍha-lakṣaṇā 19, 20
niyata 25
niyatākāṅkṣā 25
NLP viii, ix, 3, 11
node-centric 110, 119, 128

nominal 43-44, 86
  suffix 18, 35, 44
nominative 44, 48-49, 52, 70
non-congruity 87, 90-91, 136
non-congruous 90
non-determinism 4-5
non-deterministic 4
non-*kāraka* 105-06
non-finite 43, 46, 54, 66
non-planar 59, 67
non-projective 58
non-projectivity 55, 57, 67, 90, 128, 135
non-sensical 94, 104
noun *lakṣaṇa* chart 68
Nyāya xiii, 34, 59, 72, 135
Nyāyakośa 27, 76
Nyāyasiddhāntamuktāvalī 25-26, 34, 42
Nyāyasūtra 145

object 25
OCaml xii
ontological constraint 91
ontology 6, 68, 79, 86
optimality theory 7

padaśāstra 135-36
Pāṇini 2-6, 13, 47, 49, 50-52, 78-81, 86, 104-06, 135
parā–aparā 83, 106
parājāti–aparājāti 82
Paramalaghumañjūṣā 27, 149
parasparākāṅkṣā 25
parser xiv, 7, 11-12, 14, 33, 41, 51-52, 55, 69-71, 89-90, 93-95, 100-102, 110, 113, 116, 126, 127-28
part–whole 49, 87, 106
passive 43-44
Patañjali xiv, 33, 78-81, 87
planar graph 58-59
planarity ix, 54, 57, 59, 67
POS x, 7-8, 101
Prabhākara 31
pradhāna 48-49, 51, 53
prakriyā-pakṣa 135
prākṛta-dhvani 17
pramātmaka-jñāna 26
prayojana(m) 77, 85, 106
prayojanavatī-lakṣaṇā 20
precedence 53, 55, 68
predicative adjective 46, 59, 109, 115
primary meaning 18-22, 29, 70-73, 75-77, 90, 109, 136, 145
projective 115
projectivity 55-58
  constraint 58
proximity xv, 5, 13, 24, 26, 32, 35, 42, 68

qualificand 96, 99
qualified 85, 96
qualifier 78, 81-82, 96
qualitative implication 19

rhetorician 22, 30, 71-72, 137
rūḍha 18

Śābara-Bhāṣya xiv, 85
śābdabodha xiv, xxii, 10, 12-16, 18, 20, 22-24, 26, 28, 30, 32-36, 38-39, 40-42, 44, 46, 48, 50-52, 54, 56, 58, 60, 62, 64, 66, 68, 70-72, 74, 76, 78, 80, 82, 84, 86, 88, 90, 95, 97, 99, 128
śabdajagat 51
śabdakarma 104
śabdakhaṇḍa 28, 34
śabda-śakti viii, 70
sakarmaka 42, 104
śakti 15, 18, 42, 53, 70
śaktigraha 42

samānādhikaraṇa 45, 78, 84, 87, 102
sāmānādhikaraṇya 45-46, 52, 78, 85
sāmānya–viśeṣa 106
samāsa viii, 15, 18, 43, 81-82
samasta-pada 18-19, 83-84
sambaddhārtha 33
sambodhana 68, 106
saṁgatārtham 33
sampradāna 11, 13, 14, 44, 77, 85-86, 104
samprekṣitārtha 33
saṁsṛṣṭārtha 33
sandhi x, xii, 4-7, 15, 94
saṅgatārtha 33
sannidhi ix, xiii, xv, xxii, 24, 26-27, 32, 40-41, 54, 57, 59, 61-62, 65-68, 90, 103, 109, 127, 136
saptadaśāratnī 72
sāropā 19, 21-22
sarvanāma 81-83
ṣaṣṭhī 49, 77, 86-87
secondary meaning 3, 20, 28-29, 72-73, 75-77, 81, 90
segmentation 5-7, 12, 38, 93-94, 128
segmenter 6, 94-95, 126
semantic viii, 9, 11, 12, 135, 47, 49, 51, 68-69, 74, 78, 83, 86-87
  constraint 69
semantico-syntactic 83
seq2seq 7
shallow parser 12
signification 13
significative xii, 70, 90
signifié 16-17
S-selection 69
subcategorization 12, 41, 68-70
subordinate 51, 54-55, 83
substratum 80
śuddhā-lakṣaṇā 21
suggestive meaning 13, 22, 23, 73
sva–svāmī-bhāva 49, 87
syntactic 41, 69-70, 78-79, 86, 90-91
syntactico–semantic 51
syntax 51, 89, 135

tādarthya 77, 106
taddhita 43
taddhitānta 18-19, 81-84
TAG 41
Tarkasaṁgraha 18, 26-27, 76
tātparya xv, 24, 28-30, 40-41, 136
tatpuruṣa 10, 82
Tattvacintāmaṇi 27
TDIL xii
Tesniére 41
thematic
  relation 47, 50
  role 47, 49
transition-based 101, 110
Type-1 error 76
Type-2 error 77

Udyota 80
unidirectional expectancy 86
unilateral expectancy 25, 68, 90
upādhi 68-69, 78, 83-84
upamāna 42
upapada 44, 104
upasarjana 83
utthāpya-ākāṅkṣā 25, 57, 68, 86, 90
utthita-ākāṅkṣā 25, 57, 68, 90

vaikharī 17
vaikṛta-dhvani 17
Vaiśeṣika 6, 68, 79-80, 86
Vaiyākaraṇa ix, 13, 17-18, 27, 30, 34, 36, 71, 75, 96, 99, 135
vākyajam 19
vākya-karma 104

Vākyārthamātṛkāvṛtti 27, 76

Vākyaśāstra 31, 136

vākya-sphoṭa 31

valency 41

Vedic 19, 29

verb *lakṣaṇa* chart 68

verbal

cognition viii, x, xii, xv, 13, 15-16, 18, 23, 26-30, 33-34, 102, 127

suffix 14, 17, 20, 35, 43-46, 52-53, 98-99, 102, 105

vertex-centric 113-14, 128

vibhakti viii, 33, 44-46, 50, 53, 104-05

vidheyaviśeṣaṇa 46

viśeṣaṇa 10, 38-39, 46, 61, 68, 74, 77-85, 87-88, 91, 104, 106, 109

viśeṣya 10, 38-39, 77-79, 83-85, 87, 91, 96

viśeṣya–viśeṣaṇa-bhāva 77-79, 83, 88

vivakṣā viii

vocative 68

Vyākaraṇa xiii, 34, 42, 52, 59, 61, 91, 135

vyaṅgyārtha 22, 30, 73, 137

vyañjanā xv, 13, 18, 22, 40, 70, 73

weak non-projectivity 55, 57, 67, 90

weakly non-projective 58

well-nestedness 55

WordNet 6, 69, 87, 106

word-order 84

XML 3

yaugika 18

yaugikarūḍha 19

yogarūḍha 19, 20

yogyatā xxii, 13, 24, 27-28, 32, 40-41, 49, 68-71, 73-77, 88-90, 103, 106-07, 111, 127-28, 136